'Probably the most important book to l
Ireland since the foundation of the state
contain their glee. Much of what Porter ⎯ ⎯⎯⎯⎯ the nature
of the two unionisms could quite easily be transferred to the two
nationalisms. In short *Rethinking Unionism* will provoke outrage in
the two big sectarian camps. But it will do much more than that . . .
The alternative vision proposed will appeal to the growing numbers
who have already said "a plague on both your houses". It has become
something of a reviewer's cliché to say, go out and buy this book. On
this occasion it is absolutely true for everyone who really cares about
the future of Northern Ireland.'

Irish People

'In many ways this is a book we have been waiting for: a critique of
contemporary unionism by an intelligent insider which questions the
basis of policies, challenges unionism to redefine itself in terms of
modern Britain and Ireland, and offers an alternative vision for
Northern Ireland . . . a scholarly, thoughtful, penetrating and very
readable analysis of the state of unionism, providing a philosophical
basis for a new departure.'

Maurice Hayes, *Belfast Telegraph*

'Porter is unusually and refreshingly frank and honest in his appraisal
of the strengths and weaknesses of unionism. He does not attempt to
gloss over unacceptable realities. But he believes "traditional
unionists still have cards to play" . . . an intelligent and constructive
political critique . . . deserves to be widely read.'

Martin Mansergh, *Sunday Tribune*

'Porter's thesis is serious, reflective and at once personal and political.
It represents an effort to connect unionist thought with larger
understandings about the nature of political and communal life that
no serious student of the Troubles should ignore. Highly
recommended for all audiences.'

J.E. Flynn, *Choice* (US)

'One of the seminal books of the Troubles and the first genuinely visionary statement to come from the unionist community . . . an extremely daring, contemporaneous and inventive treatise in political philosophy which discovers – virtually for the first time – a concept of politics in a barren political terrain . . . A boc'; that deserves to be read well beyond the borders of Northern Ireland for its contribution to the literature on conflict resolution.'

Paul Arthur, *Political Quarterly*

'Must be read by republicans, if only for the insights it provides into unionism. It also contains a few political lessons for unionists which all political activists should take to heart also. For example, the need to clarify and articulate. Time for "Rethinking Republicanism" maybe?'

Hilda Mac Thomas, *An Phoblacht*

'Norman Porter's surprising and iconoclastic book looks to the future, equally asserting the need to recognise differences and redefine traditional boundaries . . . a powerful and imaginative contribution to the ideals represented by this Prize'

Professor Roy Foster, speaking on behalf of the judges
of the 1997 Christopher Ewart-Biggs Memorial Prize

RETHINKING UNIONISM

An Alternative Vision for Northern Ireland

◆

NORMAN PORTER

THE
BLACKSTAFF
PRESS

BELFAST

NORMAN PORTER was born in Belfast in 1952, where he was educated at Methodist College Belfast. In 1970 he and his family emigrated to Australia, where he graduated with a BA in Politics from Flinders University. He holds a D.Phil. in Politics from the University of Oxford, and he later lectured in Politics at Flinders University. In 1994 he returned to Belfast and joined the Ulster Unionist Party. His frustration with unionist politics prompted him to make a submission to the Forum for Peace and Reconciliation in Dublin and led him to write *Rethinking Unionism* (Blackstaff Press, 1996), which was joint winner of the 1997 Christopher Ewart-Biggs Memorial Prize. He is married with three children.

First published in 1996 by
The Blackstaff Press Limited
This book has received support from the
Cultural Diversity Programme of the Community Relations Council,
which aims to encourage acceptance and understanding of cultural diversity.
The views expressed do not necessarily reflect those of the
NI Community Relations Council.

This new edition published in 1998 by
The Blackstaff Press Limited
3 Galway Park, Dundonald, Belfast BT16 2AN, Northern Ireland

Typeset by Techniset Typesetters, Newton-le-Willows, Merseyside

Printed by The Guernsey Press Company Limited

A CIP catalogue record for this book
is available from the British Library

ISBN 0-85640-643-0

CONTENTS

for Lis
at last

To acquire a horizon means that one learns to look
beyond what is close at hand – not in order to look
away from it, but to see it better within a larger
whole and in truer proportion.

Hans Georg Gadamer, *Truth and Method*, 1975

To be political, to live in a *polis*, meant that everything
was decided through words and persuasion and not
through force and violence.

Hannah Arendt, *The Human Condition*, 1958

PREFACE TO THE 1998 EDITION

The core argument of this book, formulated and elaborated during 1995 and 1996, is that unionism requires a serious rethink if it is to prove capable of offering a future worth having for all citizens in Northern Ireland. Such an argument may now appear close to redundant, because unionism, or at least a significant portion of it, has succeeded in doing what seemed unlikely even two years ago, namely cutting a deal with its political opponents. In doing so, it has helped to open up a future with worthwhile prospects for citizens. This is very much to be welcomed. And obviously, if I were revising this book, I would want to amend various of its details in the light of recent events. But crucially, I wouldn't want to ditch its core argument or most of the supporting analysis upon which it relies. These are far from approaching redundancy.

There are two basic reasons why I think that the case for rethinking unionism remains pertinent, even in its originally expressed form. First, it still tells against those unionists who persist in their opposition to coming to an understanding with nationalists. Second, it provides stronger grounds for reaching such an understanding than have so far been provided by pro-deal unionists, and it thereby makes pro-deal unionism much less vulnerable to the assaults of its anti-deal critics. I want to expand a little on these reasons after taking quick stock of the new circumstances in which we find ourselves.

Since this book was first published in September 1996 significant developments have occurred in the politics of Northern Ireland. The IRA ceasefire – broken in February 1996 – was renewed in July 1997 and continues to hold, as does the combined loyalist paramilitaries' ceasefire called during the autumn of 1994. Political negotiations to secure peace and to decide durable arrangements of government have taken place and have delivered a multi-party agreement (hereafter referred to as the Belfast Agreement). This agreement, remarkably, is supported by a range of unionist, loyalist, nationalist, republican and other parties. It has been endorsed by a substantial majority of citizens in both jurisdictions in Ireland: 71 per cent in the North, 94 per cent in the South. In line with the terms of the Belfast Agreement, elections to a new power-sharing northern assembly have been held. And a new set of institutions is being created in order to reflect 'the totality of relations' in Northern Ireland – that is, relations not only internal to the North, but also between North and South and between constituent parts of Britain and Ireland. In short, a fresh political future beckons: a future promising an end to constitutional gridlock and undemocratic practices; a future heralding an era of political partnership and equality between the North's divided people.

Unionism has played its part in making such a future seem possible and has much to be expectant about as it anticipates its unfolding. Or so say those unionist and loyalist parties – the Ulster Unionist Party (UUP), the Progressive Unionist Party (PUP) and the Ulster Democratic Party (UDP) – which were involved in cutting the deal with nationalism that appears as the Belfast Agreement. For these unionists, the agreement signals conspicuous gains which inspire great confidence: it returns an important measure of self-government to Northern Ireland, it replaces the loathed Anglo-Irish Agreement of 1985, it promises the removal from the constitution of the Republic of Ireland of the South's territorial claim to the North, it recognises British sovereignty in Northern Ireland, and it establishes the principle of consent as the only legitimate criterion of constitutional change. Reassured through these gains that Northern Ireland's place in the Union is safe, David Trimble, leader of the UUP now finds himself at liberty to declare in a recent speech that the time has come to 'get down to the historic and honourable task of this generation: to raise up a new Northern Ireland in which pluralist Unionism and constitutional nationalism can speak to each other with the civility that is the foundation of freedom' ('Vision for the Future', 22 June 1998).

The suggestion, then, is that present circumstances in Northern Ireland contain the potential birth of a new political dispensation in which unionism will play a creative role. But to suppose that that is all they contain is misleading. The potential is also there to destroy any new dispensation before it has barely begun. For if it is true to say that much has changed in the politics of Northern Ireland, it is also true to say in another sense that little has changed – especially within unionism. Where Trimble sees gains for unionism, various other unionists see losses. These latter were either opposed to the political negotiations which produced the Belfast Agreement or very wary of them. They typically perceive in the agreement not so much signs of a bright political dream as those of a dark political nightmare; not so much an intimation of a vibrant Northern Ireland in the making, as a blueprint of Northern Ireland's demise as an integral part of the United Kingdom. For such unionists, the agreement plays fast and loose with democracy – not least through its alleged appeasement of terrorism – and accepts much too readily the legitimacy of a nationalist script. The fact that even Sinn Féin could support the agreement simply underscores what these unionists think is the obvious: what is really on offer – reassurances about consent and cosmetic changes to the Irish constitution notwithstanding – is

Irish unity by instalments, that is, a unity achieved not directly or suddenly but cunningly and gradually by stealth.

Thinking along such lines is not confined to some lunatic fringe within unionism, but is spread across its spectrum. It is echoed in the most recent publication of the independent unionist-oriented Cadogan group, which refers to the negotiations leading up to the Belfast Agreement as being 'locked into the fantasies and mythology of Irish nationalism' (*Rough Trade*: Belfast, 1998, p. 21). Significant traces of anti-agreement thought are also found within the UUP – despite the official stance of its leadership – and are openly articulated by six of its nine members of parliament at Westminster. And, of course, the most unreserved espousal of anti-agreement sentiment is expressed by Ian Paisley's Democratic Unionist Party (DUP) and Robert McCartney's United Kingdom Unionist Party (UKUP), both of which pulled out of political negotiations upon the arrival of Sinn Féin. The fact that, as recent referendum and election results show, close to 50 per cent of the unionist electorate oppose the terms of the Belfast Agreement indicates that competition for unionist hearts and minds is anything but over.

The reality of acute divisions within unionism makes future political outcomes impossible to predict with confidence; and it assuredly tempers the promise of the Belfast Agreement. Ironically, perhaps, this promise is also severely tempered by one of the remaining displays of unionist unity, namely that which is evoked by controversies concerning loyal order parades. The right of Orangemen in particular to march along traditional routes regardless of the objections of local residents is upheld by unionist parties of every description, whatever their other disagreements. But it is precisely this sort of show of unionist unity that endangers the possibility of an end to communal polarisation and sectarian practices and, we may now add, that strains the spirit of the Belfast Agreement. At the time this book was first published in 1996, events surrounding the most contested of all Orange parades, that at Drumcree, cast a long shadow over political affairs in Northern Ireland. At the present time of writing, events surrounding Drumcree 1998 threaten to do likewise. The point I made in 1996 is worth repeating again: a unionism that cannot disentangle itself from Orangeism, or any other form of Protestant particularism, offers grim prospects to the citizens of Northern Ireland; prospects that are a world away from those suggested in the Belfast Agreement as well as from much of the newly found rhetoric of David Trimble.

This point relates to one of the reasons why the argument of *Rethinking Unionism* is still germane: traditional modes of unionist thought and conduct are inadequate now for exactly the same reasons as I identified two years ago. Whether we are dealing with the type of 'cultural unionism' associated with Ian Paisley, or with the type of 'liberal unionism' boasted of by Robert McCartney, or with some combination of the two, we are confronted by positions that are practically inept and intellectually unconvincing. To hanker after a Protestant Ulster or to dream of an Ulster as British as Kent or Surrey is to fail to take seriously two crucial factors which circumscribe the political options open to unionism: the presence of a substantial, and politically energised, nationalist minority within Northern Ireland, and the drift of the policy initiatives of the British and Irish governments (which increasingly are moving in the same direction and which enjoy the support of international opinion). Whatever the abilities of Paisley and McCartney to impede political progress in the North – and they should not be underestimated – their positions are properly described as practically inept because the failures of which they are guilty guarantee that their most basic promise of a better future for Northern Ireland cannot be delivered upon.

Both positions reduce unionism to a form of correct thought which is ill-suited to the business of politics, however much it is suited to the mindsets of religious and/or political fundamentalists. Intellectually, their respective versions of political correctness don't impress either. As I maintain in chapter three, cultural unionism is ultimately too incoherent to provide a framework for constructive political thinking. And, as I contend in chapter four, liberal unionism, despite its amazingly overblown rational pretensions, offers a much too narrow framework which simply cannot begin to accommodate creative thinking about some of our most pressing political problems in the North. In short, both positions are deeply flawed by their futile attempts to expunge ambiguity from politics, and by their adoption of a political self-righteousness which, in its reach for the moral high ground, proves curiously blind to the moral complexity of so many of our political quandaries. That adherents of these unionist positions are predisposed to oppose the Belfast Agreement is not remotely surprising, and neither is their ability to find common cause in doing so. That their alternatives to it are destined to become political fossils hardly counts as a revelation either.

Pro-agreement unionism needs to distance itself from those cultural and liberal straitjackets which reduce unionist politics to a series of negative postures. There are hints that this is occurring, but the suggestion that we are witnessing the emergence of a new unionism is dismissed by David Trimble as 'too simplistic'. Pro-agreement unionism, he insists, is simply the latest expression of the UUP's long-standing objective of reaching 'an honourable accommodation with nationalism' ('Vision for the Future', 22 June 1998).

No doubt it is politically expedient for Trimble to stress the continuity of UUP policy, especially given unionism's current parlous state and its fear of breaking old political moulds. But there is no reason to suppose that he does not mean what he says, however surprising it sounds to many of his party colleagues. The question is whether it is sufficient for pro-agreement unionism to settle for what Trimble says. There are grounds for thinking not. If we assume that most pro-agreement unionists continue to operate within cultural and liberal frameworks similar to those of Paisley and McCartney – and I think this is a fair assumption – then the root difference between pro-agreement and anti-agreement unionist factions is a matter of pragmatism. Trimble and his supporters, it might be said, are more pragmatically attuned to contemporary political realities than are their opponents. If the Belfast Agreement is as good a deal as unionists can hope to get, then to oppose it is self-defeating for unionism. But such pragmatic considerations, welcome as they are, may not be enough to enable unionism to work the arrangements the agreement anticipates.

The difficulty is that it is hard to make sense, within the terms of either cultural or liberal unionism, of the Belfast Agreement's incorporation of an Irish dimension in its recommended solution to the problem of Northern Ireland. It is not only proposals for North–South institutions that fit uneasily here, but also proposals specific to the North: parity of esteem for an Irish identity, reform of the Royal Ulster Constabulary (RUC), early release of paramilitary prisoners, unionists sharing government with representatives of Sinn Féin. The conspicuous squirming we have witnessed among pro-agreement unionists at the mere mention of these proposals underlines the point: their support of the agreement arguably comes at the cost of coherence. And the danger is that this may prove a very high cost to pay, since it makes pro-agreement unionism perpetually vulnerable to attack from other unionists.

Succinctly put, the problem for pro-agreement unionism is that many of the new practices to which it is committed cannot be reconciled with its theory. Without at all suggesting that various of the practices envisaged by the Belfast Agreement are unproblematic, there is in my view a clear case here for abandoning the theory. Despite David Trimble's reluctance to say so, I think we very much do need a new unionism: one that cannot be held to ransom by the Orange Order or other atavistic elements within the unionist fold. If the agreement is to succeed, and if unionism is to contribute to the creation of a Northern Ireland worth having for all of its citizens, unionism has to transcend its familiar cultural and liberal frameworks. In chapter five I indicate how it may do so by embracing an alternative framework which I call 'civic unionist'. Civic unionism prioritises making Northern Ireland work rather than defending the Union. It regards self-government as a primary political good and it requires public institutions that command the allegiance of all citizens. On its terms, Northern Ireland is mischaracterised by traditional unionists and nationalists: as either merely a site of the Union or as the lost green field awaiting return to its proper owner. Northern Ireland, rather, is better depicted as a site where British and Irish factors intermingle and clash and demand mutual recognition. This depiction, together with a commitment to making our society work and a prioritisation of the goods of self-government and citizen belonging, offer a framework within which the Belfast Agreement appears intelligible and workable, whatever the practical difficulties it is likely to encounter. Civic unionism is not at all distracted by attacks from anti-agreement unionists and it provides better reasons than those presently on offer within unionism for being pro-agreement. And that is why I think again that the argument of this book continues to be deeply relevant.

NORMAN PORTER
BELFAST
JULY 1998

PREFACE

Social and political life in Northern Ireland is in a sorry condition. Some say it always has been; few dispute that it has been since 1969. Its condition is sorry not only because many citizens experience serious social deprivation but also because Northern Ireland is a deeply divided society. Conflicting political aspirations lie at the heart of its divisions and sectarianism remains an ugly blight on the social and political landscape producing as it does practices of violence, discrimination and segregation. The reality of sectarianism makes trust among opposing political actors a scarce commodity and contributes to an impasse that characterises many aspects of political affairs. One result is a politics of constitutional standoff between unionists and nationalists which drains politics of much of its meaning for citizens. It also cramps political possibilities and inhibits progress beyond the current form of undemocratic government prevailing in Northern Ireland. All political parties express dissatisfaction with the present status quo, but it persists because agreement on its alternative is extremely hard to find.

In this book I ask if unionism – the political creed subscribed to by a majority of citizens in Northern Ireland – possesses the resources to help alter such a lamentable state of affairs. Is there a unionist vision of the future of Northern Ireland capable of inspiring confidence among citizens and encouraging reconciliation with non-unionists? I suggest that there is, once we rethink what unionism means and stands for. To rethink unionism is to subject standard modes of unionist thought and conduct to critical scrutiny. These modes need replacing because they betray narrow views of politics and yield practical outcomes which worsen the divisions that plague social and political life in Northern Ireland and stifle the possibility of reaching agreement with non-unionists on permanent arrangements of government. I argue that alternative modes of unionist thought and practice which inspire an alternative vision of Northern Ireland are required, modes which embrace a broad view of politics and encourage practices designed to overcome the acute social and political divisions separating unionists from non-unionists.

Two points are worth emphasising about the kind of exercise my rethinking of unionism turns out to be. First, it is a rethinking that starts with unionists' own views of themselves, their ways of life and their basic beliefs. I take traditional unionism seriously on its own terms. Second, I try to rethink it by asking philosophical as well as political questions of its fundamental claims. Doing so runs the risk of pursuing lines of inquiry which may be unfamiliar to some readers and which they may find are not always easy to follow. But it is a risk that has to be taken, since it is only through philosophical reflections of a certain sort that we are able to become properly clear about the coherence or incoherence, the plausibility or implausibility, of what unionism has to offer. Besides, the philosophical questions I raise always have a practical point: to enable us to see better what is going on in our social and political lives. Our perceptions of what is practically possible are shaped by the horizon within which we view politics. Standard unionist practice is closed off to attractive political possibilities partly because it is constrained by narrow horizons, but I am convinced that a broadened horizon and a new set of political practices for unionism are possible to envisage, and it is these that point to the emergence of a Northern Ireland with a way of life worth having for all citizens.

In my account of the contemporary circumstances of unionism I suggest that these circumstances are largely comprised of challenges to unionism emanating from the reality of unionist disunity, from the drift of the British and the Irish governments' policies and initiatives, and from forces and trends within Northern Ireland. In my view there are three types of unionist response to these challenges: cultural unionism, liberal unionism and civic unionism. Cultural unionism is rooted in a Protestant-British way of life and operates within a political–philosophical horizon in which concepts of liberty and loyalty play a cardinal role. I argue that it is an inadequate position beset by practical and theoretical difficulties. It relies on a notion of Britishness unrecognisable in Great Britain, offers a political deal for Northern Ireland guaranteed of rejection by non-unionists, exaggerates the role of Protestantism in the maintenance of civil and religious liberties, and invokes problematic ideas of conditional loyalty. On the other hand, the liberal unionist position strips unionism of its cultural Protestant connotations, aspires to a political way of life shared in common with the rest of the United Kingdom, and moves within a liberal political–philosophical horizon. It too is not up to scratch – underestimating cultural influences in politics, it inclines towards an integrationist solution to Northern Ireland's problems which flies in the face of Anglo-Irish policy, misunderstands why nationalists are alienated from the Northern state, and trades in concepts of rights, freedom and citizenship which reveal unduly narrow and procedural political predispositions.

I turn to a third position which I call 'civic unionism'. This is the one I advocate as an alternative to the more familiar cultural and liberal unionist positions. Civic unionism anticipates a way of life in which both the Britishness and the Irishness of Northern Ireland are recognised, and structures of democracy and justice are established. It is located within a political–philosophical horizon which accommodates questions of cultural identity, liberal emphases on the entitlements of individuals and a substantive understanding of politics in which the practice of dialogue is central. I argue that the civic unionist position enables us to deal fairly with issues of parity of esteem and to embrace broadly interpreted concepts of citizenship and freedom. And it is this position that can open up political possibilities of a future Northern Ireland in which all citizens could have a meaningful stake.

NORMAN PORTER
BELFAST
JULY 1996

ACKNOWLEDGEMENTS

This book began life as a hastily constructed seminar paper delivered to staff and postgraduate students of the Politics Department at University College Dublin. I am grateful to those participants in the seminar whose questions and constructive criticisms made me think more clearly about what I was claiming, and especially to Niamh Hardiman who cajoled me into delivering the paper in the first place. The subsequent decision to write a book on unionism received a further impetus from the discussion provoked by my written submission and oral presentation to the Forum for Peace and Reconciliation at Dublin Castle in October 1995. I am indebted to everyone who contributed to that discussion, and not least to those who disagreed most with the line I was pressing. I am particularly grateful to the former Deputy Secretary-General of the Forum, Tim O'Connor, whose generous comments and enthusiasm for the idea of the book helped convince me it was worth pursuing. The ideas continued in the book are the fruit of discussions conducted over many years with many people, including Rob Bell, Bill Brugger, Steve Gadd, Martin Griffiths, Niamh Hardiman, James McEvoy, Brendan Moran, Dessie O'Hagan, Damian

O'Leary, David Plant, Vicki Spencer and Michael Sullivan. I owe all of them for their insights and friendship, even though probably none would agree entirely, and some perhaps not at all, with the argument I develop.

Intellectually, I owe most to Charles Taylor, whom I first encountered during his term as Chichele Professor of Social and Political Theory at Oxford, and whom I was fortunate enough to have as a D.Phil. supervisor in the late 1970s. Through various conversations, his memorable lectures and his many writings, he has helped to shape the way in which I understand the relationship between politics and philosophy. It is an understanding that runs through this book.

Other debts have also been incurred. I owe much to my late father, Norman Porter, with whom I enjoyed many calm and heated discussions on Northern Irish politics over the years. Were he alive today he would find plenty here to disagree with, but he would understand better than most, I suspect, what I am trying to get at and why it matters. Another debt is owed to Blackstaff Press. One of the pleasures of writing the book has been dealing with its staff. Their encouragement, interest and unflagging sense of humour have kept me going when it seemed easier to give up, and the fact that the book has appeared at all is a testimony to their considerable human (and not merely technical) skills. My greatest debt is to my family: to Shantala, Simon and Luke for putting up with more than it is reasonable to expect and, above all, to Lis, without whose patience, tolerance, good sense, sound advice, love and irreplaceable friendship the book would never have been written.

1

BAGGAGE AND PURPOSES

It is not hard to paint a gloomy picture of unionism's destiny. It
is scarcely an exaggeration to say that Ulster unionism is undergoing the most difficult period of its history since the partition of
Ireland and faces a future that is radically uncertain. Traditional
unionist solaces of unity, nationalist resignation and British support are no longer available: the so-called unionist family is
internally divided, nationalist opposition to unionism in Northern
Ireland has never been as well organised and effective as it is
currently, and there is markedly declining sympathy in Britain for
the cause of unionism. Perhaps we are living in the 'twilight of the
Union'[1] of Northern Ireland and Great Britain; perhaps the game
is up for unionism. Most unionists, though conceding that things
are pretty bad for them, refuse to admit anything of the sort. But
perhaps unionists' refusal to acknowledge that unionism is in a
state of terminal political and ideological decline amounts to little
more than a failure of nerve.

It is much harder, though not impossible, to paint a bright
picture of unionism's destiny. The changed circumstances of
unionist disunity, nationalist confidence and British indifference,
it might be said, offer not so much reasons for despair as

opportunities for redefinition and renewal. Perhaps they open up fresh space for manoeuvre which may enable unionism to develop a positive self-image unshackled by narrow Protestant or British exclusivism; perhaps they facilitate the disposal of baggage that inhibited the creation of a polity in which national- ists also felt at home; perhaps they suggest possibilities of the emergence of a new Northern Ireland rather than of impending Irish unity.

In this book I want to present a version of the bright picture. In doing so, three points should be stressed from the outset. First, my attraction to this picture is not prompted by the belief that the gloomy picture sketched above is its only alternative. I do not doubt that there are other possibilities that fall between what I am calling the bright and the gloomy. I recognise, for example, that unionist resilience is such that unionism remains capable of finding a bottom-line unity to oppose the imposition of a united Ireland; that the significance of nationalist confidence can be overestimated if not considered in the light of what it can hope to achieve in the absence of unionist agreement to significant change in Northern Ireland; and that British indifference to unionism is one thing but Westminster expelling Northern Ireland from the United Kingdom against the wishes of the majority of its inhabitants is quite another. Traditional unionists still have cards to play.

Second, my endorsement of the bright picture is not just an adaptation of unionism to my perceptions of those current realities that I think most unionists are reluctant to confront. It is not driven by a hard-headed realism that disguises a lament for the way unionism once was in the world we have lost. What I believe an appraisal of current realities does prompt, rather, is a rethinking of traditional unionist positions – positions which, on close inspection, not only appear inadequate to the circumstances of Northern Ireland in the 1990s, but have been problematic all along. My commitment to the bright picture, in short, is inspired by the conviction that unionism has an opportunity to remake itself into something it has never been. This means, of course, that what I am referring to as bright will undoubtedly strike many unionists not merely as gloomy but as deeply dark. Traditional modes of thought and action, especially within unionist circles, are not easily overturned.

Third, my version of the bright picture is drawn primarily in terms of ideas. Although of necessity I have things to say about possible practical arrangements for good government in Northern Ireland, my principal focus is on patterns of thought that serve either to open up or close off the sort of practical arrangements I consider advisable. Besides, I remain flexible about the precise form such arrangements should take, since, for reasons that will become evident, I think they are best worked out through dialogue among the major players in Northern Ireland's politics. My reflections on unionism and its future operate mostly in the realm of political philosophy.

It is probably obvious already that this book is written from an engaged perspective, that it does not aspire to be objective or neutral towards its subject. Accordingly, I should reveal a little more about the engaged perspective from which I write. Or, put another way, it may be helpful to display from the beginning the nature of the baggage I carry with me in writing this book. I attempt to do so now in the form of some personal, political and philosophical notes which may indicate both my orientation to unionism and my purposes in inquiring into it.

BAGGAGE AND PURPOSES

PERSONAL NOTES

This is a book born of frustration – frustration principally with the conduct and course of unionist politics, especially since the paramilitary ceasefires of the late summer and autumn of 1994. Such a sense of frustration and my efforts to deal with it – by suggesting how unionist politics could proceed along different lines, and v ʃ they should – become initially intelligible against the backdrop of aspects of my personal narrative.

I was born into a staunchly Protestant and unionist family in 1952. I spent the first eighteen years of my life in Belfast before emigrating with most of my family to Australia in 1970. My father was in certain respects the most influential figure in my life during my teenage years. He was an Orangeman, a Blackman, an Apprentice Boy, but never a Freemason. He represented Clifton at Stormont during the 1950s as an Independent Unionist. He lost the seat under controversial circumstances in 1958 and was defeated again – this time more cleanly and decisively – when standing for the seat of Duncairn as an anti-O'Neillite unionist in the late 1960s. Had he won Duncairn it is unlikely that we would ever have gone to Australia. Towards the end of the 1940s, Ian Paisley and he had set up the National Union of Protestants and in the early 1950s my father became director of the Evangelical Protestant Society. He was described by Michael Farrell, with probably only a touch of exaggeration, as being 'active on the extreme fringes of Unionism'.[2] I inherited from him an intense identification with an ultra-Protestantism that I took to be synonymous with 'true' unionism, but which in my case was not tempered by his evangelical faith. Prior to leaving for Australia I was by any account an extreme loyalist and an explicit Protestant bigot.

The move to Australia changed my life and, most relevant here, my attitudes to the politics of Northern Ireland. These attitudes were transformed quite early on, initially through the impact made on an impressionable teenager by exposure to a cultural and political way of life from which sectarianism had been more or less expunged. Australia quickly represented to me the chance of a fresh start: continuing in this new context to define one's allegiances in ultra-Protestant/unionist categories seemed more than faintly ridiculous. Northern Ireland and its quarrels appeared almost bizarre, and in every sense a world away. If that had been the end of the matter, of course, I would not be living in Northern Ireland now or writing this book.

Northern Ireland and my interest in its affairs and attachment to its culture and politics were not so easily disposed of. After my initial swift rejection of them they returned to puzzle and haunt me. They did so as I began to read and reflect in earnest about politics, philosophy and history, first as an undergraduate in Adelaide during the early and mid-1970s, then as a postgraduate in Oxford during the late 1970s, as a lecturer in Adelaide again through the 1980s and well into the 1990s, and finally as a dweller on the 'edge of unionism'[3] back in Belfast once more since July 1994. Over this period I regained a sense of identity with Northern Ireland that was more subtle and nuanced than the one I left behind in 1970, but which, as I now find, fits uneasily with standard unionist expressions of belonging. It was a sense of identity, however vaguely perceived at times, that disrupted my life in Australia to the point where I decided to return with my family to live in Belfast in order to come to terms with it.

Shortly after my return the ceasefires were declared and I joined the Ulster Unionist Party (UUP) and became involved in the establishment of the Unionist Labour Group. These acts reveal something about my politics, no doubt, but not nearly as much as might be expected, as I hope will soon be clear. Although an official member of the unionist mainstream, I continue to think of myself as perching on the edge of unionism. In truth, if I had not joined the Ulster Unionist Party as soon as I did after my return, I would never have bothered: I was sufficiently innocent at the time to believe that in the new circumstances of a peaceful Northern Ireland, unionist politics would witness an exploration of creative possibilities that I relished being part of and contributing to. That innocence has vanished and has been replaced by a deep-seated frustration at how stilted political thinking within unionism actually is. Extreme external pressure aside, I suspect the only language capable of disturbing unionist complacency and rigidity is that of electoral rebuffal. But to allow this suspicion to brood is to succumb to a defeatism that stultifies genuinely critical and imaginative thinking. In an attempt to stave off such defeatism and to deal more positively with my dissatisfaction with the current politics of unionism, I offer a book that refuses to accept the wisdom of the unionist status quo. Thus it is not misleading to say that a major (personal) purpose of the book is to clarify why I am frustrated with the standard fare unionism offers to the citizens of Northern Ireland and, beyond that, to discover what sense I can make of my decision to come 'home'.

POLITICAL NOTES

With regard to my political predispositions, two considerations may shed preliminary light on where I think the main problems with current unionism lie, and also give an indication of emphases that recur throughout the book.

A familiar complaint about political affairs in Northern Ireland is that they suffer from a certain abnormality which unionism is culpable in encouraging. Normal political concerns, it is assumed, have to do with social and economic questions and not with endless constitutional wrangling or disputes over conflicting identities. I agree only in part.

I accept that social and economic questions are important and that unionism has prevented them from receiving the attention they are due in Northern Ireland. It is undeniable, for instance, that unionists are too readily inclined to play the constitutional card to the detriment of other cards in the political pack. At times there have been arguably good reasons for an almost exclusive playing of this card, but at other times the playing of it has been manifestly opportunistic.[4] Whether for good or opportunistic reasons, the price exacted by unionism's constitutional overkill has been inordinately high. For one thing, it has stifled the development of non-sectarian labour politics in Northern Ireland, even if this is a drawback that bothers some considerably more than others.[5] For another, it has created within unionism a very short-sighted political view. Not only are the mainstream unionist parties bereft of any distinctive social and economic policies or objectives, but their tacit notion that a good feed of constitutionalism is sufficient to satisfy the dietary needs of Northern Ireland's citizens betrays an impoverished conception of politics. Quite simply, it is implausible to suppose that political thinking and organisation are reducible to, or that other issues of socio-political concern are *always* subservient to, maintaining Northern Ireland's constitutional position within the United Kingdom. Suppositions of this sort invite a flight of talent and imagination from political life and indifference among ordinary citizens. This is not to say that such a flight and such indifference are solely the fault of unionism. They also reflect the political peculiarities and inertia produced by over twenty years of direct rule from Westminster for which all the major political actors in Northern Ireland, and not least successive British governments, bear some responsibility.

It is impossible to deny, then, that the political situation in Northern Ireland displays abnormalities that can be traced in part to the door of unionism. But it does not thereby follow that socio-economic matters alone define the parameters of politics. On the contrary, even if we were to imagine the seemingly unimaginable – a constitutionally secure, agreed Northern Ireland – it would not necessarily mean that political attention would focus overwhelmingly on socio-economic affairs. The recent experience of other Western democracies certainly suggests otherwise. For example, liberal-democratic polities with settled constitutions, uncontested boundaries and an evident bias toward the primacy of socio-economic politics are also and increasingly becoming sites of a developing 'politics of identity' that cannot be accounted for in socio-economic terms.[6] Such a politics of identity assumes various forms, including those of gender, ethnicity, religion, and language, which span the divide between so-called left and right on socio-economic interests. What matters politically to people is evidently more than socio-economic politics alone can capture. Accordingly, it is feasible to argue that a politics of identity touches upon an irreducible feature of collective human life which appears in various guises. The dominant guise in which it appears in Northern Ireland may indeed be perplexing, but the fact of its appearance should be a cause neither of wonder nor of despair. Wrestling with political issues of identity is not in itself a sign of abnormality – though wrestling with virtually nothing else is.

On my terms, then, normal politics includes not only socio-economic issues but also, among other things, constitutional issues and issues of identity. These terms do not imply, however, that unionism is merely to be faulted for its relative neglect of social and economic concerns. Questions must be asked too about its handling of those issues that have defined its *raison d'être*. Here the political paucity of unionism is revealed in relation to its conduct and vision.

It is convenient, but short-sighted, to believe that the problem with the conduct of unionist politics consists solely in the tactical inastuteness of unionists. If this were the case, the solution in principle lies readily at hand: in the implementation of a crash training course for unionist politicians, say, and in the acquisition of better public relations.[7] Such a solution has a point, since unionists do often appear strategically inept and have been pretty awful at selling their message to an uncomprehending world audience. It is a solution that the UUP, for example, seems now intent on pursuing under the new leadership of David Trimble.[8] But the deficiencies in the conduct of unionist politics, unfortunately, are more fundamental than poor tactics or public relations and thus are not so easily fixed. They are rooted, rather, in a very limited image of what politics is about.

Put another way, unionism suffers from a lack of vision. In part this is a consequence of the minimalism of unionism's creed, which insists on little more than a commitment from its adherents to strengthen and maintain the Union. What shape the Union itself might take, or what goals might define its politics, are matters left to the British government of the day to decide. Besides seeking a constitutional guarantee, the most that unionists have required is that Northern Ireland's particular security needs and economic interests are adequately catered for. If these requirements or priorities have defined and circumscribed unionism's horizons, an attachment to cultural – and in cases religious – Protestantism has confined the range of its appeal within Northern Ireland. Although the UUP is now making belated moves to loosen such an attachment, by undoing its formal tie with the Orange Order, its efforts so far have been ambiguous and less than convincing. Taken together, unionism's restricted priorities and partial appeal suggest that mainstream unionism has scarcely a vision worth speaking of for the future of Northern Ireland. And that is largely why political conduct based on secrecy and a narrow proceduralism – exemplified by James Molyneaux's reduction of politics to working behind the scenes at Westminster and to seeking changes to the rules under which Northern Ireland is governed – seemed unobjectionable in unionist quarters so long as it was able to produce the right results, principally the security of the Union.[9] The fact that Molyneaux's tactics were not perceived to produce the desired results undoubtedly led to his replacement as leader of the UUP by Trimble and prompted questions about the efficacy of this brand of political conduct. But one suspects that such questions would barely have featured, and Molyneaux would still be leader, if the British and Irish governments' proposals for Northern Ireland contained in *Frameworks for the Future* had been more congenial to unionists.[10] If this suspicion is accurate, the fact that such questions are being raised should not blind us to the fundamental point, namely that the problem is not merely bad results but, more important, the lack of a political vision that would never have tolerated a politics of secrecy and narrow proceduralism in the first place.

In recent times, especially following the election of the United Kingdom Unionist Party candidate Robert McCartney as MP for North Down in a by-election in June 1995, talk of a new vision has been revitalised in certain unionist circles, even if it is opposed in others.[11] McCartney, a major catalyst of this sort of talk, envisages an inclusive, liberal unionism unencumbered by the cultural-Protestant baggage of traditional unionism.[12] I examine the liberal unionist vision later in the book. My preliminary assessment is that for all its welcome noises about inclusivism, it fails, like its traditional predecessor, not only to address adequately the political possibilities currently available in Northern Ireland but also to articulate a vision in which political conduct would be transformed. Its grasp of the politically possible seems slight because it fails to reckon seriously with the reasons why nationalists are so disenchanted with the political structures of Northern Ireland, with why this society is as deeply divided as it is. And, despite impressions to the contrary, its vision offers no guarantee that political conduct will proceed in the direction of what I am calling a politics of openness. For example, as I argue at length in Chapter 4, the expectations of openness raised by liberal unionism's advocacy of 'equal citizenship' are quickly dashed once we realise that it operates with a very thin notion of what citizenship consists in – a notion that, in particular, does not rate political activity highly at all.

Ill-conceived conduct which undervalues the virtue of active citizenship and which is tied to a minimalist and an insufficiently accommodating political vision poses deep problems for unionism. A corrective, I shall argue, lies in the articulation of a vision intimately connected to a politics of openness: one that puts a premium on the development of a decent civic life in Northern Ireland, recognises the entitlements of nationalists to have a meaningful stake in the society's institutions and practices, has adequate measures installed for the protection of individual and group rights, relates social and economic questions to wider considerations of social justice, and defines unionism in a positive rather than in a negative or an escapist manner.

In view of these brief reflections on politics and the problems of unionism's conduct and vision, two major political purposes of the book become clearer. The first is to show *why* unionism needs an enlarged vision of the scope and nature of politics in general, and of the peculiar requirements of the politics of Northern Ireland in particular. Without such a vision, unionism makes do with paltry forms of political conduct which betray a narrowness of mind and a miserliness of spirit, and which serve only to perpetuate the aridity of local political life and to alienate nationalists. The second purpose is to indicate *how* it is possible to entertain a suitably enlarged vision without ceasing to be a unionist, even if doing so entails revising supposedly canonical versions of what being a unionist means.

PHILOSOPHICAL NOTES

These political purposes are reinforced by specific philosophical predispositions which help to explain from another angle the approach I adopt in my analysis of unionism.

The philosophical predispositions at work in this book are most aptly described as interpretive or 'hermeneutical' in nature.[13] As I appropriate it here, this philosophical term of description connotes two central theses, a general one concerning the conditions of understanding, and a more specific one concerning an image of humans as self-interpreting beings.

A succinct formulation of the 'conditions of understanding' thesis runs as follows: understanding, in the realm of human affairs, refers to acts undertaken by historically situated agents seeking to uncover constituent features of their own situation or the situation of others. This formulation may be amplified by two related claims. One underscores the inescapably historical condition of understanding: all acts of understanding operate within some historical horizon of meaning which may be qualified, challenged or even replaced by another, but not transcended through ascension to a 'view from nowhere';[14] and while some horizons may yield a richer understanding than others, no horizon may plausibly claim a special status that loosens its attachment to historical circumstances of some sort and makes it immune from critical scrutiny. There is not available, in other words, any privileged or ahistorical vantage point from which we may deliver a transparent account of the 'true' character of historical beliefs and practices. The historicality of understanding cannot be so neatly bypassed.

The other claim deals with the types of critical probing often associated with attempts to understand what is going on in various tracts of human experience: illuminating types of probing are those that manifest an appreciation of the historicality of understanding and so resist the temptation of resorting to supposedly neutral criteria, or of canonising the criteria of one's own horizon, in order to give a definitive judgement of historical beliefs and practices. There are two assumptions at play in this claim. The first is that abandoning privileged or ahistorical criteria does not imply abandoning critical standards *per se*. The second assumption is that critical standards are integral to acts of understanding that endeavour to move beyond mere description to include, for example, elements of comparison and evaluation. These elements seem indispensable, and are arguably implicit even in purely 'descriptive' analyses, once we allow that understanding is comprised of a series of interpretive acts that have to do with becoming clearer about a particular horizon that defines the parameters of significance for those who share it, with making initially strange views and actions less opaque to us, with assessing how well or how poorly certain beliefs and practices fit within prescribed parameters, and with inquiring how modes of thought and action characteristic of another horizon bear upon modes we customarily take for granted. If it is allowed that these sorts of interpretive acts are constitutive of understanding, then critical standards are being invoked by the types of probing upon which good interpretation relies, that is, types that aim to discern, for example: (1) whether the actions and views of those subscribing to a specific horizon can be consistently contained within its parameters; (2) whether inconsistencies point not just to instances of individual or group misapprehension or wilfulness, but perhaps to restrictions of the horizon itself and so suggest that a radical overhaul, or a change of horizon, is necessary; and (3) whether a horizon is sufficiently open to facilitate changes in the world in which it is placed and to welcome 'dialogue' with different horizons, whether it is capable of rationally withstanding what such honest encounters may entail by amending and broadening its parameters, or, whether it proves too rigid to adjust to challenges and requires ditching altogether. The point is that these sorts of probes imply critical standards of judgement and rationality that are historically attuned and thus compatible with the situated nature of understanding.

My second central thesis, concerning an image of humans as self-interpreting beings, owes a great deal to the thesis on the conditions of understanding outlined above, but provides a sharper focus to the question of how individuals and groups stand in relation to themselves when trying to sort out what matters to them and why. It admits of the following formulation: our identities as individuals or groups are constituted by self-interpretations that derive from involvement in various socio-cultural contexts and are articulated through interactions with others. This thesis contains three principal facets, each of which warrants brief elaboration.

First, the idea that self-interpretations are constitutive of our identities implies that we cannot step outside them in the hope of seeing ourselves as we 'truly' are. It is through self-interpretations that we are oriented to the world and ourselves, that we acquire the contours within which we find our way around and work out what matters to us. This is not to suggest that self-interpretations remain static. Individually and collectively it is common to strive for more adequate interpretations, ones that express more authentically who we are or wish to be. The issue is how the quest for authenticity is understood. It is, I am suggesting, wrongly perceived as a drive to an interpretation-free state in which we appear translucent to ourselves, but rightly approached as an open-ended quest for better interpretations which yield deeper insights into who and what we are, and for forms of life capable of accommodating such insights. Without succumbing to acute self-delusion, it is hard to imagine a time when we think that the quest for authenticity is complete and that we have reached a state of total self-clarity.

Second, to say that self-interpretations derive from socio-cultural involvements is to deny that there can be such a thing as a purely private self-definition. It is also to intimate that our involvements shape us in myriad ways we cannot expect to become finally clear about, which is another reason why an aspiration to utter self-clarity seems so impossible. This intimation does not infer that self-interpretations are reducible to passive receptions of beliefs and practices. On the contrary, self-interpretations entail acts of appropriation whereby we make certain beliefs and practices our own. And these acts, in turn, imply a capacity of critical reflection which enables us to discriminate among the various beliefs and practices our culture and its traditions make available to us. Admitting the crucial roles played by appropriation and critical reflection in the business of self-interpretation should not, however, occlude the fact that such roles are carried out against a background of cultural practices that we can never hope to be thoroughly explicit about or completely detached from.

Third, self-interpretations, because they are indebted to socio-cultural involvements and are not private or detached accomplishments, are typically articulated and rearticulated through interaction with other interlocutors. Their primary medium is a shared language. And among the forms of language, dialogue is paradigmatic here. That is to say, it is ideally via dialogue that we become clearer about who we are, that we express what is important to us, that we check out the intelligibility and appropriateness of our goals and purposes, and so forth. Dialogue is the vehicle *par excellence* of the search for authentic self-interpretations, not least because it is constituted by relations of reciprocity and recognition. Such relations are so important because their absence goes a long way towards explaining why individually or collectively we often find ourselves struggling with frustrating self-interpretations, perhaps ones that demean us. Or, put another way, denial of opportunities to have our voices heard and a lack of recognition or misrecognition by others can inflict real damage on our sense of ourselves, as we perhaps internalise the negative self-images that they imply. And that is why dialogue presents a model vehicle for self-interpretations: it makes central a recognition of the integrity of the other interlocutor(s), it operates according to a principle of reciprocity, it allows us to engage in the process of articulating *who* we are that is crucial to the development of a healthy self-interpretation, and it opens us up to creative possibilities for the future.

My two central theses, of the historicality of understanding and of humans as self-interpreting beings, are mutually reinforcing. Both recognise the human condition as murky and yet as something that can be illuminated through historical, reflective and dialogical exercises that both shed light on our past and present and open us up to our future. Together the theses suggest that the horizons and interpretations we depend upon to make sense of ourselves should not be cut off from alternative horizons and interpretations, but, rather, that it is through openness to and interchange with alternatives that we are protected against dogmatic hubris and kept alert to the limitations of our own apprehensions of the world, society, and ourselves.

In addition to shaping the broad interpretive account of unionism I offer in the next chapter, my philosophical predispositions have political significance inasmuch as their presence is evident in the main arguments I want to advance. They run through the positive argument hinted at in the political vision alluded to earlier, as well as shaping the negative argument I develop against standard unionist outlooks.

In terms of the positive argument, a hermeneutic, or interpretive, influence is revealed in two major ways. There is, first, a discernible hermeneutic bent to the prominence I accord to the features of openness and dialogue. It is, of course, true to say that these features may be emphasised for strictly political reasons independent of philosophical considerations of any kind. In a divided society such as Northern Ireland it may be reckoned that enduring peace and stability are unlikely achievements without concessions being made in the direction of openness and dialogue, since it is too hazardous to play a game that continually closes out disagreeable voices and refuses to engage with one's political opponents. Pragmatic reckoning along such lines deserves to be taken seriously, especially within Northern Ireland. But I suspect that practices implied by openness and dialogue require rather more, in order to be viable and sustainable. For one thing, their pragmatic appeal is ill equipped to move obdurate unionists who hold out against these practices on the pretext of subscribing to principles that are allegedly not susceptible to pragmatic bartering. A hermeneutic construal of openness and dialogue, whilst not guaranteed any more success than a purely pragmatic construal, is nevertheless better designed to deal with such inflexibility. It has the advantage of tackling head-on unionist obduracy's underlying rationale. Instead of asking unionists to compromise, to bend their principles a little for the sake of peace and harmony, it disputes whether the principles in question are plausibly or coherently invoked at all. It poses an intellectual challenge that stubborn unionists cannot conveniently sidestep by arrogating rhetoric of the moral high ground. And this difference between pragmatic and hermeneutic commitments to practices associated with openness and dialogue extends into another of even greater consequence. Hermeneutically speaking, these practices are wrongly understood in pragmatic categories – as merely convenient devices of social and political life – which imply that under certain circumstances they could be satisfactorily substituted by other, more effective, devices. On the contrary, practices associated with openness and dialogue represent indispensable media of interaction, with an inherent potential to transform the views of those participating in them and to create new possibilities for a society in which they are institutionalised.

Such practices cannot be substituted without enormous loss to the quality of civic life.

There is also a pronounced hermeneutic slant to the conceptions of reason and language I draw upon to show how a dialogical politics of openness offers a fresh political vision for unionism. These conceptions are employed to overcome problems that threaten to undermine from the outset the efficacy of political dialogue in Northern Ireland. I refer, in particular, to the difficulty posed by the notion that unionism and nationalism constitute incommensurable discourses, and the challenge suggested by traditional unionism's language of last resort, namely its appeal to 'feelings' of Britishness that are purportedly unavailable to rational scrutiny and therefore unassailable.

In relation to the negative argument I construct in several stages, my philosophical predispositions are conspicuous in two of the principal modes of criticism I use to disturb deep-seated forms of unionist thought and practice. One mode focuses on the *internal* coherence and consistency of these forms. It accepts that they reflect entrenched self-understandings that have been shaped by multifaceted historical experiences and memories, and tries to take them seriously on their own terms. This mode involves recognising the sense of meaning received forms transmit to unionists who cannot imagine functioning independently of them. But such recognition does not entail uncritical acceptance of the views and practices they legitimise. To resort to the language I employed earlier, I consider the internal adequacy of the horizons of meaning and self-interpretations upon which unionists typically rely. In doing so, I argue that difficulties are confronted here that cannot be easily avoided; that the location of unionism within, say, horizons of Protestantism or liberalism proves ill-fated from whichever angle it is considered. It is ill-fated, first, since neither Protestantism nor liberalism can be convincingly appropriated for purely unionist purposes. And it is ill-fated, second, because unionist thought and practice cannot be satisfactorily contained within the parameters such horizons make available. Internal considerations of this sort prompt the conclusion that there are strains within the dominant horizons of unionism and that, as a consequence, mainstream unionist self-interpretations are under severe pressure in performing the tasks required of them.

This conclusion is supported by a second mode of criticism which examines the capacity of standard unionist horizons/self-interpretations to accommodate *external* factors, such as changes in the social and political world in which they are situated and the presence of competing horizons/self-interpretations. This mode of critical probing demonstrates unambiguously, I shall claim, that the common paradigms of unionism are too severely flawed to be redeemed and that unionism needs new forms of self-interpretation.

I should add that these modes of criticism are not developed separately but intermingle in the analysis that follows. Together, and in conjunction with the appropriation of hermeneutic emphases in my positive argument, they indicate another way of describing the purpose of writing this book: to show the possibility of fruitfully redefining unionism by drawing on philosophical insights of a certain kind. Unionists, as well as their commentators and critics, too infrequently appreciate this possibility and therefore miss out on lines of reflection and inquiry capable of taking us beyond the sterile quandaries in which too many discussions of unionism end.

ORGANISATION

Having declared the baggage accompanying me in my journey into unionism, and having introduced the major arguments I want to develop and the purposes I aim to achieve, it only remains now to sketch briefly the lines along which this study is organised.

In Chapter 2, I attempt a wide-ranging interpretation of contemporary unionism which is conducted in two major moves. The first delineates more fully the social and political background against which my analysis takes place. I suggest that the circumstances in which unionism currently finds itself – as defined by divisions within its own house, by external pressures from the British and Irish governments and the trend towards 'Europeanisation', and by the changing nature of Northern Ireland's society – pose challenges that cannot be ignored. In the second move I identify three types of unionist response to these circumstances and their challenges. I show how each employs different rankings of the challenges, and how such rankings imply different priorities and reflect different understandings of unionist identity. I maintain that conflicts over identity are crucial and that they are related to different ways of life which I refer to as 'Ulster unionist', 'British' and 'Northern Irish' respectively. I also contend that three unionist political theories – which I call 'cultural', 'liberal' and 'civic' – emerge from the different understandings of identity and ways of life. I deal separately with each of these theories in subsequent chapters.

In Chapter 3, I attend to a 'cultural unionist' theory. This is the most disparate theory of the three, and advocates of some version of it are found across the spectrum of unionist politics. Cultural unionism typically involves a defence of the integrity of Northern Ireland and an advocacy of devolved government within the framework of the United Kingdom. It is underwritten by a range of cultural, religious and political attachments. I examine the links posited between these attachments and unionism as expressed through various types of Protestantism and understandings of Britishness. I also consider how certain cultural unionists seek an intellectual justification of their position by invoking specific theories of loyalty and liberty. I maintain that although unionism cannot survive for long without a cultural component, the central claims about Northern Ireland, Protestantism, Britishness and political theory advanced within this conceptual scheme are deeply problematic. Internally they are not sufficiently coherent, and they prove unable to accommodate external features of their world and the challenge of other positions.

In Chapter 4, I deal with a second theory, that of 'liberal unionism'. This theory is not confined to any one unionist party but it is most likely to find adherents within sections of the UUP, and has a popular figurehead in the person of Robert McCartney. It also attracts support from various academics sympathetic to unionism. Liberal unionism is more theoretically sophisticated than cultural unionism and is articulated in more elaborate conceptual categories. I discuss its main claims in terms of its view of the relationship between Northern Ireland and the rest of the United Kingdom, and its conceptions of freedom, rights, citizenship and identity. I argue that liberal unionism contains insights that deserve to be highlighted, but that it suffers from an impractical vision of the future of Northern Ireland and an association with a restrictive form of liberalism which render suspect its handling of those concepts it singles out for special attention. It appears too rigid in its treatment of alternative horizons, it underestimates the significance of cultural dimensions of politics, and it is too doctrinaire in its interpretation of the circumstances in which unionism is placed. It manifests failings of internal incoherence and external blindness.

In Chapter 5, I turn to a third theory which I call 'civic unionist', and which I contend succeeds where the others fail.[15] I begin by outlining its rationale and vision of a new Northern Ireland. I show how this rationale and vision are amplified by drawing on concepts of recognition, citizenship and freedom. Throughout I claim that civic unionism offers a political vision that is not only more conciliatory to non-unionists, but is able to accommodate the insights cultural and liberal unionists have to offer.

2

INTERPRETING UNIONISM

One sign of the likely durability of any political movement or school of thought is its ability to retain its identity and yet still adapt to the changing circumstances of its environment. Atavistic tendencies have to be resisted. A problem for unionism is that its potential for adaptability – which in principle is no less than that of any comparable political movement or school – tends to be stunted by a countervailing propensity to atavism. Not only is such a propensity encouraged by the rhetorical posturing of Paisleyite fundamentalism; it is tolerated by the uncreative mini-malism of the UUP which one academic commentator, Arthur Aughey, dignifies through the euphemism 'masterful inactivity'.[1] The sobering truth of the matter is that the days in which unionism could afford either to promote or smile benignly at atavism in its ranks, though probably more fictional than real, are now incontrovertibly over. It is impossible to detect the hand of masterful genius at work in the tendency of mainstream unionism to react against trends of which it disapproves by excluding itself from the main political game. This is to run the risk of policies affecting the future of Northern Ireland and ultimately the fate of unionism being decided over its head.

Aughey now thinks that inactivity is no longer the virtue it once was, given the current predicaments of unionism, and argues that unionists need to act in order to conserve.[2] I have plenty to say about the details of Aughey's argument in Chapter 4, but at present it is sufficient to remark that even an academic as inclined as he is to justify unionist complacency recognises that the current circumstances of unionism call for new initiatives. It is these circumstances that I want to bring into sharper focus in the first part of this chapter. I attempt to do so by highlighting challenges to unionism that emerge from conditions within its own fold and, more especially, from outside. In the second part of the chapter, I give a quick sketch of important unionist responses to these challenges. I locate three such responses which I try to characterise in terms of three major differences: dissimilar rankings of the challenges, different understandings of unionist identity, and distinct conceptual articulations. The third of these differences yields separate, though occasionally overlapping, theories of unionism which become the focus of attention in subsequent chapters.

CHALLENGES TO UNIONISM

The present circumstances of unionism are constituted in large measure by three sorts of challenges unionists cannot hope to avoid indefinitely: those internal to unionism, those originating beyond the borders of Northern Ireland, and those located within its borders. Whether the cumulative effect of these challenges justifies the conclusion that unionism is in a state of crisis is a contentious point. Talk of a crisis of unionism, especially an identity crisis, is fashionable in some circles but hotly contested in others.[3] I have no wish to enter this debate directly, but it would be disingenuous to pretend that either my analysis of the challenges or the arguments I have given notice of advancing do not have ramifications that impinge on it. At least implicitly I am saying that if unionists do not perceive themselves to be in a state of crisis they ought to, but that there is a way out of the crisis, though one that many unionists are likely to chafe at. But this is to run too far ahead. What is important at the moment is to become clear on the inescapable challenges that unionists currently face, regardless of whether we think they constitute a crisis or merely some awkward quandaries.

INTERNAL CHALLENGES

Differences among unionists over such issues as party affiliation, tactics and proposed forms of government for Northern Ireland pose challenges to the coherence and direction of unionism. Each of these differences is worth reflecting upon in turn.

One quarrel among unionists concerns conflicting party affiliations, that is, the fact that a number of political parties are competing for unionists' allegiance. On the surface, this might seem an unremarkable state of affairs of no greater import than the competition that exists in other Western democracies between parties that share a commitment to the integrity of their particular polities. And up to a point this is true: it is mistaken to read too much into the presence of diverse unionist parties just as it is misleading to infer that Protestantism is imperilled by the existence of a plethora of Protestant denominations and independent churches. But simply to suppose that unionism here reflects the Western democratic norm, or that there is a strict analogy between unionist and Protestant experiences of plurality, is too facile. In particular, it has to be recalled that the proliferation of unionist parties is a comparatively recent phenomenon which coinides with unionism's decline as the all-powerful political force in Northern Ireland. From the partition of Ireland until the introduction of direct rule by Westminster in 1972, the Unionist Party enjoyed fifty years of uninterrupted government and exercised hegemonic control over social and political life. With the exception of its last years in office, between 1969 and 1972, when weaknesses began to surface in the unionist leviathan, dissenters of a unionist persuasion proved little more than minor irritants who were confined either to the old Northern Ireland Labour Party or to the relative obscurity of some independent expression. Pitched against this backdrop, the current splintering of unionism into six parties betrays traces of a worm at the heart of unionism.[4] And these traces imply a challenge to unionist coherence and direction.

If we ask, for example, about the points of differentiation that warrant so many separate unionist parties, and about the basis of attempts to forge a semblance of unionist unity in the midst of apparently wide diversity, a confusing picture emerges. On issues that typically account for a plurality of parties within a polity – social and economic priorities, law and order, the environment – or on issues long peculiar to Northern Ireland – religious composition and appeal, commitment to constitutional politics, forms of preferred government – or on issues thrown up by post-ceasefire circumstances in the North – early releases of para-military prisoners, decommissioning of weapons, and inclusive all-party talks – it is almost impossible to say that any unionist party has a distinctive line on one of these, and certainly impossible to show distinctiveness on more than one.[5] And yet despite so many shared or overlapping emphases, unionist unity remains elusive.

This depiction of unionist politics raises puzzles I do not attempt to explain. Its point here is to underscore that party divisions within the house of unionism often have no compelling rationale and are indicative of a confusion which hinders the charting of a clear course for the future. A little further light may be cast on unionism's uncertainty of direction by considering both the flimsiness of recent efforts to achieve unity and disagreements over desired forms of government for Northern Ireland.

The aftermath of the Anglo-Irish Agreement, signed in 1985 by the British and Irish prime ministers, witnessed a show of unionist unity which began to falter when the UUP was perceived by the Democratic Unionist Party (DUP) to place too much faith in the British government: the UUP's cautious welcome of the

Downing Street Declaration signed by subsequent prime ministers of the two states in December 1993 is a case in point.[6] Since the publication of *Frameworks for the Future* in February 1995, renewed efforts have been made to revive unity among unionists. If anything these efforts have been heightened by increasing requests for unionist flexibility on issues of prisoners, weapons and inclusive talks, but has been complicated by the Irish Republican Army (IRA) ending its ceasefire in February 1996. The most urgent calls for unity have been issued by the champions of unionist intransigence, Ian Paisley's DUP, followed by the ostensible liberal voice of unionist politics, Robert McCartney. These calls have been directed at the largest party in Northern Ireland, the UUP, which has responded in a decidedly lukewarm fashion.[7] The so-called 'fringe loyalist' parties, the Ulster Democratic Party (UDP) and the Progressive Unionist Party (PUP), have not been beckoned, despite the pivotal role they played in brokering a loyalist ceasefire and continue to play in keeping it on course. The Alliance Party also has not been considered worthy of much wooing, since it is regarded as superfluous to the cause of unionist unity given that its cross-community brand of moderate politics is viewed as deeply suspect, especially within DUP circles. Interestingly, the parties least wanted by proponents of unionist unity are those that showed most inclination to respond positively to requests for flexibility on issues created by the new post-ceasefire circumstances.

The call for unity is at once limited, then, in the obvious sense that it does not wholeheartedly extend to certain, admittedly minor, unionist parties. This is by no means its only, or most serious, limitation. Indeed, it is one that advocates of unity could cheerfully live with if they managed to bind together the UUP, DUP, and McCartney's United Kingdom Unionist Party, that is, those unionists with representation at Westminster who command the overwhelming support of the unionist population. But even if this situation was achieved, two other limitations would continue to expose the shallowness of the appeal for unity. One concerns its tactically negative intent: unionists are seeking unity in order to hold a consistent line of refusal to negotiate on the basis of *Frameworks for the Future*, and refusal to talk with Sinn Féin until weapons have been decommissioned, or even until the IRA's structures have been dismantled, in order to show the British and Irish governments that unionists cannot be pushed into comply-ing with policies and directives they strongly disagree with, and so forth. Exactly what is to be gained by the tactic of refusal is anyone's guess and not many lessons appear to have been learned by the DUP in particular from the failure of the 'Ulster Says No' campaign to force a British backdown on the Anglo-Irish Agreement.

Another limitation concerns the substance of the call to unity: other than affirm unionist determination to remain British, it is not clear that it has any additional ground of positive agreement. It is not obvious, in other words, that on questions of substance regarding the future shape of a peaceful Northern Ireland union-ists agree on much more than that its British character and constitutional status should be retained. The visions of unionism of Paisley and McCartney, for example, are in many respects poles apart.

The call for unity has a hollow sound. It excludes strands of unionism that are not seen as sufficiently uncompromising, and it remains tactically negative and short on substance. Beyond ob-truding the obvious – that unionists want Northern Ireland to remain within the United Kingdom – it promises little. It is doubtful if unionist unity, if ever achieved, could be sustained for long, especially since there is a substantive rift between its main proponents.

The fact that unionists find it hard to agree on the way ahead for unionism is reflected in differing views of the preferred form of government for Northern Ireland which are found within as well as between parties. Admittedly, these views share a common point of departure: the present state of direct rule from West-minster is perceived as unsatisfactory not least because it is unacceptable for Northern Irish citizens to be governed by British parties they cannot vote for or, in cases, even join, and because it results in too much power being given over to bureaucrats in the Northern Ireland Office and to unaccountable quangos. The prevailing status quo creates a 'democratic deficit' in Northern Ireland.[8] But what is its alternative?

Unionist answers divide roughly along devolutionist and integrationist lines: either Northern Ireland should have its own form of government within the framework of the United Kingdom or it should be governed similarly to the rest of Britain. But this division requires additional qualification in order to capture the different senses that attach to the options of devolution and integration. Following McGarry and O'Leary, it is possible to detect four senses in which a devolutionist case is presented, whilst we may detect three in which an integrationist case is made.[9] On the devolutionist side, we may distinguish between 'reactionary' pleas for a return to the old Stormont mode of government based upon a simple principle of majority rule; 'reformist' requests for a type of majority rule modified by such concessions as 'a Bill of Rights, proportional representation, and a role for minority parties in the committee system of any future devolved assembly';[10] 'power-sharing' proposals for a Northern Ireland assembly in which unionists and nationalists share the executive and legislative tasks of government; and 'pan-British' arguments for a devolution of power to regions throughout the United Kingdom, if not also throughout the European Union. On the integrationist side, the primary concern may be 'legal', where the aim is to see Northern Ireland accorded an identical legal status within the Union to that enjoyed by England, Scotland and Wales; or it may be 'administrative', where the purpose is to have Northern Ireland granted its own Westminster select committee; or it may be 'electoral', where the objective is to persuade the major British political parties to organise and compete for electoral support in Northern Ireland.

Three observations are prompted by this array of senses in

which the options of devolution and integration are canvassed. First, the situation among unionists is even more complicated than the one McGarry and O'Leary describe. For a start, unless devolution is advocated as a disguise to enable the establishment of an independent Ulster, any devolved arrangement would include an element of integration. Furthermore, it is possible to be a devolutionist in more than one sense – say, 'power-sharing' and 'pan-British'. More interesting, it is also possible that an advocate of one form of devolution – say, 'power-sharing' – may prefer as a second-best option a form of integration – say, 'administrative' – rather than another form of devolution – say, 'reactionary'. In short, the devolution/integration distinction, unless suitably qualified, may disguise more differences among unionists than it reveals, since certain devolutionists are closer to certain integrationists than they are to other devolutionists.

Second, various of the senses in which devolution and integration are espoused reveal improbable aspirations unlikely to cut much ice either with the nationalist population or with the British and Irish governments. 'Reactionary' devolution and 'electoral' integration are two obvious improbable candidates, but there are others. Indeed, I shall argue that some variant of 'power-sharing' devolution is the only option likely to attract enough cross-community and intergovernmental support to be worth pursuing.

Third, differences between and among integrationists and devolutionists, if pressed, disclose serious rifts over matters of political substance. At issue is not only disagreement about preferred formal modes of government but, more seriously, disagreement about how much influence citizens should have over their own affairs and about how best to organise social and political life within a Northern Ireland that contains a large nationalist minority. In other words, conflicting views of unionism's relationship with nationalism are also at stake in disputes over devolution and integration, as are competing conceptions of politics. But the cause of unionism, as exemplified in recent calls for unity, is often defined so broadly as to cover up divisions in the unionist family and minimise their seriousness. The unspoken assumption seems to be that, whatever their differences, unionists always have more in common with each other than they ever have with nationalists. Whether this assumption withstands critical scrutiny remains an open question.

Diverging opinions of the sort of government that is appropriate in Northern Ireland constitute a challenge to the long-term viability of concerted unionist action. Once these opinions are identified and we see that other substantive differences are implied by them, it is hard to believe that united unionist defiance of Northern nationalists and the British and Irish governments can be anything more than a stopgap measure. Big questions about the purpose of politics and the nature of social and political life lurk just beneath the surface, and the variety of answers they receive among unionists indicates an absence of coherent direction that cannot simply be shrugged aside as a matter of secondary importance.[11] Of course, hauling these questions out into the open also means placing them in a context that is not defined solely by the predispositions of unionists, but that is shaped in crucial respects by factors beyond unionism's control. Ultimately, the plausibility of this or that unionist answer to questions concerning appropriate forms of government, the role of politics and the character of Northern Irish society depends not merely on its faithfulness to cherished unionist ideals, but also on its ability to respond to challenges issued by larger forces in its environment. One such set of challenges comes from forces external to Northern Ireland that none the less have the power to influence decisively what happens here.

CHALLENGES FROM OUTSIDE NORTHERN IRELAND

The most serious challenges to unionism from forces external to Northern Ireland are those posed by the British and Irish governments.[12] A lesser challenge, though one worth touching on briefly, is implied by developments occurring within the

European Union. At first glance these challenges, and especially that presented by the British government, may seem the most acutely alarming. And there is no denying that this glance penetrates to a deeply troubling state of affairs if we assume the likelihood of a worst-case scenario in which the current, or some future, government of the United Kingdom decides to accede to the wishes of certain nationalists and withdraw from Northern Ireland altogether. In this scenario, whatever the fateful consequences for the North's inhabitants, unionism would have given its last gasp and be rendered redundant as a live political doctrine. Thus the future of unionism appears to rely upon the good will of Westminster, which is why the potential challenge of a hostile British government looms as the greatest threat of all.

In truth, however, Westminster's threat to unionism is of a different order and not nearly as alarmist as the worst-case scenario suggests: regardless of the private wishes of government members and officials to be rid of the nuisance of Ireland once and for all, British governments of all hues operate under constraints that cannot be flouted at whim. Possible fateful consequences of withdrawal have to be reckoned with seriously, as do constitutional procedures; and, besides, there is bipartisan support within parliament for a British governmental presence to remain in Northern Ireland so long as the majority of citizens there will it. As things currently stand, the British government's commitment to the Union is more steadfast than wilder, almost apocalyptic, unionist fears sometimes suggest. But that does not mean that it is unambiguous or that it does not constitute a challenge of some significance to many unionist hopes and ambitions. Unionists have reason to be apprehensive because they suspect that John Hume might be right in arguing that, in the wake of the Anglo-Irish Agreement, the British government has effectively moved to a position of neutrality on the Union,[13] and because there is probably more than a glimmer of truth in the philosopher Anthony Kenny's disconcerting observation that of the three grounds of attachment that historically bound Britain to Northern

Ireland – self-interest, sentiment and morality – only the latter now holds.[14]

These points of Hume and Kenny gesture at the nature of the challenge unionists face from the British government: the fact that Northern Ireland's membership of the Union is treated as different in kind from the membership enjoyed by England, Scotland and Wales. Such a challenge consists of two related issues. First, it implies a commitment to Northern Ireland that is considerably weaker than the one most unionists wish for. Second, it suggests that the sort of institutional expressions of Northern Ireland's membership that Westminster finds acceptable may not coincide with those that unionists seek.

The issue of Westminster's weak commitment is hardly new. It was present at the very inception of partition, as Lloyd George made clear when trying to reassure Michael Collins and Arthur Griffith of the temporary character of the division of Ireland:

> ... in order to persuade Ulster to come in there is an advantage in her having a Catholic population. I think you will get Ulster into an Irish unit on agreed terms. We promise to stand aside and you will not only have our neutrality but our benevolent neutrality.[15]

Political developments within Northern Ireland worked out contrary to Lloyd George's prediction and successsive British governments were content to let them take their own course up to the late 1960s and early 1970s. Since the introduction of direct rule in 1972, and especially since the signing of the Anglo-Irish Agreement in 1985, the release of the Downing Street Declaration in 1993 and the publication of *Frameworks for the Future* in 1995, Westminster's resolve to retain the integrity of the Union has been revealed as less than wholehearted. The weakness of Westminster's resolve is conspicuous in the telling phrase that the British government has 'no selfish strategic or economic interest in Northern Ireland'[16] – a phrase unimaginable in Westminster's definition of its relationship to other members of the United Kingdom. An ambivalent resolve is also evident in the elevation of the principle of consent as the benchmark of Northern Ireland's constitutional future: so long as most people in the North wish to remain part of the UK, Westminster will respect that wish.[17] This elevation of the principle of consent is not only a source of security for unionists; it is also a reminder of Northern Ireland's peculiar status, since her people seem to have an opt-out clause not as readily available to the people of England, Scotland or Wales.

The current shape of the challenge to unionism entailed in Westminster's weak commitment to its cause merely makes explicit what was always implicit and allowed to remain so until Stormont was prorogued and British governments could no longer turn a convenient blind eye to the social and political realities of Northern Ireland. Viewed from one angle, then, there is little surprise in the attitudes expressed in current British government policies on Northern Ireland: they are scarcely more than footnotes to Lloyd George.[18] Viewed from another angle, however, there is immense surprise. Handling an implicit challenge is one thing, but confronting an explicit challenge is quite another. The first sort, which is what unionists experienced during the Stormont years, is easily dealt with. So easily, in fact, that most unionists were probably lulled into a false sense of complacency by supposing that British silence implied British endorsement. Thus they were ill equipped to meet the subsequent challenge of Britain's lack of resolve to defend their corner and her apparent neutrality on the future of Northern Ireland. And thus it is that expressions of outrage, betrayal and bewilderment now characterise many unionist responses to the British government.

Unionist disaffection with the British government is increased by the kind of institutional arrangements the government is prepared to countenance and the lengths it is willing to go in their pursuit. Unique arrangements, ranging from devolved institutions at Stormont to the current institutions of direct rule, have of course been the norm in Northern Ireland. But in its attempts to project a future beyond the present provisional arrangements of direct rule, the British government seems inclined to disturb unionist sensitivities in an unprecedented manner. It envisages institutions that dilute the 'Britishness' of Northern Ireland and, in pressing its intentions, is at times undistracted by unionist misgivings.

The circumstances attending the signing of the Anglo-Irish Agreement remain the most poignant illustration of the latter point. To recall, this was an agreement with the Irish government, decided upon independently not only of unionist input but also of unionist knowledge.[19] Time and subsequent British rhetoric and assurances have done little to remove unionist apprehensions of Westminster's true designs. Unionists perceive in paragraph 47 of the second of the recent framework documents, for example, a further intimation of the British government's preparedness to impose institutional arrangements on Northern Ireland against the will of the unionist majority.[20] And there is decidedly diminished confidence in the ability of concerted unionist action to see off the threat. The Ulster Workers' Council strike of 1974 may have scuppered the Sunningdale Agreement with its proposals for a power-sharing executive and a Council of Ireland, but the structures of the Anglo-Irish Agreement which granted the Irish government a consultative role in Northern Irish affairs have withstood all forms of unionist opposition.[21]

More to the point now, the proposals laid out in *Frameworks for the Future* reveal Britain's preference for institutional arrangements that not only retain Northern Ireland's place within the United Kingdom – subject to the consent of her people – but also provide for a power-sharing devolved assembly, a strengthening of Anglo-Irish relations, and the incorporation of an explicit Irish dimension that deepens North–South relations. There is unionist unease with the details of all these arrangements, but it is towards the kind of institutions implied by a deepening of North–South ties that most antipathy is directed. So strongly felt is this antipathy that no unionist party other than Alliance is prepared to enter negotiations on the basis of the framework documents.

Rather than consolidating Northern Ireland's position within the Union, the arrangements favoured by Westminster appear to most unionists to make that position even more precarious; the favoured arrangements seem to set the North on a course bringing it closer to the South and making more likely its eventual absorption into an all-Ireland republic.[22] Now, the plausibility of the typical unionist perception that the institutional arrangements suggested in *Frameworks for the Future* represent a slippery slope to a united Ireland is debatable, as I shall argue more fully in Chapter 5. But the sheer fact that the British government recommends arrangements designed to give nationalists a more inclusive role in Northern Irish society and to entitle the government of the Republic to a say on matters impinging on areas of Northern life issues a challenge to unionism that cannot be averted perpetually. At the very least, it indicates that unless unionists can respond with convincing counter-proposals, the prospect looms of their having to accept institutions that express the Irishness as well as the Britishness of Northern Ireland.

Related to the challenge posed to unionism by the British government is that posed by the Irish government. That such a challenge exists virtually goes without saying since the government of the Republic was a partner to the Anglo-Irish Agreement, the Downing Street Declaration and *Frameworks for the Future*. But specifying the precise form of that challenge is a tricky matter. Three indicators give some clue: the claim enshrined in the Irish constitution to jurisdication over the entire island of Ireland,[23] Dublin's perceived underwriting of Northern nationalist interests, and its intention to have some involvement, however limited, in the affairs of Northern Ireland. Each of these indicators gives Dublin's challenge to unionism a different twist.

The challenge implied by the constitutional claim is potentially the most serious, though it is susceptible of a relatively benign interpretation. Rendered in its most uncompromising – irredentist nationalist – form, it calls into question the very foundations of unionism by denying the legitimacy of Northern Ireland and by inferring that the avowed Britishness of unionists is a type of false consciousness. In its benign expression, the constitutional claim amounts to an aspiration to Irish unity, legal rulings to the contrary notwithstanding, and as such finds regrettable unionists' self-alienation from the Irish state and challenges them to reconsider their position.

The challenge of the second indicator – which unionists characteristically view as the Irish government's entanglement in a 'pan-nationalist front' – is even more ambiguous. Consider, for example, three possible construals of its meaning. At one extreme the construal might be this: since the true interests of Northern nationalists can only be satisfied in an all-Ireland republic – as Sinn Féin seldom tires of reminding us – the challenge is a reiteration of that issued by irredentist nationalism. At another extreme, Dublin's underwriting of Northern nationalist interests might rather be construed as follows: in the absence of unionist consent to a united Ireland, Northern nationalist interests must be defined at present solely within the context of Northern Ireland; the challenge to unionism is to ensure that Northern society is freed from discriminatory practices against nationalists by guaranteeing that they enjoy equal opportunities across the board of social and political life; and this is a challenge the Irish government promises to make effective by acting as an advocate of nationalist interests to the British government, the European Union and the international community at large. Falling between these extremes, the underwriting of Northern nationalist interests might be construed in these terms: to be sure, Irish unity is impossible without unionist agreement but, in the absence of such agreement, the interests of Northern nationalists require nothing short of an institutional recognition of Irishness within Northern Ireland; and the challenge to unionism is to accommodate such recognition.

This in-between construal of the challenge involved in the second indicator fits with the kind of challenge hinted at in the third, where the emphasis falls on the Irish government's desire to play some role in Northern Ireland. Here the challenge to unionism to facilitate such a desire is obvious. Again this challenge admits of a number of options; these range from structures of joint authority to structures of consultation. Whatever the option, the thrust of the challenge amounts to an extension of the point that an Irish dimension should be recognised in the institutions of Northern Ireland: an adequate recognition of such a dimension entails finding space for Dublin to play some part in Northern Irish life.

It is true to say that certain of the above depictions of the nature of the Irish government's challenge are bound to offend unionists a good deal more than others. But it is also true that even the mildest depiction constitutes an affront of sorts to most unionists. The standard unionist inclination is simply to dismiss all these depictions out of hand on the grounds that a foreign state – such as the Irish Republic – has no business meddling in the internal affairs of Northern Ireland.[24] The problem is that such an inclination confronts serious obstacles. The Irish government's challenges to unionism do not appear in a vacuum and cannot be ignored just because certain forms of unionist ideology insist on screening them out. A number of them are explicitly supported by the British government as well as by the United States which, under the presidency of Bill Clinton, is taking an unprecedented interest in the politics of Northern Ireland. Accordingly, it seems short-sighted simply to lump together all the challenges listed above and to dismiss them indiscriminately. It is more prudent to distinguish among them in order to discern which reflect the actual position of the Irish government and which are likely to muster most support beyond Ireland. It is on these that unionist minds need to concentrate, even if there is no stopping certain unionist minds from detecting the darkest motives in the most innocuous of challenges.

The irredentist challenge conveyed through an uncompromising interpretation of the Irish constitution and a 'Sinn-Féin-oriented' understanding of Northern nationalist interests is the least credible. This is despite the fact that as recently as 1990 the

Supreme Court in Dublin defined the Irish state's claim to jurisdiction over the whole of Ireland as a 'constitutional imperative'.[25] Two points are pertinent here. First, even when there was no doubting the ideological commitment of successive Irish governments to the irredentist line vindicated by the Supreme Court ruling, political movement aimed at hastening the arrival of its promise was conspicuously lacking.[26] In terms of dictating courses of action, the *de facto* reality of Northern Ireland's existence as a separate entity has invariably counted for more than the Irish state's *de jure* claim over the entire territory of the island. Second, the Irish government now rejects the irredentist ideology, support of which is largely confined to Sinn Féin and sections of Fianna Fáil.[27] Thus, as *Frameworks for the Future* makes transparent, there is explicit acknowledgement that change to the constitutional status of Northern Ireland cannot be implemented without the consent of her citizens. There is also an apparent willingness to promote changes to Articles 2 and 3 of the Irish constitution in order to bring them into line with the principle of consent – a willingness that should not be underestimated given that, since being flagged, it has encountered no serious objections from within the Republic.[28] And, underlying these concessions to the validity of the unionist case, there is an accelerating recognition that the British identity of unionists has to be appreciated as such and not derisively dismissed as a distorted form of consciousness.

The real challenge presented to unionism by the Irish government is in effect an amalgam of those other construals of the challenge that fall outside the framework of irredentist nationalism. It thus consists of the following elements: first, an ongoing invitation to unionists to rethink their self-exclusion from the Irish state;[29] second, a concern that nationalists receive a fair social and political deal within Northern Ireland; and, third, a wish to see an Irish dimension accommodated within Northern institutions, a closer development of North–South ties, and a role of some sort for Dublin. Unionists should have no difficulty in principle in coping with the first and second parts of this challenge. It is with the third part, the Irish government's desire to play some role in Northern Ireland, that their most onerous tasks lie, especially given the variety of interpretations its different aspects open up. The apparent British and United States backing of the basic thrust of this objective suggests that these tasks cannot be shirked, however exacting they may prove to be.

Another external challenge to unionism, which I want to deal with briefly, stems from developments occurring within the European Union. The nature and point of this challenge is worth clarifying. In one version, it is presented as a direct and strong assault on typical unionist (and nationalist) preconceptions and promises a transformation of the ways in which we think about the problem of Northern Ireland. But this version seems somewhat overdrawn and its gloss on the significance of the 'European challenge' appears exaggerated. I suggest, on the contrary, that the challenge is more indirect, and obtains only in two milder senses.

An exaggerated version of the European challenge to unionism focuses on the idea that an emerging 'Europe of the regions' undercuts unionists' exclusive attachment to the United Kingdom and opens up the prospect of forms of North–South co-operation unencumbered by nationalist baggage. The challenge, accordingly, is for unionists to think of Northern Ireland primarily as a European region which coexists and interacts with other regions, including the Republic of Ireland and other members of the United Kingdom. If taken seriously, this is a challenge with radical consequences for unionists. It undermines the nation-state basis of their thinking, dislodges the issue of sovereignty from the central place unionists accord it in their dispute with nationalists, makes secondary the border question which they regard as primary, and shifts the locus of their political identity.[30] In the words of one of its main advocates, the challenge is to 'get beyond' the usual dichotomies unionists invoke in their quarrel with nationalists.[31]

A major problem with this explication of the European challenge is that it implies a level of 'Europeanisation' that does not exist. A 'Europe of the regions' is an aspiration and not a current reality. Moreover, it is far from evident that increased regionalisation would imply the transcending of nation-states; it seems more the case that regionalisation would occur within their ambit.[32] Accordingly, sovereignty is not so easily disposed of, borders are not so magically spirited away, and political identities are not so effortlessly relocated. Indeed, the notion that those attachments that distinguish unionists from nationalists can be transcended by the sheer appropriation of a common 'Europeanism' appears to underestimate the nature and depth of the attachments at issue: they are not cast aside so lightly. As one commentator puts it, 'one gets the curious sense that "getting beyond" the Irish Question through Europe is *cheating*'.[33] The most that may be said here is that a thoroughgoing regionalisation of Europe would perhaps encourage a more flexible approach to questions of sovereignty, borders and identities, as well as provide a further impetus for cross-border activities conducive to the benefit of both Northern Ireland and the Republic. But this is to envisage a milder sort of challenge, which comes closer to the one I think the issue of Europeanisation raises.

The present European challenge to unionism is more indirect and subtle than is admitted by those who look to Europe for some sort of quick fix to the problems of Northern Ireland. First, it is probably the case that membership of the European Union has contributed to various social, political and cultural changes occurring within the United Kingdom and the Republic of Ireland which have yet to be taken stock of in unionist thinking. Consider, for example, the divisive impact on British political life created by talk of European integration and regionalisation. Such talk has brought to the fore questions of the extent of British sovereignty and the cohesiveness of Britain, with Scotland in particular pressing serious demands for devolution, and has revealed splits over Europe within and between the Conservative and Labour parties. Now it may be that the import of this kind of talk is inflated, as I have already submitted is the case with much regionalisation discourse, and that only very minimal threats are posed to British sovereignty and unity by what is achievable on the fronts of European integration and regionalism. But what is interesting here is that the proliferation of talk about these matters has helped create a climate of debate that has exposed strains in the concept of a unitary, sovereign British state. And it is such a concept that lies close to the heart of many unionists', especially integrationists', image of the United Kingdom. And as Scottish, and to a lesser extent Welsh, nationalism threatens to fragment the integrity of the United Kingdom, the interests of an English nationalism may be implicit in attempts to halt such fragmentation. Mention of English nationalism sits most uncomfortably with much unionist ideology, as we shall notice on more than one occasion in subsequent chapters.[34]

Or consider the situation of the Irish state, which has worn its European membership altogether more comfortably than has Britain. It is not far-fetched to conjecture that the acceleration of this state's modernisation programme begun under Seán Lemass, its growing embrace of pluralism and consequent moves away from the rural, Catholic, Gaelic state of de Valera's dreams, is in no small measure due to its involvement in the European Union.[35] That such a shift in the character of the Irish state is even happening is only grudgingly acknowledged by unionists, if at all. In different ways, then, effects of Europeanisation may be detected in changes to the British and Irish states. And these constitute a challenge to unionists not in the sense that they radically undermine their reasons for wishing to remain within the British fold, but in the indirect sense that they call for a revision of standard unionist accounts of the two states and of their differences.

Second, membership of the European Union has undoubtedly contributed to an improvement of Anglo-Irish relations. The Irish and British governments have developed better understandings of each other and discovered common interests through working together in various European forums and committees. This European experience may even have led both governments to reorient their priorities to the detriment of both unionist and nationalist interests. Feargal Cochrane makes this suggestion explicit when he argues that 'the two sovereign governments are primarily concerned with maintaining good relations with *one another*, rather than with working for the achievement of more fundamental objectives such as Irish unity or preservation of the Union'.[36] Cochrane's argument is contestable[37] but, its implications for nationalists aside, it does point to a real difficulty for unionists. The British and Irish governments have since 1985 shown a resolve to reach a common position on Northern Ireland, despite occasional tensions in their relationship, and this resolve may prove very difficult for unionists to dislodge. It is a resolve that has doubtless been strengthened through common European experiences. To recognise that this is so is also to recognise that the influence of the European factor constitutes another indirect challenge to unionism.

CHALLENGES FROM WITHIN NORTHERN IRELAND

If external challenges from the British and Irish governments and from the impact of European trends comprise one set of constraints on unionist designs, challenges from within Northern Ireland comprise another. There are doubtless many ways of characterising the implications of the latter. But whichever way is chosen there is arguably a core issue which all must address and which unionists cannot duck: the requirement that the Northern Ireland whose integrity unionists insist must be respected becomes one in which all citizens may have a meaningful stake and find some sense of belonging. In other words, the ultimate challenge to unionists here, underlying all particular challenges to do this or that, is to envisage and to co-operate in creating an inclusive Northern Ireland which accommodates, as far as possible, the concerns of unionists, nationalists and others. Now as soon as the challenge is articulated in such terms, it has to be admitted from the outset that, even with the best will in the world, unionism is limited in its ability to satisfy all that it might be thought to imply. Two examples bear this out.

One relates to the nature of the concessions that may be made to nationalist concerns. If these concerns are defined in irredentist categories they are impossible for unionists to meet. The campaign of violence conducted by the IRA from 1969 to 1994 did not make them any more possible to meet, and the resumption of violence since February 1996 has not either. This is because what is being asked for is beyond giving: that unionists stop being unionists and admit that they were muddled nationalists after all. Being prepared to facilitate nationalist concerns must mean something less than signing up for a united Ireland. Another limitation relates to the restricted powers unionists have at their disposal. It is unquestionably true, for instance, that the concerns of many people in Northern Ireland are linked to structures of social and economic deprivation. High rates of unemployment, inadequate educational provision, poor housing conditions, meagre welfare benefits and so on are unfortunate facts of life for many living in certain working-class and rural areas, both unionist and nationalist. There is not, however, a great deal that unionists can do directly to alleviate these kinds of socio-economic concerns. Like everyone else in Northern Ireland, they too are subject to policies emanating from Westminster over which they have minimal control. This does not mean that policies highlighting acute socio-economic concerns cannot be developed and prioritised, and that pressure cannot be applied to government ministers, agencies and officials in the Northern Ireland Office. But it does mean that impossible demands should not be made of unionism.

If certain demands are unreasonably made, others are not. There still remain effective challenges to unionists to help promote an inclusive Northern Ireland. Not all nationalist concerns are irredentist in character, and not all social, economic or cultural concerns presuppose powers that unionists do not possess. In recent times, concerns that *prima facie* fall within the brief of unionism have been gathered under the concept of 'parity of esteem'. Picking up on this concept, which is what I propose to do, enables us to focus on what the talk of an inclusive Northern Ireland principally entails. It also permits us to identify crucial shifts that have occurred in Northern Irish society since the days of the Stormont administration or are occurring at present, and which implicitly or explicitly challenge assumptions that unionism has often been content to leave unexamined. One aspect of the challenges incorporated under the concept of parity of esteem is that unionism is in danger of being sidelined by social changes taking place independently of its areas of influence. I try to expand on this phenomenon by highlighting practices in Northern Irish civil society in which unionists play at best a marginal role, most often by choice. The challenge to unionism in this instance is to halt a gradual decline of its relevance. There is an ironical rub here, even if it is wise not to make too much of it just yet: the Northern Ireland to which unionists are deeply committed is arguably becoming one in which unionism's influence is being slowly eroded.

In considering the challenge to unionism implied by the concept of parity of esteem, it is germane to make three preliminary points which serve to underline the concept's strength. First, the very fact that this concept has entered the vocabulary of political debate in Northern Ireland is an indictment of previous unionist bad practices. For, whatever else use of the concept may involve, its present invocation suggests that a lack of even-handedness has characterised the North's social and political life, that those from minority traditions or social groups have been shabbily treated in a unionist-dominated Northern Ireland, and that rectification now has to be made to ensure that formerly discriminated against individuals, groups and traditions are accorded the respect or esteem that is their due. At the very least, a typical resort to the concept carries the inference that under the Stormont regime Northern Ireland represented a social, political and cultural environment uncongenial to nationalists; and that however much the worst excesses have been remedied under direct rule, there is yet more work to be done.

Second, and unsurprisingly, then, the concept has been welcomed within nationalist discourse, even if there is a tendency among Sinn Féin representatives to replace it with a concept of 'equality of treatment' and a belated attempt by unionists to appropriate it in defence of their own cultural practices. I do not want at this stage to consider either the adequacy of the precise formulation of the concept to convey the meanings intended by it,[38] or the plausibility of its positive use by unionists. I want to note, rather, that its employment by nationalists as a peg on which to hang their calls for further reform dovetails with the Irish government's requirements that nationalists receive a fair deal in Northern Ireland and that room be found for an Irish dimension. As we have seen, these are emphases with which the British government is sympathetic, as indeed is the US administration. This convergence of Northern nationalist, Irish, British and US interests is very powerful evidence of the seriousness of the challenge to unionists captured by the concept of parity of esteem: it is no longer tolerable to have a Northern Ireland created solely in unionism's self-image.[39]

Third, it should also be pointed out that it is not only nationalists who have latched on to the concept in order to press for improvements in the quality of social and political life in the North. It has been approvingly cited by political parties, social institutions and community groups whose *raisons d'être* are not inherently nationalist. In short, the concept has proved amenable to wide-ranging uses, and is often called upon in attempts to destabilise customary practices of discrimination and domination. And that is why unionists cannot convincingly deflect the challenge the concept poses as a purely nationalist ploy to subvert the integrity of Northern Ireland. The fact that the concept has acquired non-nationalist connotations means that the challenge to unionism's designs for Northern Ireland appears in another form which, even if not so well organised and powerfully backed, warrants attention.

Taken together, these preliminary points suggest that the concept of parity of esteem provides a focal point for expressing inescapable challenges to many unionists' views of Northern Ireland. But exactly what do these challenges amount to? I think they amount to three things.

The first challenge is to end discriminatory practices against individuals. This is the sense in which the concept of parity of esteem translates most uncontroversially into the language of rights. Each individual regardless of his or her race, religion, culture or gender has a right to be treated with a respect equal to that due to every other individual. An application of this sense appears in fair employment and equal opportunity legislation recently implemented in Northern Ireland. It also lies behind the request supported by most local political parties for the intro-duction of a bill of rights. There are, however, two rather more controversial extensions of this 'individual-rights-based' con-strual of parity of esteem. First, there is the call for affirmative action in favour of those belonging to groups that were system-atically disadvantaged by earlier bad practices – say, Catholics and women. The beneficiaries of such action, it should be noted, are individuals who are deemed worthy of special treatment by virtue of their membership of a disadvantaged group, whether or not such membership figures in their own self-definitions. Se-cond, there is the idea that doing justice to individuals or respecting their rights requires the state to take interventionist action in the marketplace to correct injustices done to certain individuals through no fault of their own. This derivation of redistributive policies from respect for individual rights is an idea that is prominent in much contemporary liberal political theory.[40] These controversial extensions of a rights-based notion of parity of esteem may complicate the challenge to leave behind dis-criminatory practices, but its overriding concern remains unal-tered: to secure the rights of individuals as individuals.

In the second challenge, the emphasis shifts from individuals to cultural groups, traditions and social movements. Here the guiding motivation is to curb the real or potential all-pervasive power of the dominant culture from which various minorities feel excluded. And this motivation energises a conception of 'cultural parity of esteem' which insists on adequate scope being given to the expression of minority voices. The challenge, then, is to create sufficient spaces in civil society for a plurality of cultural forms to flourish, for their adherents to articulate their own thoughts and to pursue their own ways of life. Or at least that is the general challenge. But given the peculiar circumstances of Northern Ireland, a concern with cultural parity of esteem issues a particular challenge too: of being prepared to encourage understanding of, and accord equal respect to, the two main traditions in the North, whether we describe these as unionist and nationalist or as Protestant and Catholic. Such a challenge is responded to in schools in Northern Ireland in the Education for Mutual Understanding programmes. Facing up to the implications of this challenge is integral to the rationale of the government-sponsored Community Relations Council and its offshoot the Cultural Traditions Group, and to the activities of ecumenical and reconciliation groups within the churches.

Not surprisingly, the challenge to accord parity of esteem to Northern Ireland's two major traditions admits of controversial interpretations. Take, for example, a situation that may obtain when the notion of cultural parity of esteem is depicted in the language of rights: just as individuals have a right to equal respect so too have cultural groups and traditions.[41] Given such a depiction, when a tradition – or more exactly a group claiming to represent a tradition – chooses to exercise its right to cultural expression, it is simultaneously demanding that others respect that right. But it may happen that that demand is not acceded to because the cultural expression in question is perceived as offensive by those from another tradition, especially when it is imposed in a manner they cannot avoid encountering. In such a situation it is possible for both contending parties to invoke a concept of parity of esteem in defence of their respective positions, and to call upon conflicting claims to rights. On one side, the argument might be that cultural parity of esteem means tolerating traditional expressions different from one's own, and that all citizens have a general duty to respect others' right to such expressions. On the other side, the counter might come that cultural parity of esteem does not involve riding roughshod over the traditional attachments of a minority by asserting a dominant cultural form in areas where it is not welcome, and that minorities have a right not to have their lives interfered with in ways they find deeply offensive. Controversies over the routing of Orange marches bring into play both sets of arguments and provide a poignant illustration of the difficulties involved in confronting the challenge posed by an idea of cultural parity of esteem. For our purposes here, though, the relevant question is whether unionism is prepared to concede that those arguments developed by its political opponents have any credibility whatever.

Confronted by the apparently intractable nature of the conflict between rival traditions, there is a temptation to give the idea of cultural parity of esteem a 'neutral' twist, at least whenever possible. Seemingly, such a temptation proved overwhelmingly attractive to the Queen's University Senate when it decided in 1994 to stop playing the British national anthem at graduation ceremonies. In the interests of parity of esteem, it was considered prudent to cease privileging symbols of the majority tradition. The subsequent furore this decision provoked among unionists indicates that ostensibly neutral responses to the challenge posed by the idea of cultural parity of esteem are not guaranteed a smoother reception than others. But the mere fact that a university institution was willing to meet the challenge in a fashion destined to arouse unionist ire is very revealing. It shows the discomfort unionists experience when faced with interpretations of parity of esteem that call into question their preconceptions. Beyond that, it also reinforces a general point I made earlier:

cardinal assumptions of unionism are being disturbed not just by some 'pan-nationalist front', but by broader forces and movements within Northern Irish society. The challenge to unionism's adaptability and credibility runs deep and wide.

Unionism's difficulties are compounded by challenges engendered by a third sense of the concept of parity of esteem which is appropriately dubbed 'political'. This sense is intimated in a recommendation of the Opsahl Commission's report which conceived of parity of esteem 'between the two communities' entailing 'legal recognition of Irish nationalism' without denying the 'Britishness' of unionists.[42] Given acceptance of such a conception, the report envisaged achieving what it termed 'absolute parity of esteem' in the government of Northern Ireland – a situation in which, as a matter of principle, 'each community has an equal voice in making and executing the laws or a veto on their execution, and equally shares administrative authority'.[43] At a minimum, such 'absolute parity of esteem' anticipates power-sharing arrangements within Northern Ireland to which significant legislative and executive capacities are devolved. But as the recommendation of a 'legal recognition of Irish nationalism' infers, much more is anticipated besides. Here there may be a foreshadowing of the conviction lying behind the anthem decision made by Queen's University Senate – that it is inappropriate in a divided society to privilege the symbols of one tradition. Accepting such a conviction as basically sound does not, of course, necessarily imply a commitment to the kind of neutral alternative pursued by Queen's. Recognising the validity of both nationalism and unionism suggests, rather, the presence of public institutions reflecting the Irishness and the Britishness of Northern Ireland, an extension of North–South ties, and perhaps a role of some sort for Dublin as well as for Westminster. As we have seen, these are suggestions already favoured by the Irish government, tacitly supported by the British, and echoing the desires of many Northern nationalists. But again it is worth remarking that they are suggestions for the future of Northern

Ireland that are attractive not only to nationalists. Support for them also comes from an independent body such as the Opsahl Commission as a result of its canvassing of citizens' opinions within Northern Ireland.

Each of the above suggestions prompted by a political rendering of the concept of parity of esteem constitutes a separate challenge to unionists. But each in its own way also contributes to the overall challenge such a rendering forces upon unionist attention: to imagine a political future in Northern Ireland where matters of power and public identity are wrested from exclusively unionist control and expression and shared with nationalists. This is a challenge issued not just by external forces or nationalist 'fifth columnists', but by actors within Northern Ireland who are not working from a nationalist script.

It is, however, relatively easy for unionists to caricature or to turn a blind eye to a non-nationalist challenge precisely because it neither makes much of an impression on unionism's electoral fortunes nor receives powerful external support. Indeed, with so much intergovernmental and international attention being devoted to mediation between the 'two traditions' and to reconciliation of the 'two communities', there is a (perhaps unwitting) tendency to marginalise even further those whose agendas are neither strictly unionist nor strictly nationalist. Accordingly, the danger is that the significance of non-nationalist concerns about parity of esteem will simply be trivialised.

This danger is hard to avert if it is assumed that all that counts politically is conducted at formal levels of government, state institutions and political parties. It is on the basis of such an assumption that many unionists think they can ignore criticisms from non-nationalist sources. But the assumption is questionable, and a non-nationalist challenge may prove more formidable than is initially supposed.

At first blush it seems odd to regard as formidable a challenge that is barely perceptible to many unionists. Its oddness diminishes, however, once we recognise that its real sting lies not so much in a direct confrontation of unionist sensitivities – as, say, in the Queen's University example – as in its indirect whittling away of unionist influence in various areas of civil society. As I have suggested, moves to end practices of discrimination and domination, to create spaces for cultural plurality, and to initiate in the manner of the Opsahl Commission new forums for discussion of Northern Ireland's future, raise important issues connected to the concept of parity of esteem. But that does not exhaust their significance. In addition, such moves reveal the emergence of forms of action and debate that transcend the confines of typical unionist forms. They attest to the growing importance of what may be termed 'a politics of civil society' that is separate from those formal levels of politics with which unionism is used to dealing.[44] It is because unionism is not accustomed to engage seriously in a politics of civil society – as evidenced, for instance, in its begrudging attitude and paltry contributions to the Opsahl Commission[45] – that it may be oblivious of the real strength of the non-nationalist challenge and thus ill equipped to meet it. And the essence of this challenge consists in the unsettling possibility that the character of Northern Irish society is increasingly being shaped independently of unionism; that various matters of social and political import within Northern Ireland are being pursued without regard to unionist opinion.

It could be objected that I am making something out of nothing here, since unionists can afford to be perfectly relaxed about a developing politics of civil society. That is to say, to the extent that unionists genuinely believe that Northern Ireland should be a fully pluralistic society, it is entirely acceptable to them that various modes of social, cultural and political expression flourish independently of their control. More forcefully, it could be said that there is something insidious about attempts to keep too strict a check on the activities of civil society, as the awful instances of political authoritarianism in the twentieth century amply demonstrate.[46] Such an objection has a point if it is assumed that the alternative to a civil society independent of unionist influence is a civil society under unionist control. But this is not the only alternative, and it is not the one I have in mind. In spite of its apparent plausibility the objection falters on two counts, the second of which I think is decisive.

First, it is doubtful whether all unionists are so generously disposed to full-blooded pluralism as the objection supposes. Unionist practice during its years in power at Stormont gives us reason to doubt, as does the current practice of the DUP in particular. At least for those unionists whose vision of Northern Ireland includes that of a society bearing the religious and cultural stamp of Protestantism, the non-nationalist challenge issued through a politics of civil society remains a powerful threat.

Second, the sanguine attitude the objection implies to the prospect of a politics of civil society being conducted beyond the reach of unionism betrays a cavalier approach to unionism's ongoing viability and a limited conception of politics. It is cavalier to suppose, for example, that unionism can thrive without loss even as it is marginalised from a raft of social and cultural issues that are being debated and acted upon within civil society. Being reduced to the role of spectator as socio-cultural dramas are played out before its eyes hardly constitutes evidence of unionism's vibrancy. It suggests, rather, a tacit admission that various concerns of social life are beyond unionism's ken. And this sort of admission arguably hastens the arrival of unionism's sell-by date. At work here is also a very restrictive notion of unionist politics which pares down unionism to a single-issue, constitutional creed. The idea that such a minimalist creed equips unionism to tackle the range of social and political responsibilities required of a political movement, party or government is of course absurd. But so long as a notion of political minimalism is fostered, it means that when unionism is forced to handle wider sorts of responsibilities, as it always has been, it can only do so either in an *ad hoc* way or in a way that is overdetermined by its constitutional priorities. To declare, even if only implicitly, the politics of civil society to be out of bounds is to suffer from myopic vision or perhaps a failure of nerve. And it is a declaration that derives small comfort from an invocation of pluralism once we eschew the simplistic distinction of 'total autonomy' and 'total control' regarding the life of civil society. That is to say, to advocate that unionism should participate in the affairs of civil society is not to urge that it should endeavour to control those affairs; it is, rather, simply to say that in the absence of serious participation unionism consents to its own undermining and has few grounds for complaint if it is viewed by non-nationalists as a creed aspiring to obsolescence.

To summarise, the non-nationalist challenge to unionism transmitted indirectly through a politics of civil society has a significance that far exceeds the electoral strength of non-nationalist political parties. Its general thrust is to query whether unionism has anything to offer to aid the resolution of the manifold social, cultural and political problems increasingly surfacing in the arena of civil society. If taken seriously, this non-nationalist criticism, considered in general terms, issues a formidable challenge on two fronts: by casting doubt on the long-term possibilities of a unionism that avoids meaningful engagement with large tracts of social life in Northern Ireland; and by raising searching questions about the range and depth of unionist politics, including its guiding principles and strategies for non-constitutional political activity and its understanding of the relationship between a politics of the state and a politics of civil society. To allow such doubt to linger, and to carry on as though these questions do not need answering, is tantamount to confessing that unionism's political imagination is severely withered. It is also to add an element of credibility to the ironical prospect, gestured at earlier, of a Northern Ireland whose integrity may, as unionists wish, be respected, but whose character bears less and less resemblance to typical unionist images. And this is to open up another can of worms.

UNIONIST RESPONSES

The sheer array of challenges unionism faces from within its own ranks as well as from outside and inside the borders of Northern Ireland is daunting. It is a tall order to expect all these challenges to receive equal attention. Needless to say, they do not. Certain challenges are seen as vitally important and others as not. Opinions differ within unionism, however, about which challenges cannot be avoided and which can. I want to throw light on these differing opinions by laying out three unionist responses that reveal sometimes conflicting estimations of where the real challenge to unionism lies. Before doing so, I start with some general remarks.

CHARACTERISING THE RESPONSES

Differences over how the challenges faced by unionism should be ranked, what the locus of a unionist identity should be, and the sort of conceptual articulation unionism should be given, distinguish the three responses and provide the focal points of my characterisation of them. What warrants initial clarification is what my characterisations presuppose. Accordingly, I lay out now the basic meanings and interconnections of the terms 'ranking', 'identity', and 'conceptual articulation' at work in my characterisations.

By claiming that different unionist responses rank the challenges to unionism differently, I may seem to be assuming that unionists generally recognise the challenges to be as I have described them, and that they have engaged in an explicit analytic exercise that permits them to delineate which challenges are more significant than others. But this is not so. The first assumption is not necessary, since to allow different rankings is also to allow different slants being put on the challenges up for ranking. The second assumption is not strictly required either. To clarify, the claim that ranking occurs does not necessarily entail that it does so explicitly, as it may go on whether or not particular unionists are reflectively aware of it. Ranking is implicit in unionist practice and is discernible when the direction of unionists' energies suggest certain challenges are treated with the utmost seriousness, others with moderate seriousness, and still others with no seriousness. Making explicit what is implicit – in this instance the ranking of challenges – is a requirement not of unionist practice but of unionist theory. But ranking in itself is not an invention of theory. This is not to say that practice can get by adequately without theory. On the contrary, the ranking embedded in practice is refined and, in cases, altered by theory, and the move to make the implicit explicit is properly seen as illuminating in two senses. First, it brings into clearer view the understanding of unionism tacitly invoked by the priorities expressed through unionist practice; and, second, it recognises that reasons need to be offered for such priorities, for taking unionism's principal tasks to be these rather than those, and so forth. Otherwise put, making explicit what is involved in ranking brings to the fore questions of identity and conceptual articulation, that is, of how unionists understand themselves and of which concepts best articulate their self-understandings.

The issue of identity is of the essence here. It is the touchstone of any coherent ranking process and establishes the contours of the type of conceptual articulation deemed appropriate for unionism. But the term 'identity' is notoriously slippery and it is not always clear what is meant by it. Although this is not the occasion to discuss its manifold meanings, it is important to indicate the main connotations associated with my use of the term. Three in particular stand out.

The first, and most rudimentary, has to do with what questions of identity are *about*. I take it that they are principally about 'who' we are either individually or collectively. Questions of identity are bound up with questions of self-understandings or self-interpretations. They refer to how we make sense of ourselves and to what matters to us. There are, of course, many ways in which we try to make sense of our lives in order to imbue them with significance, just as there are many things that matter to us. If taken in their fullness, questions of identity range across the whole gamut of human experience, from the intimate to the formal, and seem to raise an impossibly large number of issues. It is not, however, my intention to attempt the impossible by taking these questions in their fullness. A second connotation of my approach to the theme of identity makes plain its restricted *focus*. I am concerned only to explore what is involved in having a *political* identity. Even so, such a restricted focus admits of narrow and broad interpretations. As we shall see, for some unionists a political identity relates primarily to a legal status and a set of procedural rights and entitlements, whereas for others it also relates to a series of substantive cultural or religious commitments and attachments. Limiting the focus on identity to political issues, then, certainly has the advantage of making matters more manageable, but it does not foreclose the possibility of having to examine multifaceted dimensions of human experience.

A third connotation refers to the *source* of unionists' identity. There is a widespread tendency to think of identity mostly in psychological terms and thus to locate its source in the psyche, consciousness, perceptions or mindsets of individuals or groups. This tendency is evident even when the focus is on a political identity. We see it, for example, in familiar attempts to discover the source of unionism's identity in its renowned 'siege mentality'.[47] It is also present in John Whyte's influential study *Interpreting Northern Ireland*, where the concept of identity is introduced as a key 'psychological aspect' of social and political life in the North. Whyte discusses its importance in relation to theories in social psychology that highlight how group identities emerge through competition with other groups and involve some claim to superiority.[48] He goes on to surmise that 'those who are insecure in their identity are precisely the ones who will feel most strongly about the issue'.[49] And he concludes that, as a crucial psychological aspect, an emphasis on identity is useful as 'an explanation of the intensity of feeling engendered by the cleavages in Northern Ireland'.[50]

Now there is no doubting in general that psychological components of identity formation are important. And there is little arguing in particular that feelings of insecurity, of superiority, of emotional intensity and, in sum, of being under siege are features of many unionists' identities. But there is ample disputing that these feelings take us to the heart of any unionist identity and, moreover, that questions of identity are reducible to psychological explanations. Take, for example, two problems encountered by accounts of a unionist identity that accord a central explanatory role to those feelings mentioned above. One is that they overlook the fact that such feelings are unevenly distributed among different expressions of unionist identity. As I shall argue later, they are highly concentrated in one expression, mildly present in another, and almost without trace in a third. Another problem is that even where they have most going for them – in that expression of unionist identity in which a siege mentality looms largest – these accounts tend to distort what is at stake. At their most uncharitable, they virtually give the impression that to bear a unionist identity is to suffer from a pathological condition. In their slightly more charitable vein, they add a psychological spin to the idea that unionism only can define itself in terms of what it is not, by depicting unionists' identity in negative psychological categories, such as insecurity and the like. In either case we have a distorted story, since what is missed or severely downplayed is the significance unionists attribute to those positive features of their world that they, rightly or wrongly, perceive to be threatened. And it is only when pitched against the backdrop of their 'world of significance' that unionists' negative psychological reactions become properly intelligible.

This latter point raises the bigger issue of whether psychological descriptions, positive or negative, point us to the source of unionist (or any other) identities. I do not think they do. When trying to get clear about the constituent features of a political identity such as unionism there are good reasons to trace back to what I have called the world of significance that forms the indispensable background to psychological expressions of one sort or another.[51] It is this that puts us in touch with what matters to unionists. Their world of significance consists of institutions and practices with which they identify, of memories, commitments and allegiances that define who they are as unionists. In short, the unionists' world of significance amounts to a political, if not also a social and cultural, way of life that is valued for the meanings and purposes it makes available. It is such a way of life that is the source of a unionist identity and that provides unionists with an orientation to politics. It is when they face disorientation through their way of life being disturbed, threatened with disturbance, or imagined to be so threatened, that elements of a siege mentality are conspicuous among certain unionists. But these are derivative elements and to treat them as though they are primary, as though they are the source of a unionist identity, is to misunderstand who unionists are and what they stand for.

The final question I want to address in order to clarify how I propose to characterise different unionist responses or positions concerns what I mean when I say that unionism warrants conceptual articulation. The need to tackle this question received a prompt from the requirement of unionist theory that it provide reasons why it ranks challenges to unionism the way it does. The question now can be approached in a more informed manner given the preceding remarks about identity. I claimed that the contours of an appropriate mode of articulating the concepts underlying unionist self-understandings are set by an understanding of identity. And it is this claim I want to make good in a way that also links up with the philosophical emphases I raised in Chapter 1. There are four brief points I wish to stress.

First, by conceptual articulation I do not mean an explanatory theory written about unionism from an outsider's perspective. There are already more than enough such theories.[52] I mean, rather, a theory or number of theories that start from unionists' own senses of identity and try to articulate in appropriate conceptual categories the political vision these senses of identity warrant. This is to envisage a theoretical enterprise that – as in the case of ranking challenges – endeavours to make explicit in conceptual form much that is implicit in practice. Otherwise expressed, it is one that begins with unionists' own self-understandings and attempts to articulate what they imply.

Second, this enterprise is made easier to pursue once we think of unionism's identity as residing in a valued way of life rather than in psychological feelings. A way of life is open to conceptual articulation and rational debate in a manner that feelings often are not thought to be.[53] It now becomes harder to avoid challenges to unionists' senses of identity by retreating to an inner sanctuary that is supposedly impervious to rational contestation. It will not suffice, for example, simply to greet challenges to unionism from Irish nationalists with the retort that I, as a unionist, 'feel British'. And it will not suffice precisely because unionists' identities are tied to a political way of life that is constituted by institutions, practices and relationships that exist in public space and, there-fore, are open to public scrutiny and debate. It should also be borne in mind that amenability to conceptual articulation and debate is incumbent on unionist identities since ways of life are not static and are interpreted differently, not least by unionists themselves.

Third, by virtue of its connection to basic issues of identity, a conceptual articulation of unionists' self-understandings is ap-propriately conceived of as an integral part of delineating their horizon(s) of meaning. In giving an account of what matters to unionists, a unionist theory is thus cast in a highly significant role, one that bears little resemblance to that played by supposedly arid academic exercises. In trying to bring to theoretical light the nature and ramifications of unionists' commitments and attach-ments, it provides at its best a conceptual framework within which unionists can understand more clearly and deeply what they stand for. It also affords a set of conceptual tools with which unionists can engage others. Of course, not all unionist theories are equally successful, and I have already intimated that I think one is vastly superior to others. In making judgements about the various unionist theories on offer, the crucial questions are how well the horizon of meaning captured by a specific conceptual framework enables unionists to see what ultimately matters to them, and how adequately it equips them to deal with the serious challenges they face. It is because the tasks of theory, or conceptual articulation, are so important that these questions must be pressed relentlessly.

Having stressed the indispensability of theory, I should add, finally, a word of caution about its limits. There are two limits, one extrinsic and the other intrinsic, which together counsel against having inflated expectations of what conceptual articulation can achieve. An extrinsic limit pertains to the likely influence on conduct of good theoretical arguments. Take, for example, the difference that exposure of weaknesses in a unionist theory can be reasonably hoped to make to those who subscribe to it. There is, it is true, little way of calculating the difference that might be made in the long term. But in the short term it is prudent not to anticipate too much given what is at stake in many unionists' attachments to a particular theory. It is not just that some have substantial emotional investments in seeing things from a certain angle. It is also that giving up a specific theoretical view may also imply a need to abandon customary facets of a familiar way of life. Even if the argument is lost, or perhaps especially if it is, existential as well as psychological resistance may remain entrenched. To risk being disoriented – which is sometimes what is entailed in admitting theoretical defeat – is not, after all, an enticing prospect. Settling a theoretical argument, in short, rarely settles all that requires settling. An intrinsic limit consists in the inability of any theory, however comprehensive, to capture everything involved in a way of life or a horizon of meaning, to render explicit all the background practices that shape our identities. To imagine that theories can make our lives utterly transparent and unmysterious is probably to succumb to an

Enlightenment-derived prejudice of which it is better to be sceptical.[54]

Neither of these limitations, needless to say, is sufficient to justify dispensing with the service of theories. And unionism, which has muddled through with minimal conceptual reflection, needs their service more than most contemporary political positions.

The above understandings of ranking, identity and conceptual articulation run through the rest of the book. It is against the backcloth they afford that I turn now to note how different responses to the challenges to unionism exhibit different ranking priorities which derive from different construals of what a unionist identity consists in, construals that in turn call for different conceptual articulations of unionism. In subsequent chapters, I explore each of these responses in more detail, paying particular attention to their conceptual articulations.

AN 'ULSTER' UNIONIST RESPONSE

One response is inclined to put more weight than others on challenges from within unionism. It also accords considerable importance to challenges from the British government, but thinks these are best met through a show of unionist unity. External challenges from the Irish government, much like challenges from Northern nationalists that openly refer to Northern Ireland as 'a failed political entity' or that appear more subtly under the name of 'parity of esteem', are not seen as intrinsically serious. That is to say, they neither derive from sources unionists recognise as authoritative nor entail content unionists regard as compelling. Their seriousness as challenges lies only in their propaganda value; in their ability to influence international opinion, especially American, and to sway on occasions the British government. And like challenges from the British government, these challenges are seen as being most effectively dealt with through concerted unionist opposition and unionist counter-persuasion of the British government of the rightness of its cause. Non-nationalist non-unionist challenges, if recognised at all, do not rate much mention.

This response is one that evidently disputes the interpretation I have given of the challenges to unionism, especially because I devalue the importance of unionist unity and appear to grant too much credence to nationalist-inspired challenges of one sort or another. Here I must seem to miss the point, since my interpretation does not sufficiently grasp that the current circumstances of unionism are defined above all else by uncertainty over the constitutional future of Northern Ireland. As a consequence, I underplay the threat to that future posed by the irredentist nationalism enshrined in the Irish constitution, the subversive influence at home and abroad of unionism's new bogeyman – 'the pan-nationalist front' – the vacillations of Westminster, and in general the readiness of the British and Irish governments, with considerable encouragement from the United States administration, to pander to nationalist aspirations, placate republican terrorists, and squeeze unionists into compromising their principles. To understand that a threat to Northern Ireland's constitutional future appears in such multiple forms is also to understand that unionism occupies a beleaguered position susceptible to the betrayals of untrustworthy allies and the attacks of conniving enemies. These are understandings that my interpretation lacks, not least when it allows itself to be diverted by such distractions as non-nationalist challenges in the realm of civil society. Hence, it is no surprise that it fails to appreciate why the achievement of unionist unity is such a priority: in the absence of unity unionism is ill equipped to fend off such powerfully backed challenges to its defence of the integrity of Northern Ireland. Unionism's most urgent tasks, on this reading, must be to heal its own divisions and shore up its collective resources in order to defend itself against blatant and subtle attempts to undermine the justness of its cause. And crucial to successful defence here is convincing the British government to pursue its own unionist-oriented agenda independent of the machinations of Dublin or Washington.

It is tempting to say that if my interpretation of unionism's circumstances is wide of the mark in the manner just suggested, it is because it does not manifest many signs of a siege mentality. For a siege mentality is exactly what is on display in the ranking priorities favoured by this first unionist response. As I have argued, however, the locus of a unionist identity is not to be found in such a mentality. What the above response to the challenges to unionism points to, and what its siege mentality is symptomatic of, rather, is an identity that is appropriately described as 'Ulster' unionist. I do not use this descriptive term in any party political sense, although those to whom it applies are more likely to be members of the DUP than of any other unionist party. The term refers simply to those unionists whose primary allegiance is to an 'Ulster' way of life that has been shaped by an intermix of Protestant and British institutions and values.

A familiar belief of those bearing an Ulster unionist identity is that its distinctive features are by and large peculiar to Northern Ireland. Its combination of Protestantism and Britishness has long since ceased to characterise political life in the rest of the United Kingdom, even if it lives on at the margins in areas of Scotland. It is unsurprising, then, that Ulster unionists regarded Stormont as 'their' parliament and that the preference of many is for a form of devolved government in which the unionist majority is able to play a dominant role once more, even if it is one that falls short of that enjoyed during the Stormont years. Given the constrained circumstances in which unionists currently find themselves, however, other options may also be considered. Full integration with the rest of Britain, if ever offered, would have attractions, principally because of the constitutional peace of mind it would bring. At a pinch, some power-sharing arrangement with nationalists might be acceptable, but only on the proviso that Dublin is uninvolved in the affairs of Northern Ireland. Whatever the arrangement, public institutions would be expected to express a British political identity alone. And there should be no embarrassment in acknowledging that symbols of Britishness are simultaneously symbols of Protestantism. For Ulster unionists the two quite properly belong together, although they also concede the possibility of being Catholic and British in Northern Ireland.

It is the dual Protestant and British character of Northern Ireland that is perceived to be threatened by the Irish government and Northern nationalists and, through pan-nationalist influence, by the US administration and the British government. In all the fine talk about parity of esteem and respecting the two traditions, what is being proposed are concessions to Irish nationalists that, in effect, undermine the basis of an Ulster unionist identity. And the fear is that it will become so emaciated that there will be little resistance in the long run to its ultimate loss as Northern Ireland is absorbed into a united Ireland. That is why vigilance is required now, and it is also why unionism's siege mentality is alive and well. Those institutions, practices and values that uniquely embody Protestantism and Britishness are under assault.

What calls for conceptual articulation here are the various senses in which Protestantism and Britishness are regarded as constitutive of unionism proper. Here opinions differ among Ulster unionists, not least between those whose attachments to Protestantism are primarily religious and those whose attachments are mainly secular. But despite differences, there is a shared view that a Northern Ireland in which an Ulster unionist identity gains rightful expression is one whose institutional life is shaped by a Protestant-British ethos. Accordingly, it is appropriate to refer to the type of conceptual articulation consistent with this identity as 'cultural unionist'. It should also be pointed out that cultural unionism involves specific political claims to the effect that the source of liberalism and democracy lies in Protestant-Britishness. The irony here is that it purports to offer a political deal to those Catholics and nationalists who value liberal democracy that the resources of Catholicism and nationalism cannot match. To the chagrin of its critics, then, it presents itself not as a rationalisation of bigotry and supremacy but as a theory of a free society. And integral to this theory are specific concepts of liberty, loyalty and legitimacy. It is with these concepts, as well as with the general connections drawn between unionism and Protestant-Britishness, that my discussion of cultural unionism is concerned.

A 'BRITISH' UNIONIST RESPONSE

A second unionist response prioritises the challenge from the British government. It does so not merely because this challenge is potentially the most serious of all but, more important, because it is with the politics of Westminster, rather than with the internal politics of Northern Ireland, that its main interest lies. Put another way, it acts on the assumption that the surest way to secure the integrity of Northern Ireland is to convince the British government that there is a convergence of British and unionist interests, inasmuch as maintaining the Union is in principle the priority of both. Other challenges pale into insignificance in comparison with this one; or, at least, they must be judged in its light. Thus unionist fragmentation may seem a big problem, as it did to the first unionist response, or it may seem a relatively minor matter, depending on the circumstances. Unionist unity may be crucial, for example, if it is clear that without it unionists are likely to be railroaded into accepting arrangements they find unpalatable; but it may on occasions be a hindrance if the cultural Protestantism of Ulster unionists serves to convince the British government that its interests and those of unionists do not coincide. In other words, tactical astuteness and flexibility guided by the primacy of the challenge of the British government dictate how seriously challenges from within unionism are to be taken.

What I call British unionists adopt a similar attitude to Ulster unionists when rating most of the challenges issued by the Irish government and Northern nationalists: they count only to the extent that they are heeded by the British government. It is unionism's task to ensure that the British government ceases to give them as much credence as it has tended to, at least since 1985. An exception here applies to one, and possibly two, of the senses in which the concept of parity of esteem is used. There should be nothing grudging about acknowledging nationalists' entitlements to equal civil rights and to having opportunities to express their cultural identity. There is objection only to the idea that cultural nationalism is entitled to political expression within the institutional life of Northern Ireland. As for non-nationalist challenges in civil society, these should not be considered a threat at all to a unionism that wholeheartedly embraces pluralism, though just how much unionist involvement in a politics of civil society is deemed necessary remains unclear.

From another unionist angle, then, it appears again that my interpretation of unionism's circumstances is less than satisfactory. Other than giving a quick nod at its potentially devastating impact, I end up not attributing much more significance to a challenge from the British government than I do to one from the Irish. And in seeming inordinately concerned about nationalist and non-nationalist challenges from within Northern Ireland, I give the impression that unionism needs to be more apologetic and concessionary than is either warranted or healthy. Put in slightly different terms, on this reading I go seriously astray on two fronts. First, I assume that in trying to make the face of unionism more agreeable to nationalists I increase the prospect of their acceptance of the integrity of Northern Ireland. But this is wishful thinking which succeeds only in weakening unionism and encouraging nationalists to believe that the arrival of a united Ireland is almost at hand. Second, in chiding unionism for its relative neglect of aspects of the internal politics of Northern Ireland, I misunderstand what really matters. This misunderstanding is communicated in various ways, including a sarcastic dismissal of the notion of 'masterful inactivity' at the beginning of the chapter, unduly harsh criticisms of Molyneaux's political tactics in Chapter 1, disdain at the lack of unionist interest in the Opsahl Commission and, it could be added for good measure, disagreement with mainstream unionism's decisions not to participate in all-party talks until preconditions are met or to attend the Irish-government-sponsored Forum for Peace and

Reconciliation at Dublin Castle. What such negative appraisals of unionist attitudes and conduct fail to understand is that persuading Westminster to take seriously the idea of the Union is where unionist energy is most profitably directed. Appreciating that this is unionism's priority puts a quite different gloss on talk of masterful inactivity, Molyneaux's tactics and unionist indifference to nationalist- and non-nationalist-inspired political initiatives. To suppose that energy would be better spent trying to convince nationalists or non-nationalists of the virtues of unionism risks sending the wrong signals to Dublin about the sort of involvement in the affairs of Northern Ireland unionists might be prepared to tolerate of it, making unionism needlessly vulnerable, and squandering resources playing a game where the prize is small beer compared to that on offer in the game at Westminster.

Given such reasoning, the ultimate culpability of my interpretation, of which the flaws described above give hint, lies in its failure to perceive what the ranking priorities of this second unionist response manifestly point to, namely that a unionist identity is primarily located in a 'British' political way of life. It is crucial to emphasise that this identity is political, not cultural, in kind and therefore drawn more narrowly than an Ulster unionist identity. Those who define themselves in terms of it may differ widely in their religious and cultural attachments. They may equally be Protestant or Catholic. They may consider themselves Irish, Northern Irish, English or whatever. The point is that unionism as a political identity is *culture-blind*. It is bound up with the life of citizenship made available by the institutions of the British state – a life that delivers a genuine pluralism unavailable in an Irish state whose institutions remain mired by the cultural particularity of Irish nationalism. So many of the challenges to unionism conspire to put this unionist political identity even further beyond the reach of unionists. That is why they must be opposed and efforts must be concentrated on showing the British government that unionists are entitled to enjoy the full benefits of an identity taken for granted elsewhere in the United Kingdom.

And that is why the challenge from the British government is of supreme importance, since it is in the power of this government alone to give unionists what they want and what is rightfully theirs.

The arrangements that would give British unionists what they want are clearly those associated with Northern Ireland's full integration with the rest of Britain. In contrast to Ulster unionists, there is little lament here for the demise of Stormont, since such an experiment in devolved government is regarded as having been an unfortunate mistake from the start. If devolution of some kind is all that is ultimately available in Northern Ireland, however, British unionists prefer that it should involve as minimal a transfer of powers from Westminster as possible. An administrative local assembly would find greater favour, for instance, than a legislative assembly. It is accepted that any such assembly would have to be organised along power-sharing lines. What is not accepted is that any new structures of government in Northern Ireland should entail a dilution of its political Britishness. Thus, as with Ulster unionists, British unionists reject entirely any claim for political parity of esteem between unionists and nationalists, and refuse to entertain any diminution of British sovereignty in Northern Ireland through a role being found for the Irish government.

Conceptual articulation is required here to elucidate more fully the sense of political Britishness being called upon. In particular, we need to know more about the notion of the state said to be embodied in the United Kingdom's institutions and practices but not in the Irish Republic's. We also need to explore the concepts typically invoked in support of this notion, such as citizenship, pluralism, rights, freedom, and legitimacy. When we examine the treatment accorded to these concepts by British unionists, it becomes clear that they fit within a theoretical scheme appropriately described as 'liberal unionist'. And, we are told, the political way of life articulated by liberal unionism affords unrivalled benefits to all citizens in Northern Ireland, regardless of their religious, cultural or ethnic affiliations.

A 'NORTHERN IRISH' UNIONIST RESPONSE

A third response puts most emphasis on challenges to unionism arising from within Northern Ireland. The range of issues raised under the banner of parity of esteem as well as the questions asked of unionism through a politics of civil society are taken to introduce considerations of the most searching sort. These are considerations that penetrate to the core of what unionism has to offer. Other challenges do not carry the same intrinsic importance even if many of them appear in more powerfully endorsed packages. But this does not mean that they are not taken seriously at all. On the contrary, to prioritise internal Northern Irish challenges, or at least those gathered under the heading 'parity of esteem', is simultaneously to face up to the external challenges of the British and Irish governments. It is only internal unionist challenges that are given relatively short shrift. The price demanded by unionist unity, for instance, is too high to contemplate paying. Given the current state of unionism, it means effectively shutting out the crucial issues raised by nationalist and non-nationalist challenges. And this is to accept the unacceptable, namely that a politics of the tunnel vision is unionism's lot.

The way in which this third response ranks the challenge to unionism fits with my interpretation of unionism's circumstances. Little else should be expected, of course, since this response is the one I advocate. To extend its rationale a bit further, it assumes that the British and Irish governments would gleefully underwrite any settlement in Northern Ireland that was mutually acceptable to unionists and nationalists. Encouraging a process of reconciliation that brings together the major political actors in the North is precisely what the thrust of the external challenges to unionism amounts to. The glaringly obvious point that the British and Irish governments force upon unionist attention is that there is no possibility of permanent structures of government being introduced in Northern Ireland that do not accommodate (at least some) nationalist concerns. Other unionist responses contrive ways of having their attention diverted and so miss the obvious. They have their reasons for doing so, of course, but none is sufficiently compelling. There is ultimately no escaping the requirement to engage nationalists in order to secure a future for Northern Ireland with which everyone can live. And to recognise that this is so is to acknowledge that challenges to unionism from within Northern Ireland cannot be dodged.

Such a conclusion captures the inner logic of the external challenges to unionism. But that is not the main reason for adopting it. As I have intimated, challenges emanating from within Northern Ireland deserve to be prioritised because of their content. All of the questions prompted by the concept of parity of esteem are important, including those connected with its cultural and political senses which other unionist responses have most difficulty entertaining. The task of allowing these questions to occupy centre-stage cannot be shirked if it is accepted that all citizens in the North are entitled to have a say in how the character of their society is shaped. At stake here is the crucial matter of what sort of deal unionists are prepared to offer nationalists to convince them that Northern Ireland is a polity with which they may fully identify – a matter that involves the sort of accommodation unionists are willing to find for an Irish dimension. Challenges emerging from non-nationalist sources also have a vital role to play. These have the virtue of shifting the focus away from a politics of constitutional standoff by asking the probing question of why wider issues of democracy and justice in civil society should always play second fiddle to unionism's constitutional preoccupations. Or, put sharply, is there not something terribly awry with notions of unionism that are not defined as much by their commitment to create a democratic and just society in Northern Ireland as by their constitutional commitment to the United Kingdom? If any question commands serious deliberation it is this one.

A ranking procedure that privileges challenges from within Northern Ireland relates to a unionist identity bound up with what I want to call a 'Northern Irish' way of life. This identity is less obviously captured than other unionist identities, partly because it is more complex and partly because it is still in the process of making itself. It is a cultural identity but not in the exclusive sense of Ulster unionism, and it is a political identity but not in the narrow sense of British unionism. Its cultural meaning is rooted in an understanding of Northern Ireland as 'a place apart' that is defined by its ties to both the rest of Britain and the rest of Ireland, and also by the distinctive stock of experiences and meanings its inhabitants share, as a result of their peculiar history, which distinguish them from their counterparts elsewhere in Britain and Ireland. The political meaning of this 'Northern Irish' identity also appreciates Northern Ireland's apartness, but within the constitutional context of the United Kingdom. It is an identity shaped in part by those institutions of the British state that deliver benefits of citizenship and a pluralist society, and which cannot legitimately be surrendered against the democratic wishes of Northern Ireland's citizens. But it is also an identity that anticipates facilitation of the North's major cultural strands in public institutions, and the development of social and political institutions that are sustained by the actions of citizens and afford new forms of citizen identification.

The arrangements capable of expressing a Northern Irish identity are most likely to be found (1) in a form of power-sharing devolved government that enjoys a substantial transfer of legislative and executive powers from Westminster; (2) in an interrelationship between the politics conducted at this level and the politics conducted in civil society; and (3) through an accommodation of Irishness, as well as Britishness, in the institutional life of Northern Ireland. On the third suggestion, two points bear emphasising. First, nationalism's hijacking of Irishness, not least through its attempts to identify it with Catholicism, should be repudiated by unionists. Second, there should be openness to certain claims of political parity of esteem, although openness should not be mistaken for compliance with every nationalist request. On the other suggestions a common rationale is at work: citizens in Northern Ireland are entitled to maximal control over their social and political affairs and require institutions that recognise their entitlement. This rationale stresses the indispensability of citizens' actions to the health of a polity. And from its perspective a notion such as 'masterful inactivity' must always appear as a political oxymoron.

Conceptual articulation is required here on several fronts. More needs to be said, for example, about the possibility of combining the various strands that constitute a Northern Irish unionist identity, and about the institutional arrangements they imply. The relationships between culture and politics and between the state and civil society that a way of life informed by this identity involves also demand clarification, as do the specific concepts of citizenship, freedom and legitimacy that underpin them. Given the central role accorded to the activity of citizens in this view, it is appropriate to describe the theory that derives from a Northern Irish identity as 'civic unionist'. It is this that provides the conceptual resources to project a future for Northern Ireland beyond a zero-sum game played out between so-called pan-nationalist and pan-unionist fronts, by suggesting that the only 'front' unionism should be interested in joining is a pan-democratic one.[55] It is only when the interests of democracy are made primary that Northern Ireland will have a future worth having.

Before arguing in detail why the conceptual framework afforded by civic unionism alone opens up a future worth having, I need to show why the frameworks provided by cultural unionism and liberal unionism do not. I deal with these in separate chapters, starting with the theory of cultural unionism.

3

CULTURAL UNIONISM

A cultural unionist theory derives from an 'Ulster unionist' way of life which is characterised by institutions and practices reflecting a Protestant-British ethos. Or so I claimed in the previous chapter. I also claimed that it is these institutions and practices and this ethos that are perceived by cultural unionists to be at risk in the uncongenial circumstances in which unionism currently finds itself. In this chapter, I make occasional references to the latter claim but concentrate mostly on the former, which points to the substantive core of what I am calling cultural unionism. It is a core that I try to extract in two major ways. First, I articulate the forms in which an Ulster unionist way of life appears by exploring the sorts of institutions and practices that are taken to embody a Protestant-British ethos, and by highlighting the horizon of meaning that the ethos implies. Second, I consider the type of political theory with which cultural unionism is associated, the conceptual scheme that the institutions and practices and the horizon of meaning implicitly or explicitly invoke. This scheme relies heavily upon a cluster of ideas that may be usefully discussed in relation to the concepts of loyalty and liberty.

Although, as I have already indicated, I am unconvinced that cultural unionism offers a fruitful way forward for unionists, I want to start with a defence of a cultural unionist position against a type of attack that would discredit it *in principle*. Doing so enables me to distinguish between forms of criticism that properly tell against it and forms that do not. It also helps to lay the foundation for a conception of culture's relation to politics that I build upon in chapters 4 and 5. Here, though, I try to establish that in principle cultural unionism represents a legitimate theoretical stance and that its problems are ones of substance.

CULTURAL UNIONISM AND ITS CRITICS

A constant refrain of liberal unionists is that unionism is done a disservice by its association with cultural and religious connotations of Protestantism. It is precisely such an association that they think makes unionism needlessly vulnerable to the charge of sectarianism. Thus Robert McCartney, for example, urges that unionists should oppose 'the forces of an irrational and sectarian Unionism which sees the Union merely as a convenient constitutional device for maintaining a non-Catholic ascendancy'. This is of the utmost importance, he continues, because the 'true and essential Union is not an exclusive union of loyalists or protestants, but a union between peoples who believe in liberal democracy and civil and religious liberty for all in the fullest sense of a pluralist society'.[1] And, according to Arthur Aughey, to grasp this point properly means refusing to reduce unionism to matters of 'religion, identity or security'[2] and distinguishing sharply the issue of political allegiance from issues of 'cultural values or identity'.[3]

THE ANTI-CULTURALISM THESIS

These remarks of McCartney and Aughey point to a political vision of unionism that I consider in depth in the next chapter. But they also introduce two points of immediate significance: that a unionism that is too closely identified with Protestantism is not only sectarian but irrational, and that cultural attachments of whatever sort are superfluous to the essence of unionism. These points are at the heart of disputes between liberal and cultural unionists and it remains to be seen whether the latter are sufficiently equipped to answer them. But taken in a certain way – which ultimately extends beyond the particular agenda of liberal unionism – the points potentially settle matters in advance by discounting the possibility of cultural unionism coming up with effective rejoinders. The die is already cast, so to speak, if the charges of irrationality and superfluousness predispose us to a general anti-culturalist thesis that may be put as follows: political commitments – such as unionism – are not primarily explicable in cultural/religious categories if due deference is to be paid to rational criteria. If correct, this thesis cripples cultural unionism from the outset. Cultural/religious arguments for unionism are reduced to implausible rationalisations of bad (sectarian) practices, or to disingenuous smokescreens, or perhaps to self-deceiving forms of advocacy.

Now it may be true that cultural unionists are unconvincing rationalisers, disingenuous disguisers, or sincere yet self-deceived advocates; or then again it may not be. That decisions of these kinds can be made *a priori* is what is at issue. But is an *a priori* line, with its in-built negative judgements, as central to the anti-culturalist thesis as I have inferred? And if it is, what justifies it? In relation to the first question, it should be admitted that there is possibly more to the thesis than I have implied inasmuch as arguments that are not purely *a priori* may also be at work in it. For example, the points made by McCartney and Aughey could be taken to reflect in part their assessments of the damage inflicted on the cause of unionism by cultural unionist practices. And much the same could be said of another instance of anti-culturalism upon which I want to focus: the debunking by McGarry and O'Leary of culturalist interpretations of Northern Ireland. In some measure that debunking is informed by the judgement that these interpretations have been tested and found wanting, as misgivings about the explanatory value of, say, Padraig O'Malley's culturalist account of republican hunger strikes purportedly demonstrate.[4] The anti-culturalist thesis, then, is not unreservedly *a priori*; it contains *a posteriori* elements too.

This much may be granted without dislodging the central *a priori* plank of the thesis. That such a plank is central almost goes without saying. It is revealed in the call made by both McCartney and Aughey for unionism to transcend its cultural affiliations not redefine them, and in their arrogation of the label 'rational' to a unionism that has (ostensibly) succeeded in transcending Protestant culture. It is also manifest in a similar ploy, though not one made in the name of unionism, that is adopted by McGarry and O'Leary. Although prepared to allow that there are better and worse sorts of culturalist interpretations of Northern Ireland, they consider all of them inferior to 'rationalist' explanations. The striking feature of the anti-culturalist thesis thus remains *a priori* in kind: it consists in a commitment to rationality not available on culturalist terms. But what justifies this feature? Or, now more precisely, what is it about rationality that makes it both superior to culture and inaccessible to culturalists?

These questions are profitably considered against the backdrop of distinctions drawn between rationalists and culturalists by McGarry and O'Leary. Rationalists, we are told: (1) concentrate on the interests at play in any cluster of social and political preferences; (2) incline towards economic explanations which show how agents are 'pulled' by material incentives; (3) regard human actors as 'strategists'; and in sum (4) think that we act in the ways we do because it is in our interests to do so. Culturalists, by contrast: (1) concentrate on values and norms; (2) conceive of agents being 'pushed' by 'quasi-inertial forces'; (3) consider humans as creatures of habit; and ultimately (4) suppose that our perceptions of our interests, as well as the normative codes governing how interests are pursued, are culturally determined.[5]

With these distinctions in mind, the question of why rationality is superior to culture admits of easy answers, at least according to McGarry and O'Leary. Two of these answers are worth a quick mention. One is that rationality is superior because it enables us to understand political action in Northern Ireland not as a baffling replay of outmoded (irresolvable) historical dramas, but as an entirely modern pursuit of (conflicting) interests. Rationality delivers us from the mind-numbing assumption that 'people are mindless executors of historic cultures'[6] by projecting an altogether more compelling image of us as calculating, strategic, interest-driven agents. And thus we are given a grasp that eludes culturalist analysis of what was going on in such important events in recent Northern Irish affairs as the republican hunger strikes. For whereas 'knowledge of Brehon, Catholic, or Gaelic cultures does not enable anybody to predict how Sands and his colleagues would have reacted', with recourse to rationality we break through to the explanatory insight that 'the whole saga of the hunger strikes can be seen as a rational short-term game or manoeuvre in a long-term political war of position; and as more rational and political, and as less shrouded in culture and psychology, than O'Malley and others suggest'.[7]

Another instance of rationality's superiority to culture is afforded by the focus it invites on institutional design to account for the experiences of loyalty and disloyalty, obedience and disobedience, and peace and violence that have characterised political life in Northern Ireland. Ideally, institutions should be designed to facilitate as wide a spread of citizens' interests as possible. The fact that Northern Ireland's institutions failed the facilitation test by privileging unionist and Protestant cultural modes – and thus evoked expressions of disloyalty, disobedience and violence from nationalists – reveals that they were bedevilled by the problem of 'inappropriate institutional design'.[8] The point here is that rationality once more shows us why instability has occurred and what is required to overcome it in a manner that cultural analyses, with their 'vague appeals to historic cultures',[9] cannot match. And, in doing so, we are reminded again of the secondary role of culture in social and political life: 'cultures do not just happen, and do not just persist of their own accord. They persist because they are institutionally supported or because they serve people's interests.'[10]

On the question of why rationality is inaccessible to culturalists the response is now obvious. Rationality, as defined by McGarry and O'Leary, is hard-headed. It has to do with strategic and institutional planning, with how we may as calculative actors maximise our interests. Used astutely, it instructs us on how we may most efficiently marshal the means at our disposal to achieve our ends. Rationality thus turns out to be a tool or instrument we deploy to impress our design on the world. The stuff with which culturalists deal – values, norms, customs, traditional understandings and the like – falls outside the domain of rationality proper. This is the soft stuff about which rationality necessarily remains silent and which if prioritised leaves culturalists closed off from the benefits of rationality. Accordingly, rationality is inaccessible to culturalists to the degree that they persist in being culturalists.

To return to the point of this exploration of the concept of rationality at the centre of the anti-culturalist thesis two remarks are in order. First, if McGarry and O'Leary are right, my proposal to take seriously culturalist arguments for unionism is misguided. I risk falling for the trap into which they think O'Malley tumbles and to avoid this I should, rather, be looking behind these arguments to discern the interests they are serving. Second, it follows on McGarry and O'Leary's terms that those unionists who define themselves in culturalist categories are, to reiterate what I stated earlier, either manipulating or self-deluded agents. And if they are the latter, there is an implicit prescriptive message in the analysis of McGarry and O'Leary which echoes the message of McCartney and Aughey: for political purposes at least, put matters of religion and culture on the back burner, emerge from the misty world of cultural preoccupations, and become enlightened, rational political advocates.

I want to resist these implications and to do so effectively requires challenging the assumptions upon which McGarry and O'Leary rely. I suggest, in particular, that we should be sceptical of the either/or scenario they depict in relation to rationalists and culturalists, and that we should oppose the canonical status they attribute to a very narrow notion of rationality.

The either/or scenario is susceptible to a number of objections. First, it is possible, if not highly probable, that both culturalist and (strategic) rationalist factors are involved in many instances of political action, including those pertaining to the IRA hunger strikes. To elucidate the cultural context within which Bobby Sands and others operated is not *in itself* to be blind to the strategic dimension of a decision to die in such a harrowing way. What is hard to credit is the supposition that the hunger strikers' actions are properly explicable without recourse to the cultural images, memories and norms that sustained them. At one point McGarry and O'Leary appear to draw back from this supposition by conceding that 'culture may be invoked to explain the preferences of paramilitaries, whereas rationality may be used to explain the means chosen to achieve the cultural preferences'. But they seem to suspect that this concession may give too much credence to culturalists and immediately add that 'unique cultural explanations should only be resorted to in the last instance, rather than in the first instance'.[11] This is too meagre a concession and one that is designed to leave undisturbed precisely what needs disturbing, that is, the sovereignty of strategic rationality.

Consider what McGarry and O'Leary have to offer here: a plausible account of how the strategy of hunger strikes served the IRA's overall interests. What they do not offer, however, is a decent understanding of why the IRA has the interests that it does. And this is not a trivial oversight. On the contrary, understanding what informs republican interests is constitutive of appreciating why republican goals are what they are, and of grasping how it is that these goals are able to be pursued by a variety of means – including those as extreme as hunger strikes. In short, once we set about filling the gap in the McGarry and O'Leary account we are back on the turf occupied by O'Malley and others and culturalist considerations are brought out of the background and into the foreground. And this in turn opens up the possibility of a pattern of reasoning that might run as follows: (1) strategies may be judged as more or less rational to the degree that they succeed in advancing certain interests; (2) interests thus establish the parameters for strategically rational action; (3) but interests are shaped by cultural factors such as values, norms and memories as well as by calculations of self-advantage; (4) accordingly, cultural considerations cannot be bypassed by attempts to explain thoroughly why individuals or groups act as they do, and to assess whether this or that course of action is strategically rational. This pattern of reasoning subverts the dichotomy between the cultural and the rational by emphasising their interrelation and by casting doubt on the alleged sovereignty of strategic rationality.

It is a pattern of reasoning that also calls into question not only the claim that culture is a secondary social and political concern that is parasitic upon institutional and interest-based support, but also the notion that institutional design can be effectively undertaken independently of cultural influence. On the notion of institutional design's independence, it is sufficient to remark here that McGarry and O'Leary simply assume what needs to be shown: that the designers of social and political institutions are capable of working as culturally unencumbered actors, that it is possible to design institutions in a cultural vacuum, as it were, and that it is desirable to try. I deal with these sorts of assumptions in more detail in Chapter 4 when discussing liberal unionism. I also develop another point there that is worth stating baldly here, namely that the presumption that culturally neutral institutions are a good thing is itself a product of a 'liberal-Enlightenment' cultural package, as indeed is the general preoccupation with strategic or instrumental rationality.

The claim that culture requires institutional and interest-based support in order to survive is obviously valid in one sense. That is to say, it is hard to imagine how any cultural expression could exist indefinitely in the absence of any institutional recognition or correspondence with people's interests. But it is not valid to infer from this that culture is therefore a secondary political factor. If culture's dependence on institutions and interests is one side of the coin, *their* dependence on culture is the other side. Quite simply, it beggars belief that institutions and interests are not related to values and norms, or that they do not reflect certain customs and historical traditions, at least to some degree. It is equally hard to accept that cultural changes at the level of values, norms, customs and traditions do not impact upon institutional life and upon how interests are both perceived and pursued. In the end, it is tempting to conclude that not to recognise the interdependence of so-called rational and cultural dimensions is to fall victim to a very strained form of philosophical contrivance.

Acknowledging such interdependence undermines the anti-culturalist assertion that rationality is superior to culture. The other part of the anti-culturalist thesis – which holds that rationality is inaccessible to culturalists – remains relatively intact, however; and construed in a certain manner it is hard to oppose. If, as McGarry and O'Leary stipulate, rationality is defined exclusively in instrumental–strategic terms then it is unlikely to figure prominently in typical culturalist investigations. Explorations of the roles, meanings and perhaps justifications of values, norms, traditions and customs in social and political life, for example, are not characteristically dictated by criteria of efficiency and interest-maximisation. So if rationality is indeed the preserve of instrumentally oriented, calculative activity, it is quite appropriate to conclude that it lies outside common culturalist concerns.

But why should we accept that this is the case? McGarry and O'Leary simply take it for granted and thereby confer canonical status on a specific variant of rationality. And, having done so, they then presume the liberty to pass sweeping, pejorative judgements on culturalist emphases. These emphases are 'vague' and 'shrouded in culture and psychology'. Cultural values and norms are little other than 'preferences'. And culturalists apparently believe that humans are 'pushed' by 'quasi-inertial forces', that they are 'mindless executors', that they are merely creatures of habit whose interests and norms are culturally determined, and so forth. In sum, culturalists, it appears, do not believe in human agency and make claims that are rationally or epistemically empty.

Two big issues emerge here. Can it be demonstrated that rationality is unreservedly instrumental or strategic in kind? And must culturalist predilections imply a denial of human agency and an absence of practical reason? These issues raise philosophical queries beyond the scope of this study. But I should indicate very briefly why I think the answer to both is an emphatic no.

In a nutshell, rationality cannot be held to be unreservedly instrumental because instrumental rationality itself relies upon principles that are not instrumentally derived. To elucidate, rationality in its instrumental sense entails a clear-sighted thinking through of 'preferences' – setting out their relation to one another, weighing up their relative importance, ordering them in some fashion – and a rigorous calculation of the means best suited to their maximisation and of the most efficient implementation of these means. What is involved here are two different sorts of activity: a sifting through or ordering sort and a calculative sort. And it is evident that the latter sort, with which instrumental rationality is typically identified, is intelligible only against the backcloth of the former sort. The problem for an 'immodest' instrumentalism which thinks of rationality as instrumental to the core is that it cannot show that the principles invoked in sifting through or ordering preferences are themselves the fruit of instrumental calculations.[12] And inasmuch as it cannot, it manifestly overreaches itself and requires a more modest formulation that allows that there is more to rationality than instrumentalism can ever capture.

Once we recognise that instrumental–strategic pursuits do not exhaust the scope of rationality, we are in a position to reconsider the pejorative judgements McGarry and O'Leary pass on culturalist concerns. The possibility remains, of course, that their judgements may be apt: certain culturalist interpreters and certain apologists of a particular cultural persuasion may regard human beings as so thoroughly constituted by their historical circumstances that neither agency nor practical reason are rated very highly. But these are judgements that cannot appeal for their justification to an *a priori* criterion of instrumental rationality. And, more important, they are judgements that run foul not only of the self-understandings of countless historical actors, but also of longstanding philosophical traditions. In rather different ways, admittedly, followers of, say, both Aristotle and Kant are convinced that issues of values and norms are susceptible to the investigations of practical reason, that they do amount to more than arbitrary preferences, and that one's historical heritage is as amenable to critical reflection as it is to passive reception.[13] Or, to reinvoke the spirit of the hermeneutic orientation introduced in Chapter 1, it is perfectly plausible to think of humans as beings who are situated *and* reflective, historically implicated *and* historically creative, culturally embedded *and* critically engaged. Accordingly, to admit that we are persons for whom traditional understandings matter is not equivalent to confessing that we are hostages to tradition. On the contrary, in hermeneutic terms it is also to say that understandings have to be appropriated by us, not merely transmitted to us, and that they have to be refined, adapted and perhaps even radically revised over time, not least through their contact with other understandings. And, in so saying, it is to affirm that agency counts as indeed does practical reason and its deliberations.

To clarify, I am not claiming that all culturalists do think along Kantian, Aristotelian, or hermeneutic lines, but that culturalist considerations are in principle open to such lines of thinking, especially a hermeneutic line. Stated succinctly, a rejection of the anti-culturalist thesis returns to centre-stage the role played by cultural understandings in social and political life, and leaves open the prospect that these understandings have rational warrant.

INTERNAL QUESTIONING

The above conclusions are of considerable consequence for the main remit of this chapter. They permit us to take seriously cultural unionists on their own terms, they permit us to allow the possibility that matters of religion, culture and history are as crucial to unionism as the cultural unionists maintain, and they permit us to probe whether the normative and evaluative scheme(s) they espouse are rationally defensible. Cultural unionism is, then, in principle a legitimate theoretical position. And the types of criticisms to which it is vulnerable are those pertaining to the substantive details of both institutions and practices it upholds and of arguments proffered in their defence. This means, in particular, criticisms that expose flaws in its internal rationale by questioning the ability of the horizon of meaning it makes available and the conceptual framework it affords to enable unionists to see what ultimately matters in Northern Ireland and to handle challenges from other sources. It is with critical questions of this sort in mind that I turn now to probe the adequacy of some central features of a cultural unionist outlook.

A WAY OF LIFE AND A HORIZON OF MEANING

Cultural unionism is bound up with a way of life sustained by memories and comprised of institutions, practices and values displaying a Protestant-British ethos. By virtue of being so, it is associated with certain attachments to the British state and to governmental arrangements in Northern Ireland, as well as with broader religious, social and cultural affiliations. It is typical of cultural unionism to link these kinds of association; to say that political attachments and arrangements are properly informed by broader affiliations and vice versa. State institutions, in other words, set the boundaries within which religious, social and cultural forms of Protestant-Britishness operate; but they, in turn, should also reflect the norms and values of these forms.

Discerning and evaluating what this particular link of politics and culture consists in is the principal task of the remainder of this chapter. To set about accomplishing it, I start with a brief sketch of basic facets of an 'Ulster unionist' way of life that attest to an intermingling of the two. These facets also give a glimpse of the horizon of meaning accessible to participants in such a way of life. They show the range of vision made available by a Protestant-British ethos regarding those things of greatest significance to cultural unionists. But, I shall argue, examination of the role played particularly by Protestantism in shaping this horizon of meaning reveals serious practical strains in the way of life from which cultural unionism emerges. It encourages blind spots which create political problems not easily resolved. These problems are compounded by intellectual strains in the conceptualisation of the horizon of meaning which I then proceed to discuss in relation to the sort of political theory cultural unionism engenders.

AN 'ULSTER UNIONIST' WAY OF LIFE

To describe a way of life as 'Ulster unionist' is at once to indicate one defined by dual referents: the institutions, beliefs and practices of a people living it out within a location in Ireland – Ulster – but doing so in part through bonds to a larger entity – the United Kingdom. The constituent elements of these particular 'Ulster' and more general 'British' referents may on occasions be mutually reinforcing, or they may exist in creative tension, or they may diverge sharply. Arguably, the quandary of current cultural unionists is how to maintain allegiance to both referents when the signs are that their relationship is increasingly becoming one of serious divergence, rather than of creative coexistence or mutual reinforcement. To grasp why this quandary is as it is, we must first delineate what the constituent elements of the two referents are and how they inform an Ulster unionist way of life.

This way of life is underpinned by political elements that contain basic British and distinctively Ulster connotations. The British elements are in this case of the essence since, in addition to contributing to its character, they amount to nothing less than constitutional guarantees of the way of life. These are delivered through three great historical events in particular, namely the so-called 'Glorious Revolution' of 1688, the Act of Union of 1801, and the Government of Ireland Act of 1920. The benefits yielded through such events are presumed to include at least the following: British institutions of state ensuring a Protestant monarchy, parliamentary sovereignty or the sovereignty of the Crown in parliament, the rule of law, religious toleration in particular and a bundle of civil and religious liberties in general; a Union of England, Scotland, Wales and Ireland in which each member is granted a comparable stake in British institutional life; and, following the secession from the United Kingdom of what is now the Republic of Ireland, an arrangement underwriting Northern Ireland's constitutional status as part of the Union.[14]

The terms of this arrangement, of course, also placed Northern Ireland's position within the United Kingdom on a unique footing through the establishment of a devolved government in the region. Although British sovereignty was not relinquished and fundamental powers were reserved by Westminster, such crucial powers as law and order were transferred to the new local administration.[15] And it is here that tangible political expression is given to something that may have been there all along, but that had certainly been imposing itself on the political scene since opposition was organised to Gladstone's first Home Rule Bill in 1886, namely the distinctive Ulster element in the unionist way of life in Ireland.[16] Perhaps not surprisingly given the circumstances of Northern Ireland's troubled birth, when a significant minority of those who found themselves under its jurisdiction refused to give active consent to its legitimacy, the devolved parliament that embodied this distinctively Ulster element reflected the views of the consenting majority. And this meant Protestant views.

Britishness in Northern Ireland was intertwined with Protestantism. That powerful slogan of unionist opposition to Home Rule in
Ireland – 'Home Rule is Rome Rule' – was intended in earnest,
however much it suited the interests of capital besides.[17] And it is
tendentious to deny that Stormont did develop in significant respects into a 'Protestant parliament for a Protestant people'[18] with
which cultural unionists identified strongly.

Since the end of this particular experiment in devolution in
1972, the political dimension of an Ulster unionist way of life has
been left searching for adequate institutional recognition. Direct
rule from Westminster offers modest consolation inasmuch as it
maintains a British connection which many in Ulster continue to
interpret in predominantly Protestant terms. Just as important,
it protects this way of life from the extinction its adherents fear
would be its lot in a united Ireland. But direct rule frustrates, not
least because cultural unionists are essentially devolutionists.
What they will not accept, however, is devolution at any price.
Arrangements for government in Northern Ireland that are
perceived to undercut their way of life, to dilute the 'Britishness'
of Ulster, will not be countenanced. Just as they stood against the
Sunningdale Agreement in the 1970s and the Anglo-Irish
Agreement in the 1980s, so in the 1990s they look suspiciously
at the Downing Street Declaration and reject outright *Frameworks
for the Future*. It is probably true that many cultural unionists
would prefer a form of devolution based on majority rule but
know that nothing of the sort will be on offer.[19] Precisely what
they might settle for remains an open question given the
uncertainties that afflict political life in Northern Ireland. Some
variant of power-sharing between unionist and nationalist parties
might eventually win their reluctant approval, especially if the
alternatives seem bleaker. But what they appear implacably opposed to is any devolved arrangement that includes a role for
Dublin in the internal affairs of Northern Ireland, or that
envisages institutions reflecting nationalist as well as unionist allegiances. These points are taken to be non-negotiable.

They are non-negotiable for cultural unionists because to concede ground on them is tantamount to accepting a violation of British sovereignty in Northern Ireland, it is tantamount to depriving the Ulster unionist way of life of its legitimate claim to exclusive institutional expression, and it is tantamount to signalling a fateful step on the path to Irish unity. The insistence on non-negotiability here is expressed with considerable feeling. To plumb its depths, we have to understand that the way of life such insistence is ultimately designed to defend is one nourished by historical memories that retain contemporary salience.

These memories reinvoke a number of apparently disparate events which are linked together and retold in the service of a collective identity. Thus we have vivid reminders of such seventeenth-century events as the massacre of Protestants in 1641, the Siege of Derry in 1689 and the Battle of the Boyne in 1690.[20] To these we may add events in the second decade of the twentieth century: the signing of the Ulster Solemn League and Covenant in 1912, say, and the losses incurred by the 36th Ulster Division at the Battle of the Somme in 1916.[21] Or, to bring matters up to date, we may include the successful Ulster Workers' Council strike in 1974, along with remembrances of the deaths suffered by ordinary British citizens and members of the security forces at the hands of the IRA since 1969. The point is that these memories and more interweave in a sort of grand cultural unionist narrative which emphasises three themes: the precariousness of Protestant experience in Ireland, the right of Protestants to belong in the North as a distinctive British presence, and the ongoing willingness of Protestants to make ultimate sacrifices for the sake of Britain in general and the Ulster unionist way of life in particular. Quite simply, then, to contemplate negotiating a deal for the future of Northern Ireland that would vitiate the above-mentioned memories and the themes they convey is not part of the script in this cultural unionist story.

If this story lacks a proper political home or sufficient institutional recognition given the demise of Stormont and the reality of Westminster indifference, it does not want for other kinds of expression in Northern Irish society. Significant traces of it are evident in all the unionist political parties and its presence is conspicuous in the more sinister media of loyalist paramilitary organisations.[22] The story is carried in undiluted form by the loyal institutions, especially the largest – the Orange Order – which stands steadfastly for the Protestant faith and loyalty to the Crown.[23] It is also transmitted in a more diffuse way through various popular rituals and cultural symbols that proliferate in Protestant areas of Northern Ireland, from bonfires to wall murals, from painted kerbstones to the display of Union and Ulster flags, and so on.[24] The story is still communicated via many Protestant churches, not only through sermons but also more subtly through church organisations such as the Boys' Brigade. No doubt the political theology of Ian Paisley provides the cultural unionist narrative with its most explicit religious endorsement. Indeed, in Paisley's view, the narrative is virtually given a divine imprimatur. Ulster, we are informed, 'has had the peculiar preservation of divine Providence'. And 'when it seemed humanly impossible to extricate Ulster from seeming disaster, God intervened'. He did so, apparently, because he 'has a purpose for this province, and this plant of Protestantism sown here in the north-eastern part of this island'.[25]

So Northern Ireland is special. The interconnection of Protestantism and Britishness, though perceived as integral to the *raison d'être* of Britain's constitutional arrangements, has become the almost unique hallmark of an Ulster unionist way of life. And the specific ethos to which its various symbols, memories and political aspirations attest is one deriving from a set of religious and/ or political commitments that make central the primacy of individuals and the defence of civil and religious liberties. It is one that manifests itself in a distrust of centralised ecclesiastical or political authority, and that, doubtless due to the influence of Presbyterianism, values democratic responsibility, law and order, and individual judgement.[26] To borrow Charles Taylor's term, it is an ethos that follows the Puritan 'affirmation of ordinary life'[27] in its denial of hierarchical orders and its acceptance of the intrinsic dignity of social, economic and domestic transactions. And these transactions are characteristically carried out through a sparing and direct use of language and a straightforward manner of dealing with people. Bearers of the ethos also tend towards a legalistic and literalistic interpretation of documents and agreements, not least in their insistence that promises must be honoured and that the strict letter of the law or of a contract must be upheld.[28] In sum, the Protestant-British ethos inherent in the Ulster unionist way of life is taken to point to a set of political, religious and social arrangements that are unavailable on the terms of Irish Catholicism and nationalism. That is why, again, any move perceived to bring closer Northern Ireland's incorporation within a united Ireland must be resisted.

References, such as those we have seen, to Northern Ireland's special status or to the uniqueness of a way of life embodying a Protestant-British ethos bring back into focus the quandary for cultural unionists I gestured at earlier: how is it possible to maintain an equilibrium between their British and Ulster referents when the two seem to be drifting further and further apart? One response is simply to give up trying. And those who are so tempted might avail themselves of a form of reasoning that runs roughly as follows. Ulster people have a distinctive Ulster-Scots identity. This identity traces back not merely to the seventeenth-century plantations of Ulster, but to a pre-Celtic past where it finds its source in the 'ancient people of Ireland' – the Cruithin.[29] Appropriating such an identity inclines us to an ethnic nationalism that requires for its full expression an independent Northern Ireland.[30]

The singular appeal of an independent Northern Ireland lies in its promise of a definitive resolution of the ambivalence plaguing many Ulster Protestants' experience: the delivery of a sense of belonging unencumbered by a siege mentality and a new set of arrangements whereby the people of Ulster are treated as first-class citizens of their own state, rather than as second-class citizens of a state that does not want them – the United Kingdom – or of a state to which they do not want to belong – the Republic of Ireland. Leaving aside the practical difficulties of establishing an independent Northern Ireland and of coping with nationalist antipathy, two points are worth making. First, the chain of reasoning invoked in its support is not comprised of necessary links. We may quite consistently accept, for example, that we bear an Ulster-Scots identity and buy the Cruithin thesis without concluding in favour of an independent Northern Ireland; or we may simply view ourselves as Ulster-Scots and remain highly sceptical of talk of either the Cruithin or an independent Ulster; or, indeed, we may, even as Ulster Protestants, balk at the ascribed ethnic label, its historical antecedent and the political recommendation and decide that none of them tallies with our self-definitions. Second, it is doubtful if the ambivalence of Ulster Protestant experience can be so neatly resolved. The price it asks – that unionists should effectively cease to be unionist, that they should concede that Britishness is not constitutive of their identities and is thus discardable without loss – is too high for most unionists to contemplate paying. Although the idea of an independent Northern Ireland has been flirted with by prominent unionist politicians,[31] it remains for the vast majority a fallback option at best. It is to be entertained seriously only if Northern Ireland faces expulsion from the United Kingdom and incorporation within the Irish Republic.

And so the quandary persists. At its heart lies the disconcerting realisation that a Britishness mediated through the peculiar experiences of an Ulster unionist way of life has become significantly unrecognisable to British citizens outside Northern Ireland. Accordingly, it is entirely plausible to think of those whose Britishness is so mediated as constituting a distinctive ethnic group. And, whatever the claims about many unionists' Ulster-Scots ancestry, it is also plausible to locate the source of the identity of this group in a particular notion of Protestantism. This is a Protestantism that, in certain hands, can result in such British symbols as the crown and the flag being used 'as badges of ethnic rage', as Michael Ignatieff so vividly puts it.[32] Or, more generally, it is a Protestantism that ties a certain construal of Reformed or evangelical faith to allegiance to Britain, as the example of Ian Paisley amply demonstrates.[33] Either way, it is the link between Protestantism and Britishness that seems incomprehensible to most British citizens, including most members of the Westminster parliament, and that is at the root of the practical and intellectual strains to which cultural unionism is susceptible. I want to begin exposing the more practical of these strains now by considering the horizon of meaning implicit in the Ulster unionist way of life which cultural unionism takes for granted.

A PROTESTANT HORIZON OF MEANING

Protestantism, whether religiously expressed or not, provides the horizon of meaning within which cultural unionists interpret their world and define their sense of themselves. As we have observed, it is integral to their Britishness and is the chief source of their values; it pervades their rituals and symbols and is the focal point of their shared memories. Protestantism runs through the way of life cultural unionists consider their own and marks out their difference from other inhabitants of the island of Ireland. And it is this sort of Protestantism that is more or less unintelligible in other parts of the United Kingdom.

That a horizon of meaning, in terms of which one understands one's Britishness, should be opaque to the majority of those one considers as fellow British citizens is close to tragic. Translated politically, it certainly indicates a very worrying state of affairs at the level of dealings between cultural unionists and the British government. As political experience over the last quarter of a century has shown, it is a state of affairs that proves too conducive to distorted communication, mistrust, recriminations and bitterness; that wrings concessions cultural unionists can scarcely admit   to   having   given;   and   that,   reluctant   concessions notwithstanding, produces little other than stalemate. But the painful truth for cultural unionism is that British neutrality on Northern Ireland, having been stirred from its prolonged slumber during the Stormont years, is not about to transform itself into pro-Protestant advocacy. And here there is no escaping the reality that the arrangement with Westminster that led to the formation of Northern Ireland was, as John Fulton puts it, 'an alliance rather than a consolidated interest or a genuinely shared culture'.[34]

Here too there is no dodging the deep practical strains in cultural unionism. These are of two kinds. One refers to the practical disturbance of cultural unionists' self-understandings implied by an unsympathetic reception of their views in Britain at large. The absence of a 'genuinely shared culture' binding British citizens in Northern Ireland to their counterparts elsewhere in the United Kingdom cannot be lightly shrugged aside in a post-Stormont era. For cultural unionists to have their way of being British barely recognised and treated as a liability at Westminster is tantamount to their having their basic sense of themselves called into question. It is to have the way of life in which Protestantism affords the dominant horizon of meaning undervalued, if not also undermined. It is to leave cultural unionists isolated and mostly friendless within Britain, and increasingly turned in upon themselves. And thus arises the haunting thought that there might in fact be a deep contradiction within an Ulster unionist way of life: instead of vouchsafing the untrammelled Britishness of Northern Ireland, it seems to render it more problematic than ever.

Another, related, kind of practical strain refers to the diminishing stock of political capital with which cultural unionists have to trade. Given that their brand of unionism strikes a discordant note at Westminster, and given that it is primarily with the British government that they are manoeuvring to cut a deal for Northern Ireland, it appears fanciful to believe that their resources allow them to buy much of what they want. At most, they can expect that what capital they have is sufficient to block certain outcomes, and to force the odd short-term, largely procedural, concession from Westminster. But what has to be given up as forlorn – rousing rhetoric notwithstanding – is the hope that Northern Ireland will ever again have political arrangements that unambiguously underwrite cultural unionist ideals and privilege an Ulster unionist way of life. The gulf between Westminster and cultural unionism ensures that the political efficacy of the latter's voice is waning irretrievably.

It is easy to sigh at these kinds of practical strain and to take refuge in analyses that explain the historical origins of the misunderstandings that underlie them. It is by now commonplace to be informed that the perceptions differentiating cultural unionists from their fellow citizens in Britain are a product of diverse historical experiences. The British in Ireland persevered under siege conditions from which the British elsewhere were spared, and Protestantism remained a badge of loyalty to the Crown in Ireland in a way that is only a distant memory in Britain. Analyses that tell us this, and a lot more, are illuminating. But it is what we infer from them that matters most. A debilitating, and I think an unwarranted, inference is that cultural unionist perceptions of siege and the like – shaped as they are by a distinctive historical experience – have to be treated as sacrosanct, even if we do not agree with them. In this vein O'Malley, for example, argues as follows:

> Protestant fears are endemic. They encapsulate the entire Protestant experience in Ulster. They are so deeply rooted, so pervasive, so impervious to the passage of time that it is almost possible to think of them as being genetically encoded – a mechanism, like anxiety, necessary for the survival of the species.[35]

This is an unconvincing argument on two counts. First, by its use of the dreadful metaphor of genetic encoding, it asks us to accept what it nowhere proves and to ignore experiences that it cannot accommodate. What we have to accept on faith is startling: that Ulster Protestants are victims of their history since their fears are virtually determined, and that, as a consequence, practical reason is impotent to do anything about it. To accept these propositions, incidentally, is to vindicate the jibe of McGarry and O'Leary about culturalists treating people as 'mindless executors of historic cultures'. What O'Malley's argument effectively asks us to ignore are the experiences of those Protestants whose thinking has ceased to be dominated by the categories of siege, who have loosened the grip of traditional fears on their lives and have started to articulate alternative modes of being Protestant in Northern Ireland.[36]

Second, and by extension, an argument like O'Malley's leaves uncontested the conceptual apparatus through which Protestant experience has been mediated. Thus we are tacitly invited to suppose that cultural unionism's horizon of meaning is the only one available to it. But this invitation deserves to be refused and its supposition rejected. Understanding how a certain conception of Protestantism has been integral to the distinctive historical experience of cultural unionism is one thing, but regarding it as given is quite another. Irish history did not make it inevitable. It is this point I now want to expand upon by asking hard questions of the horizon of meaning embedded in an Ulster unionist way of life. It is only by doing so that we see that cultural unionism suffers from intellectual as well as practical strains.

LOYALTY, LIBERTY AND PROTESTANTISM

To ask hard questions of the intellectual credentials of a horizon of meaning defined by a Protestant-British ethos in which Protestantism plays the key role requires, in particular, scrutinising the concepts of loyalty and liberty that are at the heart of cultural unionism's political theory. In broad terms, via these concepts I am concerned to explore the adequacy of those reasons cultural unionists adduce in support of their basic beliefs about Northern Ireland. I ask why they have the commitment they do to the United Kingdom and what its nature is, why they see

Protestantism as integral to their commitment and as indispensable to liberty, why their loyalty to the British government is tied to certain conditions, and why these conditions are understood in the particular ways they are. Old problems and new appear through these explorations. The practical strains I have already located in a cultural unionist way of life are seen to cut even deeper. In addition, fresh difficulties are detected regarding both the quality of a number of cultural unionism's theoretical arguments and the internal consistency of its conceptual framework. What emerges with particular clarity is the inability of its conceptual scheme sufficiently to accommodate nationalist concerns, and to provide compelling reasons why nationalists should be untroubled by the demand that they must respect the integrity of Northern Ireland.

LOYALTY AND SOVEREIGNTY

At a glance, there is no special difficulty in answering why cultural unionists are committed to the United Kingdom and in saying what the nature of their commitment consists in: to have their way of life protected and to remain loyal to the British sovereign for so long as that protection is ensured. But these quick answers need unpacking. They presuppose views of sovereignty, liberty, political obligation and disobedience that require drawing out.

To think of loyalty to Britain as a hallmark of cultural unionists is to beg the question of what precisely they are loyal to. Any vagueness we may have here is apparently dispelled effortlessly. A member of Paisley's DUP, for example, gives a characteristically blunt response which aims to leave us in no doubt:

> My loyalty is to the British Throne being Protestant. I have no loyalty to any Westminster government. I have no loyalty to a government which prorogued a democratically elected government, destroyed our security forces and left us prey to the IRA. Nor have I loyalty to a British government going over the heads of our people, conniving and double-dealing behind our backs with a foreign government.[37]

This testimony, which is typical of a significant strand of cultural unionism, fixes loyalty firmly to a Crown that carries the promise of a Protestant ascendancy. And, it should not be forgotten, it is a Protestant Crown that is taken to copperfasten civil and religious liberties. All this seems plain enough. But there is a lingering ambiguity which still needs clearing up and a dispute worth noting about the character and locus of British sovereignty which sets cultural unionists on a collision course with the majority of the British population.

The ambiguity concerns the entailments of loyalty to the Crown. Is loyalty so unswerving because the Crown yields benefits or because it possesses intrinsic qualities that command loyalty? For some cultural unionists this is possibly a puzzling question, inasmuch as it projects a distinction between the Crown's benefits and its qualities which they do not recognise. They might reason that what I call benefits – civil and religious liberties – are among the Crown's qualities. By virtue of its being Protestant such liberties necessarily follow, since a commitment to them is constitutive of what being a Protestant monarch means; and any monarchy not characterised by such a commitment would prove itself unworthy of the label 'Protestant' and of our loyalty. The plausibility of this line of reasoning hangs on the customary cultural unionist supposition of a necessary connection obtaining between Protestantism and liberty. But as I shall argue in relation to the concept of liberty, the supposition is contestable: it is required to bear too much weight and the political connection that can be posited here is contingent at best.

Even laying aside the issue of the nature of Protestantism's relation to liberty, matters are not necessarily settled as simply as the above response might lead us to think. Let us take a case where it is presumed that civil and religious liberties are integral to Protestantism but where media other than the Crown are deemed capable of delivering them. If what really matters is the enjoyment of these liberties then it is possible to decide that it is of no great consequence whether the Crown happens to be

Protestant, or, more radically, whether there is a Crown at all. The precedent in English history for the latter view was accompanied by a very strong attachment to Protestantism in the period of Cromwell's time as Lord Protector, during which we witnessed the development of a Protestant republicanism articulated, for example, by John Milton.[38] In a more contemporary vein, we may say that the safeguarding of the British people's civil and religious liberties is part of parliament's brief which it is hard to imagine it relinquishing should the monarchy ever be abolished. Whatever the rhetoric, it stretches credibility to accept that the Protestant Crown is currently the guarantor of civil and religious liberties that would inevitably be imperilled should the Crown either cease to be Protestant or cease to exist.

This sort of talk goes much too far for most cultural unionists. It overlooks the symbolic function of the Crown and the deep emotional investments Ulster Protestants have in it. The Crown exercises such a powerful grip on their imaginations because it symbolises the unity of the British state through its transcendence of the particular interests of its member nations, and because Protestantism is perceived to be interwoven in the idea of unity it expresses. This is to say, then, that although civil and religious liberties matter, other things matter too. It is the Crown's capacity to embody and interconnect all these things that matter – in short, Protestantism, liberty and unity – that marks it out as a unique institution. And it is such uniqueness that explains why it, and not parliament, is the object of cultural unionists' loyalty. The fact that this explanation makes sense, at least to many Ulster Protestants, does not mean, however, that the Crown is entitled to arrogate to itself exclusive criteria of loyalty. Yet it is only by such an act of arrogation that cultural unionist expressions of loyalty can be made unambiguous. But this is unsatisfactory. Ambiguity is kept at a distance at the cost of avoiding certain realities: that loyalty to Britain can be expressed without insisting that Protestantism is essential to liberty, as I shortly aim to show is the case, and that it is not a sign of disloyalty to admit that the

Crown is not necessary for an enjoyment of civil and religious liberties.

An extension of the latter point brings us to the problem of sovereignty involved in the cultural unionist fixation with the Crown. The reluctance to concede the sufficiency of parliament's role in guaranteeing civil and religious liberties reflects a view that qualifies the idea of parliamentary sovereignty by stipulating that, strictly speaking, the locus of sovereignty is the Crown in parliament. This qualification is of capital importance in general because the will of parliament is fickle and susceptible to influences subversive of the cause of unionism, and only the constitutional safeguards inherent in the Crown can be relied upon to keep these in check. It is of great consequence in particular because the Crown is the custodian of the Protestant character of Britain's constitutional arrangements, and thus of the liberties that are part of the warp and woof of Protestantism. If we once more ignore the claim of Protestantism's indispensability to liberty, cultural unionism has *prima facie* an impeccable case. According to the strict letter of the law of the Williamite Settlement, Britain's constitution is indisputably Protestant and the locus of sovereignty is the Crown in parliament. The trouble is that conventional wisdom outside Ulster does not operate according to the strict interpretation of the constitution to which cultural unionists appeal. And upon inspection it is easy to understand why it does not.

Consider the issue of the constitution's Protestantism. Picking up on the Act of Settlement, for instance, Paisley can declare that its wording is 'unambiguous and crystal clear. Those that hold communion with or are reconciled to the Church of Rome are incapable to inherit, possess or enjoy the Crown and Government of the United Kingdom.'[39] And thus he can spot constitutional violations in meetings between the Archbishop of Canterbury and the Pope and between the Queen and the Pope, and go so far as to view the latter as a threat to British liberty.[40] Such constitutional exactness is often accompanied by a febrile imagination gifted in detecting constitutional perils to Protestantism of which others are serenely oblivious. An article in a recent edition of the *New Protestant Telegraph*, for example, warns as follows:

> The modern European movement is a new Counter-Reformation disguised in economic garb. If Britain were to become absorbed into a European Superstate, she would undo with a stroke of the pen what our forefathers won through the Reformation and enshrined in British constitutional law – the principle of Protestant ascendancy over papal supremacy.[41]

The fact that such an interpretation of the British constitution is considered bizarre outside certain cultural unionist circles indicates two points especially. First, it shows that an inflexible insistence on the constitution's Protestant character is out of kilter with social and political realities in Britain as we approach the end of the twentieth century. Catholicism has long since ceased to be regarded as a political danger to the British state, and the Protestant trappings of the Crown are mostly viewed by citizens of a multi-cultural, multi-faith Britain as matters of historical curiosity and traditional ceremony. Second, the fact that constitutional exactness is seen as anachronistic suggests that what counts elsewhere in Britain is the spirit of the law rather than its letter. If the letter were to be insisted upon, it is a fair bet that the pressure to change its Williamite formulation would be irresistible, since to stick to a literalistic application of its privileging of Protestantism would be considered intolerable. To fail to see this, in the manner of Paisley and his followers, is to remain blinkered by a theological dogmatism that refuses to concede that sixteenth-century versions of Protestantism and Catholicism are rather less than canonical.

A similar conflict over the spirit and letter of the law is at the bottom of different construals of the locus of British sovereignty. In terms of the letter, the Crown in parliament is the locus and parliament, accordingly, is limited by powers reserved to the Crown. The spirit suggests that the people represented through parliament are sovereign, and that royal prerogatives are a matter of form not substance; or at least that they are not exercised contrary to the will of parliament.[42] Since it is through such a rendering of the spirit of the constitution that the business of governing Britain is conducted, disputes about its letter are treated as arcane affairs except at times of constitutional crisis. Whether current disquiet about the role and future of the monarchy in contemporary Britain – prompted by the antics of members of the Royal family – is likely to precipitate a constitutional crisis remains to be seen. But if it does it is hardly going to result in a strengthening of the Crown's position *vis-à-vis* parliament; and it is not going to herald a retreat back to the letter of the constitutional provisions of the Williamite Settlement. Consolation for an Ulster Protestant reading of the constitution will be an even scarcer commodity than it is already.

At present it is certainly scarce enough. We have noted the practical difficulties cultural unionists face on account of the misunderstandings that typify their relationship with Westminster. Now we can see that the central problem for cultural unionists of how to maintain an equilibrium between their Ulster and their British referents is even sharper. The misunderstandings are made more acute by conflicting interpretations of the character and locus of British sovereignty. Sympathy for the constitutional predicaments of cultural unionism – exacerbated by uncertainty about Northern Ireland's future – is in short supply in Britain, not least because its constitutional claims are associated with expressions of loyalty to a Protestant Crown but decidedly not to parliament. And this is to appear impossibly arcane.

What are we to make of cultural unionism's seemingly defiant unpreparedness to shift its thinking here in order to bring it more into line with the British mainstream? Ignatieff answers by tracing back the conflicting interpretations to different appraisals of the significance of 1688. Whereas the Glorious Revolution entered British myth as 'inaugurating the imperial high noon of parliamentary sovereignty, religious toleration and constitutional monarchy', in Ulster, he says, it became 'the founding myth of ethnic superiority. Ulstermen's reward, as they saw it, was permanent ascendancy over the Catholic Irish, whom they now conceived, once and for ever, as potential rebels against the British crown.'[43] This answer implies not only that it is hard to shift an entrenched myth, but that Protestants' views of themselves and their interests remain tied to a notion of 'ethnic superiority'. So whatever the discomfort experienced by the lack of receptivity in Britain for their gloss on the Glorious Revolution, too much is at stake to back away from it. Cultural unionists are not likely to accept Ignatieff's answer. The point of their 'myth', they might say, is not to dominate Catholics but, rather, to underscore the indispensability of Protestantism to what he calls the 'British myth'. That this goes generally unappreciated in Britain and creates difficulties for cultural unionists are matters of regret. But matters of regret are not enough to move matters of principle.

In view of the range of problems that I have already suggested afflict a cultural unionist position, this sort of reply to Ignatieff's analysis smacks too much of special pleading. And yet it might have a point in the sense that the unpopularity of certain beliefs and the practical difficulties they encounter are not sufficient proofs of their untruth. And the core of the cultural unionist claim to truth resides in its thesis that Protestantism is essential to liberty.

PROTESTANTISM AND LIBERTY

The thesis may be interpreted in two different senses: as referring to a necessary condition of a free society, and as referring to an indispensable medium of individual freedom. Expressed negatively, what is significant in the first sense is to prevent a despotic government which would force society to live under tutelage, whereas what counts in the second is to protect individuals from external interferences that would constrain them from living their own lives. Taken in either sense the thesis as formulated is absurdly overstated. It amounts to claiming that in the absence of a

Protestant constitution no society ever has been or could be free, and that without Protestantism the liberty enjoyed by individuals would be jeopardised. I have already intimated why I think claims like these are dubious in relation to how we read Britain's constitution and understand its mode of government. Pressing further, I do not know how claims of such strength would begin to be defended. And if it is in terms of them that cultural unionists intend us to construe the link they posit between Protestantism and liberty, there is nothing more to say except that they are wrong.

Whatever their intentions, however, it is possible to reformulate the thesis in more modest ways that are worth discussing. It could be read to mean, for example, that Protestantism is peculiarly conducive to liberty and has played a vital role in its development in Western civilisation since the Reformation. Or it could be taken to infer that Protestantism has proved essential to liberty within the context of Irish history and politics. An upshot of this latter reformulation is that Protestantism has protected the flame of liberty and prevented it from being extinguished by its 'natural enemy', Catholicism. The burden of proof here lies in showing that Catholicism is as much antithetic to liberty as Protestantism is sympathetic.

I propose to work with both of these reformulations, since together they capture the broader European and the narrower Irish dimensions of cultural unionists' claims about Protestantism and liberty. I argue that their thesis, even in its reformulated guises, does not hold in connection to that sense of liberty that pertains to the idea of a free society. But I concede that it does have pertinence to the sense of liberty that relates to individual freedom, although only in a more circumscribed way than cultural unionists want to suppose.

To start with individual liberty, a case for Protestantism is easily made. By means of the Reformation doctrines of justification by faith through grace alone and freedom of conscience, a spiritual image is conjured both of direct communication by individuals with God, unmediated by the Church, and of direct accountability to God. Accommodating this image entails a transformation of ecclesiastical structures. As the image gains widespread acceptance, its implications permeate and reshape ways of life in which an ethos, already touched upon and typified by Presbyterianism, develops around ideals of individual independence and dissent. These ideals cultivate an attitude of suspicion toward hierarchical and centralised authorities. Now, manifestly, the various revolutions in spirituality, ecclesiastical organisation and ways of life – initially triggered by theological breakthroughs that accorded a primacy to the concept of the individual – require political recognition. For Ulster Protestants, such recognition was definitively delivered through the Williamite Settlement and its guarantee of civil and religious liberties. And its delivery was taken to be directly attributable to Protestantism. Thus we find the common association of Protestantism with such freedoms as those of conscience, worship, assembly, opinion, speech and so forth. Moreover, the incorporation of these freedoms into a modern vocabulary of rights – which reinforce the claims that individuals may legitimately make against a sovereign authority – is generally greeted enthusiastically as an extension of the principle of individual liberty that Protestantism has championed.

That Protestantism played an important role in the development of Western understandings of individual liberty, from the spiritual insights of the Reformation through to the modern language of rights, cannot be denied; and that Catholicism not only has not played a comparable role in this development, but has on occasions opposed it is also not open to serious dispute. But it is disputable to say much more than this. Unfortunately, that is what cultural unionists are habitually inclined to do. It is not enough for them to stick to the historical advantages Protestantism can claim over Catholicism in the development of Western conceptions of individual liberty. Instead they want to add the further claims that Catholicism remains the opponent of liberty and that a state, such as the Republic of Ireland, in which

Catholicism has exerted considerable influence is necessarily inhospitable to the civil and religious liberties valued by Protestants. These claims contribute to a sense of suspicion about Catholic demands in Northern Ireland, the hint being that some sinister intent must lurk within them.

I want to put aside for the moment cultural unionists' unease about the motives of Northern Catholics and concentrate on the additional claims they make. These may be challenged indirectly and directly. An indirect challenge questions the amount of credit that Protestantism is entitled to claim for the importance attached to ideals of individual liberty in Western civilisation. I have of course intimated that there is nothing to be said for an excessive grasp at credit that makes Protestantism indispensable to such ideals. The mere fact that the ideals have become the common possession of liberals of all religious persuasions and none, and that they are derived from a range of premises, demonstrates that their survival and justifying rationale do not depend upon Protestant allegiances. But what is left open here is the retort that non-Protestants who value individual liberty incur debts to Protestantism even if they do not acknowledge them; or even that those who uphold the strong connection between Protestantism and liberty are more authentically in touch with what liberty hangs on than are those for whom the connection is inconsequential.

Perhaps there is something to retorts like these, but they are prone to exaggerations that need curbing. They tend to overreach themselves in their disregard of the fact that Protestantism provides only one route among others that lead to our ideas of individual liberty. Take, for instance, a philosophical route that leads from Descartes, say, through the Enlightenment into contemporary Western culture.[44]

Reflecting on the irreparable damage modern science inflicted on the ancient notion that the universe embodied a meaningful order to which humans properly resorted to discern their true ends, modern philosphy inaugurated an introspective turn which saw philosophers endeavour to locate the basis of certainty and meaning within their own consciousness. From this turn there emerged a new image of humans as self-defining subjects which inspired fresh understandings of freedom. On one understanding, for example, freedom is taken to consist in the removal of obstacles that inhibit individuals' opportunities to live as they choose on the basis of their desires. Or, on another, freedom is conceived in terms of a life lived on the basis of autonomous, rational choices. Either way, there is a philosophical impetus to achieve political arrangements that respect what we are as self-defining, free subjects; that is, arrangements that acknowledge individuals' liberties and their entitlement to live their own lives. And this is an impetus that owes nothing to Protestantism.

Now telling a philosophical story like this one does not of course subvert the claims that cultural unionists are keen to make against Catholicism and the Irish state. It does, however, bear indirectly upon them inasmuch as it assaults their more extravagant boasts about liberty's marriage to Protestantism. It implies that the contrasts drawn between Protestantism and Catholicism should at least be tempered by a degree of circumspection.

A direct challenge goes much further. It accuses cultural unionists of employing outmoded, stereotypical caricatures of Catholicism and Ireland, and of being undistracted by evidence that these caricatures cannot accommodate. The obvious, it seems, has to be obtruded when dealing with cultural unionist distortions here: Catholicism has changed since the Counter-Reformation, and especially since the Second Vatican Council, and Ireland in 1996 is not identical to Ireland in 1937. This is not the place to explore in depth Catholicism's relation to liberty or the Irish Republic's record on civil and religious liberties. But without wishing to deny that there are illiberal tendencies in Catholicism (as there also are in Protestant fundamentalism) or that the Irish Republic would benefit from more liberalisation, it seems to me that cultural unionist charges against both fail to take into account three sorts of factor. First there are those internal to Catholicism that suggest a narrowing of differences from Protestantism: in general, a proliferation of diverse political and theological views scarcely under Vatican control, and, in particular, an increasing emphasis on freedom of conscience and an openness to Reformed doctrines of justification and the like.[45] Second, there are factors pointing to the decline of Catholic influence in the South of Ireland: the Church's loss of constitutional privilege, its official acceptance of a separation of Church and state, and a steady erosion of an exclusively Catholic ethos through forces of modernisation, pluralism and Europeanisation.[46] Third, there are factors relating to the nature of the Irish state: its respect of the basic civil and religious liberties valued by Protestants, and its possession of liberal-democratic credentials comparable to those of the United Kingdom.[47] Until cultural unionists attempt to engage seriously with such factors, there is little reason to accept their charges against Catholicism and the Republic of Ireland.

If, when suitably qualified, there is a case for saying that Protestantism is instrumental in safeguarding individual liberty, it is not clear that there is a comparable case for saying that it is instrumental in safeguarding a free society. To avoid confusion, a maximisation of individual liberty does not in itself yield a free society or state, since it is perfectly possible for individuals to have many freedoms under the rule of a benevolent dictatorship. Minimally, then, a free society is one not subject to despotic forms of government. Certain cultural unionists think that this is tantamount to saying that a free society is Protestant, given the Reformation's success in Western Europe in dislodging Catholic 'tyranny' politically as well as ecclesiastically and spiritually. To restrict this argument to its historical claim, let us accept that Catholicism in the sixteenth and seventeenth centuries was politically absolutist in character and did pose a despotic threat at the level of government. The question thus becomes whether Protestantism offered a guaranteed, non-despotic alternative. It is hard to think that it did, as two quick historical excursions with substantive ramifications for our present circumstances indicate.

That Protestantism secures what Catholicism destroys only

begins to appear a feasible boast if we ignore the reality that Protestantism often proved in practice every bit as authoritarian, intolerant and despotic as Catholicism. Calvin's Geneva is a case in point.[48] Moreover, the religious wars that ravaged post-Reformation Europe gave little prospect of any creed serving as the basis of a free society. If anything, the achievement and maintenance of a free society was, arguably, made more precarious as a consequence of the political impact of the Reformation. The appearance within the same society of rival authoritarian and salvationist religions whose members were prepared to fight each other to the death created an acute problem for civil order. As John Rawls puts it, under such circumstances the searching question became 'how is society even possible between those of different faiths?'[49] So instead of serving as a necessary condition of a free society, Protestantism constituted an obstacle to its actualisation. And, as Quentin Skinner remarks, it was largely as an attempt to overcome such an obstacle that certain post-Reformation political thinkers proposed that 'the State would have to be divorced from the duty to uphold any particular faith'.[50]

In any event, the most impressive endeavours to stave off the threat of despotism in the late medieval to early modern period of European history derived more from Renaissance than Reformation sources. These centred on efforts by various writers, among whom Machiavelli was the most prominent, to defend the political liberties of Italian city-republics against the encroachments of the *signori* and the imperial designs of the Church. Drawing on earlier Roman thinkers such as Livy and Cicero, what emerged was an articulation of a civic republicanism that viewed the deliberations and commitments of the whole body politic as integral to the realisation of a free society; that is, a political theory that considered citizen self-rule as the necessary condition of political liberty. Free states, Machiavelli tells us, are those 'which are far from all external servitude, and are thus able to govern themselves according to their own will'.[51]

At the very least, these cursory references to the Reformation and the Renaissance suggest the implausibility of appealing to Protestant experience in the sixteenth and seventeenth centuries as a religio-political golden age. More pointedly, the inability of Protestantism to provide the basis of a free society in early modern Europe retains a salutary lesson for any presumption of its capability to do so today. As I have already contended, even where Protestantism appears to perform a constitutive role – as in the Williamite Settlement – it transpires that the appearance masks the reality: the political glue holding together the British state and halting a lapse into despotism owes little to Protestantism *per se*. Attempts to claim Protestantism as the decisive factor of a free society – as in Northern Ireland during the Stormont years – lack credibility. In Northern Ireland such attempts merely sowed seeds of a divisiveness that has reaped a whirlwind of disorder and violence since 1969.

An even more fundamental objection to claims regarding Protestantism's ability to safeguard a free society is that it does not in itself afford a sufficiently strong commitment to the value of public life. As the example of Renaissance civic republicanism illustrates, it is the actions of citizens operating as a concerted body that proves a necessary condition of a free society rather than adherence to a particular set of beliefs. The idea of citizen self-rule presupposes involvement in the public life of society for the sake of the common good that an emphasis on Protestantism does not strictly require. Indeed, such an emphasis is as compatible with our being (passive) loyal subjects of a Protestant Crown as it is with our being (active) citizens striving for the good of society. And if securing a free society is what is at stake then Protestantism as such does not possess the necessary wherewithal to secure it.

A conclusion such as this one, especially when pitched against the backdrop of the preceding discussion of liberty, cuts at the intellectual heart of cultural unionism. It challenges the core justification for insisting upon the Protestant character of the United

Kingdom in general and Northern Ireland in particular. It also challenges the tendency to rationalise a cavalier approach to non-unionist demands for civil rights under Stormont or for parity of esteem today on the pretext that they disguise subtle ploys to destroy the free society that Protestantism makes available. But these challenges have to be pressed further yet. Cultural unionist assumptions about Protestantism's privileged relationship with liberty appear in other forms that need to be examined on their own terms. This becomes clear if we turn to consider the conditions attached to cultural unionist loyalty to the British government. Here we see from another angle why Protestantism is unsuited to provide the basis of a free society, and why, when it is assumed to, it can easily result in a denial of the rights and concerns of those considered enemies of such a society. *En route* we also see other things, including the various contractual arguments upon which cultural unionists often draw, their inability to make these arguments cohere, and a deepening of their practical difficulties.

CONDITIONAL LOYALTY

Cultural unionists understand their relation to the British state in contractual terms which suggest a conditional loyalty. Stated abstractly, this is to say that they will remain loyal to the state, and assume the burdens and responsibilities such loyalty requires of them, in so far as the state fulfils its duties towards them. Such a statement conjures up the image of a contract, real or hypothetical, entered into by two parties – say, the sovereign and the people – whereby each agrees to promises and to be bound by them. And this image in turn calls to mind the great contractarian, or contract-based, theories of political obligation developed most famously in the seventeenth century by Thomas Hobbes and John Locke.[52]

Common to the theories of both Hobbes and Locke is the notion that we can become clear about what politics is for, what its purposes are, if we imagine people in a pre-political situation –

the 'state of nature' – and ask why, and under what conditions, such people would agree to submit themselves to a common authority or sovereign. Reduced to skeletal form, among the basic answers to emerge are these: (1) politics is a useful convention created to afford human life with a measure of security it would otherwise lack and to protect those things we value most – self-preservation (Hobbes) or our natural rights of 'life, liberty and estate' (Locke); (2) these things are precarious possessions in the absence of a common political authority either because there are no moral laws constraining our dealings with one another in a state of nature (Hobbes), or because the moral laws that do exist are difficult to apply impartially and to enforce (Locke); (3) accordingly, people living in a state of nature – either as atomised individuals (Hobbes) or as individuals who have already formed social relations (Locke) – would agree to establish a political authority for the sake of those things that are most valued; (4) involved in this agreement is their willingness to transfer all ex-ecutive, legislative and enforcement functions to a common auth-ority; (5) also involved is an acknowledgement that such an agreement obliges them to obey, and to perform duties aiding the preservation of, this authority on the proviso that it, in return, protects those things for the sake of which it has been established; (6) its failure to fulfil its protective role releases people from their obligations and duties toward it; and (7) may even warrant their resistance to it, although Hobbes strongly cautions against such a conclusion and the support Locke lends to it is somewhat ambivalent.

Such a contract-based scheme, especially its Lockean variant, has had an enormous impact upon Western political thought and, as we shall see, has exerted a discernible influence on liberal unionism. Given that Locke's theory has been read as an in-tellectual justification of the Glorious Revolution,[53] it might be expected to provide the theoretical underpinnings of cultural unionism's idea of conditional loyalty. But matters are not that simple. The cultural unionist idea is sometimes conveyed through the language of contract, in a manner reminiscent of Locke, but more often through the language of covenant. And this latter language is appropriated from Calvinist theology in general and a Scottish Covenanters tradition in particular.[54] To make matters even more complex, the term 'covenant' is at times invested with a specific theological content and at other times not. So the idea of conditional loyalty is presented in a variety of forms, not all of which appear to sit easily with each other. To help us work through a potentially confusing situation, let us pick up the major emphases arising from the quick snapshot I gave of the theories of Hobbes and Locke in order to detect the extent to which cultural unionists agree and disagree with them. In doing so, it becomes easier to clarify and evaluate what they are saying about their relation to the British government.

To begin, there is the view of politics as a useful convention, the purposes of which are largely, if not exclusively, protective. In espousing this view, Hobbes and Locke distance themselves from the old, Aristotelian view of politics as natural, as essential to the fulfilment of what we are as human beings,[55] and from the civic republican view which is close to Aristotle's. There are many ways of drawing the contrasts between these alternative views of politics, but the following must suffice. According to the contractarian view, politics has instrumental value: it exists for the sake of external goods by creating the conditions – such as peace and order – under which they may be enjoyed. Politics thus serves limited ends. According to the Aristotelian or civic republican view, however, politics has intrinsic as well as instrumental value: in addition to providing stable conditions that permit us to attend to those things that matter to us, it affords internal goods – such as the development of certain character traits bound up with devotion to maintaining a free society – that are available only through participation in public affairs. Politics here serves larger ends.

Cultural unionists tend to share the contractarian view of politics. For many of them this view is reinforced through their understanding of biblical teaching – an understanding that attained its most painstaking treatment in Saint Augustine's *The City of God*[56] and received further mediation through the Augustinian influence in the writings of Luther and Calvin and other Reformers.[57] In its bare essentials, this understanding conceives of politics as a product of original sin, and of government as necessary only to compensate for the weaknesses of human nature and keep them in check. Moreover, as a sign of human fallenness, politics is perpetually open to corruptions and not much should be expected of it. This is especially the case since the future of human perfection anticipated in the 'heavenly city' is decidedly apolitical in kind. And with the full realisation of the kingdom of God humankind will be well rid of politics. Political purposes are therefore entirely protective and in themselves do not conduce to human improvement or perfection.

The distance between this view of the origins and purposes of politics and an Aristotelian or civic republican view is considerable. And, in noting it, we can see another reason why a Protestantism permeated by Augustinian influences is not equipped to provide a necessary condition of a free society: for it, upholding a principle of citizen self-rule is at best an incidental affair. By contrast, there is a happy coincidence between cultural unionist and contractarian views of politics at this general level, even between views that are theologically disposed and those that are not.

A rather different situation obtains, however, when we consider the constituent features of the human beings who are conceived to agree to a contract or covenant and the rationale involved in depicting these features in a specific way. On the surface, the divergence of views here is obvious: Hobbes and Locke invoke fictional agents operating under the conditions of a hypothetical state of nature, whereas cultural unionists invoke real agents like themselves operating under the conditions of particular historical circumstances. But it is what lies beneath the surface here that is most interesting. And this is something we can get at by asking what Hobbes and Locke are up to when they resort to the hypothetical device of a state of nature.

Take two of the principal things they are up to. First, despite their different characterisations of the human condition in a state of nature, they are both inviting us to perceive ourselves as we 'truly' are independent of the contingent effects of a particular civilisation upon our self-interpretations. By accepting the invitation we are able to focus on what matters to us as persons considered as persons, rather than as members of a certain tribe, nation or state. The idea is that if we strip away the influences of culture and history and imagine ourselves without them, we may arrive at a translucent vision of ourselves as we are 'by nature'. And on the basis of such a vision we can decide with unrivalled clarity why we need government, what we should expect of it, and under what conditions we would recognise its authority as legitimate. Second, what is being introduced through such a pattern of reasoning, especially as employed by Locke, is a doctrine of popular sovereignty. In divesting individuals in a state of nature of any specifically religious features – even if they are subject to a moral law of divine origin – and in making consent the basis of legitimate authority, Locke inaugurates a decisive shift towards a secular grounding of the state which relieves government of its putative duty to maintain 'true religion'.

If cultural unionists on occasion seem sympathetic to the second contractarian argument, it is not because they have already bought the first. And, in truth, they have difficulty with both. In what follows I suggest reasons why they are entitled to reject the 'state of nature' argument, but I then show how their reliance on covenant theory tempers their acceptance of the 'secular consent' argument (which secularises authority by basing it on consent) and leaves them in a deeply confusing, if not a flatly contradictory, situation.

Objections to the type of 'state of nature' argument I have associated with Hobbes and Locke are commonly of two kinds. First, there are doubts about the possibility of peeling back the layers of culturalisation to the point where we can identify human nature in its acultural, raw state. C.B. Macpherson controversially expresses such doubts when he discerns in the depictions of Hobbes and Locke images of a 'possessive individualism' that fitted neatly with the requirements of an emerging bourgeois society.[58] Or, perhaps less controversially, the doubts may be aired by noting of Locke, for example, that the meanings he attributes to 'life, liberty and estate' reflect the influence of a Western tradition of thought. Second, there are reservations about what Hobbes and Locke think the most important features of our humanness consist in. What both leave out are those features that impinge upon what may be termed our sense of belonging, that is, features we acquire from moving within a certain history, living in a certain place at a certain time, believing certain things to be true, seeing things within a certain horizon of meaning. In short, they set aside those features without which we would not recognise ourselves to be the particular persons we are. It is one thing to say, as I do, that these features are open to investigation, deliberation and debate, that they may contain distortions that we would be better off without, but quite another to say that we only relate to them contingently and that to make progress politically we should transcend them. As Michael Sandel argues with particular force, to think of such features as only contingently ours is to ignore the fact that they are the stuff of our 'constitutive attachments'.[59]

This second set of reservations about the 'state of nature' argument is especially relevant to the position of cultural unionists. It is as bearers of a specific history and culture that they envisage entering into contracts or covenants. And this is an entirely defensible position.

The question is whether it is possible to reject the 'state of nature' argument and yet accept the 'secular consent' argument. In Chapter 5, I contend that it is, especially if the latter argument is detached from a contractarian framework. But it is not clear that cultural unionists inspire much confidence in the possibility, partly because their commitment to the 'secular consent' argument is half-hearted and compromised by other commitments.

On contractarian terms, there are two central suppositions at work in the 'secular consent' argument: that the basis of legitimate authority is popular consent and not divine right, and that a contract between citizens and government involves all citizens and not just a privileged group bearing certain traits. This latter supposition is crucial in all societies, but especially in those that are diverse or divided where ethnic or religious homogeneity cannot be assumed. Contemporary cultural unionists use language that implies their acceptance of these two suppositions. The fact that all unionist political parties freely endorse the principle of consent as the basis of any agreement for future arrangements in Northern Ireland seems to suggest nothing less, as does Paisley's avowed willingness to concede the legitimacy of a united Ireland should the majority of citizens in the North decide that that is what they want.[60] But if we inspect the terms of cultural unionists' covenant theories a different picture emerges.

Take the strongly theological theory of covenant espoused by Paisley.[61] It has three parts. First, we are told that God has entered into a covenant with his people (Protestants) whereby they can be assured of his unswerving faithfulness if they honour his ways by, among other things, living according to the Ten Commandments. Second, we learn that the British sovereign, by virtue of the coronation oath – in the swearing of which a promise is made to 'maintain the Laws of God, the true profession of the Gospel, and the Protestant Reformed Religion established by Law' – and the Declaration upon Accession, incurs covenantal obligations to God. These include not only upholding 'true religion' but opposing 'false', which is to say Catholicism, since not to do so is to invite God's curse upon the nation. Third, we should understand that as part of their covenantal obligations, Protestants are required to obey the sovereign and to abide by the laws of the state in so far as they reflect or are not in conflict with God's laws.

Now on these covenantal terms, there is not much space for the suppositions of the 'secular consent' argument. Ultimate authority still derives from a divine principle, the sovereign is presumed to have a divinely ordained duty to uphold a particular faith and to oppose another, obedience is tied to a government's faithfulness in maintaining and implementing God's law, and it is Protestants who are envisaged as the covenanting partners of God and of the sovereign. In short, it is impossible to hold consistently both to such a version of covenant theory and to the 'secular consent' thesis of contractarianism. The two are incompatible.

Matters improve in one respect (but only marginally overall) if we turn to another, less theologically loaded, version of covenant theory. This is one that derives from the long-standing Protestant practice of forming 'public bands' – of which the Orange Order is an early example – in order to protect a valued way of life against perceived threats from Britain's or Ulster's enemies. Ulster's Solemn League and Covenant, together with the women's Declaration, signed in 1912 by close to half a million citizens in opposition to Irish Home Rule afford a memorable testimony to the practice. Other, more recent, testimonies may be detected in events such as loyalist workers' opposition to the Sunningdale Agreement in 1974 and mass opposition to the Anglo-Irish Agreement of 1985. The covenant theory at work in these testimonies to the practice of public banding is one that appears capable of accepting unproblematically the contractarian supposition that in the modern era a principle of popular consent has replaced a principle of divine right as the ground of political authority. At any rate, it can be read this way if we take a charitable line on the intermix of religious and political language often present in covenanting statements, as captured succinctly by the original Ulster Volunteer Force motto – 'For God and Ulster' – which is retained by the force's self-appointed contemporary heirs. We can attribute to such statements an acceptance of the supposition of popular consent if we think that religious language is being employed more loosely than Paisley would require,[62] and that for some at least it amounts to little more than excusable hyperbole designed to make an ethnic–political claim rather than a serious theological one.

Charitable interpretations are in scarcer supply, however, once we focus on the contractarian position which effectively assumes that *all* citizens stand in a similar contractual relation to political authority, regardless of their cultural and religious allegiances. This supposition is hard to reconcile with a covenant theory that rests upon two premises: that Protestants have formed a covenant with each other and have incurred mutual obligations to defend a way of life they cherish; and that, since their way of life entails loyalty to Britain, the British state should recognise that it has a unique relationship with those who have pledged themselves to defend British sovereignty in Ireland/Ulster against those who would destroy it. Indeed, according to David Miller, unionists seemed to think that British compliance with such premises led to the formation of Northern Ireland:

> A band had been entered into, its adherents had stood their guard against the enemy, and in the end the sovereign authority seemed to have contracted with the banded community to exercise its sovereignty in the territory in question: to hold the pass against the king's enemies and their own.[63]

Since 1972, of course, it has been obvious that Westminster did not perceive itself to have undertaken a special contractual relationship with Ulster Protestants. But that does not mean that cultural unionists have ceased thinking in covenantal terms. It means, rather, that we witness here yet another source of their alienation from mainstream British thought.

To sum up, given the presence of contractarian and different covenantal themes in their thought, cultural unionists' understandings of their contractual position *vis-à-vis* Britain seem to include three different formulations. First, there is the 'secular consent', or what I now simply refer to as the 'contractarian' formulation: political authority derives from popular consent and therefore all citizens *as* citizens stand in an identical contractual relationship to the state. Second, there is what I call the 'political covenant' formulation: political authority derives from popular consent, but those who have formed a covenant among themselves to express their loyalty to this authority enjoy a special contractual relationship with the state. Third, there is what I term the 'religious covenant' formulation: political authority ultimately derives from God and, since the sovereign is obliged to maintain true religion and to oppose false, those who are covenanted to God also possess a peculiar covenantal relationship to a state whose constitution underwrites its divine obligations. I have suggested that the positions represented by these formulations are at odds with each other. The curious question is why this is not so obvious as to have cultural unionists scuttling off to re-define their contractual theories and make them more cogent. Speculation on possible answers would be premature, however, prior to noting how the above formulations shed light on the cultural unionists' approaches to the other major emphases of the theories of Hobbes and Locke, namely, what it is that government is contracted to protect and the grounds of political disobedience.

If we run together the emphases on protection and disobedience and consider them from the perspectives of the three contractual formulations outlined above, we may quickly see the different sorts of claims cultural unionists are making. On contractarian terms, government is contracted to protect those things that matter to individuals *as* individuals: security, say, and basic rights or, as unionists prefer, civil and religious liberties. A government's failure to honour its contractual obligations to individuals, to protect those things that matter, provide grounds for possible disobedience. On political covenantal terms, government is also contracted to protect the way of life of a covenanted band or community which, whatever the diversity among its members, is bound in loyalty to the state and in opposition to those who would undermine it. A government may fail to fulfil its protective role here by not recognising that it has one; by denying, that is, that it incurs contractual obligations of the sort implied. It is when such failure ceases to be tacit and becomes explicit that the problem sharpens. When a government is perceived to adopt measures corrosive of the valued way of life and insulting to the covenanted community's loyalty, not least by appeasing the state's enemies, serious grounds for disobedience appear. On religious covenantal terms, government is contracted to protect its citizens or subjects against false teaching and practice by upholding true faith and ensuring that the laws of the state do not conflict with God's laws. In the face of a government abandoning its divinely ordained duties, those whose primary covenantal relationship is to God have reason to contemplate disobedience.

As we can see, then, cultural unionism's idea of conditional loyalty which shapes its orientation to the British state is quite complex. It appears in more than one form and admits of various claims, not all of which seem to cohere. But perplexing though a lack of coherence is in an intellectual sense, it is possibly considered advantageous in other, practical and tactical, senses. Advantageous possibilities may be calculated upon, especially given what we have noted about the different angles opened up on protection and disobedience by the contractarian, political covenantal and religious covenantal strands in cultural unionism's thought. Instead of cultural unionists appearing merely confused on questions of whether or not popular consent is the basis of political authority and on whether or not all citizens count equally in contractual arrangements with government, these angles suggest two other possibilities. One is that they reveal cultural unionism's subtle practical grasp of the entailments of politics; of the fact that dealings with the state are not satisfactorily conducted merely on the bland liberal assumption that we are all undifferentiated individuals, but must also be based on the assumption that we are bearers of specific cultural, political and religious identities which demand different sorts of recognition. Another possibility is that the angles make available a tactically astute and flexible approach to politics that enables different strands to be emphasised on different occasions in order to achieve maximum political advantage. If such practical and tactical benefits have to be bought at the price of a bit of theoretical untidiness then so be it. Thus there is no urgency among cultural unionists to attend to the task of redefining their conceptual arguments regardless of what I suggested earlier.

This is perhaps the most positive gloss that can be put on cultural unionism's inconsistent conceptualisations of its understanding of loyalty. But it is one that wears thin very rapidly. Inconsistency may be rewarded through tactical advantages but the scope for these to amount to much is severely diminished by Westminster's indifference, if not antipathy, to cultural unionism. And the notion that inconsistency may be compensated by practical subtleties and nuances unavailable to theoretical rigorists is plausible only if we assume that consistency is always narrowly drawn and never broadly, and if we ignore how cultural unionism's facilitation of subtleties and nuances appears in a grossly distorted form – one entailing vacillating arguments that respect the entitlements of individuals at one moment and sanctify intolerant practices in the name of a privileged political or religious identity at others. In Chapter 5, I try to show how it is possible to accommodate the practical insight in this notion without either decrying the value of consistency or rationalising the intolerable.

Let me bring to a close this discussion of loyalty by vindicating these negative assessments of attempts to put a positive spin on cultural unionism's inconsistencies. I do so by highlighting practical difficulties suggested by its views of contract, protection and disobedience which add to those noted previously, and by arguing that these views betray a defence of Protestant exclusiveness that is neither practically nor intellectually benign.

The practical difficulties I want to highlight fall into two categories and can be dealt with fairly briskly. First, there is the familiar difficulty of cultural unionists relying upon understandings that are foreign to the British government. This difficulty appears in an almost absurd form when cultural unionists cite contractual arrangements that are met with blank stares or are given short shrift at Westminster. To state the obvious, a contract requires the mutual agreement of two parties and in its absence there is no contract. To proceed as though a contract exists by appealing to contractual obligations that one party denies were ever incurred is simply to embark upon a futile course of political action. And this, I suggest, is precisely the predicament in which cultural unionism finds itself. Following Miller, I have already remarked on how the proroguing of Stormont demolished the contractual assumptions of political covenantalism. And there is no doubt that the contractual terms of religious covenantalism fail to raise the merest flicker of recognition at Westminster, reflecting as they do an utterly arcane reading of the British constitution. The only chink of light for cultural unionism's contractual claims lies in the direction of its contractarian strand. But it is far from evident that the British government understands its relation to its citizens in a contract-based way, and even if it does it is of no special consolation to cultural unionists since contractarian terms apply indiscriminately to all citizens.

Second, difficulties are posed by the sort of disobedience that it is prudent for cultural unionists to consider undertaking. Such difficulties are nothing but heightened by the realisation that the British government is hardly going to be impressed by acts of disobedience aimed at bringing it to account for welching on contractual commitments it does not believe it has agreed to. That aside, unionist disobedience is constrained in principle by its attachment to the notion of loyalty and by a fear of overplaying its hand. Although loyalty may be conditional, it would be massively counterproductive to insist upon its conditionality to the point where Ulster risked excluding itself, or being excluded, from the United Kingdom. The purpose of disobedience is not to undermine the authority of Westminster, but to make that authority more amenable to the loyalty claims of cultural unionism. And, ironically enough given their literalistic interpretation of so much else, that is why the strict requirements of cultural unionists' contractual understandings are rarely enforced in practice.

For instance, in religious covenantal terms, the British government is so far away from meeting its obligations to maintain the Protestant faith, oppose Catholicism, and implement laws based on the Ten Commandments as to be close to qualifying as an illegitimate authority. Yet this is a point that Paisley, say, chooses not to push too assiduously. He contents himself for the most part with rhetorical denunciations of the government's failure to satisfy its constitutional duties and on occasions conducts, or condones, small-scale acts of civil disobedience primarily intended to disrupt ecumenical gatherings.

In practice, cultural unionist disobedience has concentrated on violations of the terms of political covenantalism. Asquith's Home Rule Bill fell into this category as did the Sunningdale Agreement, and successful acts of disobedience saw off the threat of both. But the Anglo-Irish Agreement, seen by cultural unionists as another such violation, remains intact. And, given its hostile reception among unionists, it seems that *Frameworks for the Future*, if ever acted upon, would be deemed to violate political covenantalist principles too. More generally, British failure to defeat the IRA allied with perceptions of the gains made at home and abroad by the pan-nationalist front, add to cultural unionists' sense of uncertainty and create a climate in which the option of resorting to disobedience for the sake of a way of life in which loyalty to the Crown is central lies close at hand.

It is an option, however, that seems deprived of any compelling justification. Granted that every major political party in Ireland, with the exception of Sinn Féin, agrees that Northern Ireland will not be removed from the United Kingdom without the consent of the majority of its citizens,[64] disobedience cannot be justified on the pretext of safeguarding Northern Ireland's constitutional position. A cultural unionist decision to exercise this option can only appeal to the assumptions of political covenantalism by claiming that too many concessions are being given to nationalists and that, as a consequence, the British character of Northern Ireland is being eroded. On the terms of cultural unionism these are of course sufficient grounds on which to appeal. The trouble is that outside unionist ranks few others, and least of all the British government, concur. Accordingly, the efficacy of acts of disobedience undertaken on such a basis is likely to be limited. This likelihood is enhanced by the perception that unionism is revealed at its intransigent worst in its resort to political covenantalism – digging in its heels at the prospect of having to share Northern Ireland with nationalists without being able to invoke special privileges.

This perception evidently has a salience beyond issues of disobedience. Cultural unionists, none the less, might seek to counter it by arguing that the political covenantal strand of their thought is qualified, say, by the contractarian strand. But this is a difficult counter to sustain. It is impossible not to conclude from cultural unionist practice that the covenantal strand has priority and that contractarian considerations are too readily sacrificed for its sake. It is also hard to resist the further conclusion that cultural unionism's priorities attest to its embrace of an exclusivism that is considerably less than benign.

The priority of the political covenantal strand was manifested clearly in the old Stormont regime and in cultural unionist overreaction to the civil rights campaign of the late 1960s. The regime's shameless maintenance of discriminatory practices against Catholics, and the tendency of many Protestants to dismiss claims for equal rights as a subversive threat to Ulster and to organise protests against a campaign calling for an end to gerrymandering, unfair housing policies and so on stand as telling indictments of cultural unionism. They show just how easy it was to sideline the contractarian strand, on the terms of which discrimination and a denial of equal rights are hard to justify.

These instances of bad practices raise two curious features of cultural unionism's understanding of government's relation to its citizens. As we have noticed, unionists are keen to stress Westminster's contractual obligations to citizens in Northern Ireland, including its duty to accord citizens in Northern Ireland the same rights and entitlements as those enjoyed by citizens in Britain. In dealing with Westminster, in other words, the contractarian strand is an important weapon in cultural unionism's armoury. But a quite different understanding of government–citizen relations apparently came into play when attention was focused not on Westminster but on Stormont. First, as I have suggested, the contractarian strand was marginalised to the detriment of non-unionists. And, second, contractual language ceased to be employed at all. It was as though such language only had currency when relating to a government that was not to be fully trusted. When relating to one that embodied political covenantal ideals a different logic obtained: loyalty was not conditional on contractual obligations being honoured, but rather was taken for granted as unproblematically given, as unreflectively assured. Stormont enjoyed 'diffuse support', to use Miller's term, and not merely contractual support.[65] Loyalty was assumed because it derived from the shared understandings of the covenanted band which was entrusted with power.

That those outside the covenanted band were disloyal by inclination was equally assumed. Not sharing the same understandings, drawing on different historical memories and traditions, being opposed to partition in the first place, they were by definition suspect. Accordingly, it was relatively easy for cultural unionists to caricature any demand Catholics made for a better deal in Northern Ireland as a token of their disloyalty, even if the rationale of the demand was identical to that which unionists used when making requests of Westminster. Catholics did not properly belong and never could, given the explicitly Protestant nature of the political covenantal strand that was in the ascendancy at Stormont. Or, to put the point in terms of the earlier discussion of liberty, when Protestantism is assumed to be a necessary condition of a free society – such as when political and/ or religious covenantalist principles are privileged in the state – there is a tendency to rationalise both an exclusion of non-Protestants from the source of power and a less than even-handed treatment of their claims to equal rights or liberties.

This sort of privileging of Protestantism and the ascendancy it encouraged lie of course in a past that is buried forever. There will be no return to an old Stormont, majority rule in Northern Ireland is unlikely to be reinstigated, cultural unionism's star is on the wane. Fair employment and equal opportunity legislation prevent the use of what I have called political covenantal arguments to override the entitlements of individuals. A devolved government with power-sharing arrangements is probably the best cultural unionists can hope for. The odds may be stacked against them, their day may have come and gone, but this does not mean that cultural unionists are an utterly finished force or that their thinking has been transformed. They frequently complain about biases toward Catholics in fair employment and equal opportunity legislation, and, as the commitment of Paisley and his followers indicates, hold out against the principle of power-sharing. But, more important, they have drawn a fresh set of lines in the sand which often have the support of liberal unionists. No role for Dublin in the internal affairs of Northern Ireland, public institutions and symbols expressing only the Britishness of Northern Ireland, and the right to hold traditional parades along traditional routes are among the new rallying cries of cultural unionism. And in them we discern the continuing influence of political covenantalism, and with it the retention of an exclusivism that justifies itself in majoritarian terms and still regards non-unionists as 'other', as the enemies of Ulster who have no legitimate claim to a political expression of their identities within the borders of Northern Ireland. As Peter Robinson says of parity of esteem, it 'is a cunning maxim behind which the republican minority argue that equality must be given, in terms of a political outcome, to a minority *vis-à-vis* a majority'.[65] And that of course is unthinkable.

CONCLUSION

Various of the threads of our discussion may be tied together through three general conclusions which point to the difficulty of sustaining a cultural unionist position. First, a way of life embodying a Protestant-British ethos not shared by other British citizens finds itself placed under enormous practical strains. These strains are exacerbated by the employment of conceptual arguments on liberty and loyalty that underscore even more radically the gap between cultural unionist and mainstream British self-understandings. Second, such conceptual arguments also run into two other sorts of problems: there are frequent doubts about their consistency and about their credibility. Third, cultural unionism's way of life and conceptual articulations squeeze out non-unionist concerns and so contribute to an exclusive political and intellectual position that is ill prepared to wrestle seriously with views it finds inconvenient or uncongenial. It is hard to see how such a position permits those who embrace it to grasp what matters in a Northern Ireland no longer under unionist control, or how it offers compelling arguments designed to settle the doubts of those in Northern Ireland who remain suspicious of unionist intentions. A political vision restricted to the horizon of meaning that is offered by cultural unionism fails to recognise too much that counts for the future of Northern Ireland.

4

LIBERAL UNIONISM

Liberal unionism purports to overcome the major difficulties plaguing cultural unionism. It offers a 'rational' political position unhampered by sectarianism and uncluttered by esoteric interpretations of history and religion. Instead of exclusiveness and special covenants, it recommends inclusiveness and plain contractual arrangements. Rather than requiring specific cultural attachments, it relies only on strictly political considerations. Its promise of a better future for Northern Ireland is uncompromised either by traditional prejudices or by pleas for different treatment, but, rather, is characterised by a determined resolve to see social and political life in Northern Ireland placed on a par with that in the rest of Britain – where the rights and freedoms and other benefits of a pluralist society are fully available to all citizens whatever their traditional affiliations.

Expressed succinctly, liberal unionism boasts two major advantages over cultural unionism and, correspondingly, two sets of reasons why everyone in Northern Ireland should accept its proposals: a political vision without confessional bias and a political theory based solely on rational principles. Its political vision reflects a rootedness (or at least an aspiration to be rooted) in what I earlier called a British political way of life. This is one that fixes on the idea of the Union, emphasises a modern concept of the state, claims cultural blindness in political affairs, celebrates plurality, and thus appeals across the sectarian divide in a way cultural unionism never could. And if liberal unionists seem at times to agree with their cultural unionist cousins on the inadmissibility of various nationalist designs for Northern Ireland, it is not because they retain any residual attachment to Protestant privileges. Such designs are deemed inadmissible given the requirements of sovereignty, rationality and liberal principles alone. In the words of John Wilson Foster, defence of the Union and antipathy to key nationalist demands do not betray 'an historic supremacism taking ill the challenge to its political power', since 'unless unionism is reasonable it is not worth defending'.[1]

Liberal unionists, assured of the reasonableness of unionism, accordingly draw upon meanings that are different in kind from those invoked by cultural unionists, and narrower in focus. If the cultural unionists' arguments often appear loose and baggy, liberal unionists claim theirs are tight and tailored. These arguments issue in a lean political theory trimmed of cultural excess and uncoupled from any specifically Protestant view of the world. All the theory asks is that we look beyond cultural distractions and obfuscations, whether unionist or nationalist in origin, and concentrate on the rational case for the Union. In doing so, we may appreciate an intellectual strength in liberal unionism that unionist and nationalist culturalists have trouble matching.

In claiming these sorts of advantages, liberal unionists are engaging three political and intellectual opponents: cultural unionists, the British government and Irish nationalists. I want to examine what they are up to here by considering, first, some fundamental aspects of the British political way of life that they are devoted to defend. Whatever the coherence of the defence, I argue that the horizon of meaning implied by their way of life contains notable occlusions. As a consequence, liberal unionists encounter grave practical quandaries as a result of their inability either to convince Westminster radically to change course or to handle the inconvenience of a sizeable and unpersuaded non-unionist minority in Northern Ireland. I suggest that the latter difficulty poses the greatest challenge to the cogency of liberal unionist political theory, and I examine how the challenge is met through the 'rational' conceptual arguments at liberal unionism's disposal. I discuss in turn arguments appealing to concepts of history, sovereignty and liberty and arguments appealing to concepts of citizenship and identity. Although not without insight, these arguments prove inadequate to the tasks set and, beyond that, illustrate a worrying restrictiveness in liberal unionism's understanding of politics in general and of the requirements of Northern Irish politics in particular. Its political vision is, I shall contend, severely flawed and offers little prospect of moving beyond the impasse created by a politics of constitutional standoff.

A 'BRITISH' POLITICAL WAY OF LIFE

I wish now very briefly to explicate the differences between liberal and cultural unionists from another angle, as well as to remark upon some similarities. Doing so provides an entrance into the British way of life from which liberal unionism emanates and opens up various of its features to which I want to draw attention.

LIBERAL AND CULTURAL UNIONISTS

Liberal unionists may at times cite approvingly key events in Irish history from the plantations of Ulster onwards. With cultural unionists they may derive consolation from such events as the Williamite Settlement, the Act of Union and Ulster's Solemn League and Covenant, as well as from the show of unionist opposition to the Anglo-Irish Agreement and, to a lesser extent, to *Frameworks for the Future*. But these events and shows of opposition are divested of their explicitly Protestant or covenantalist connotations. They are to be recalled and applauded principally for their rational and liberal implications.

What matters about the Williamite Settlement, for example, is not its guarantee of a Protestant ascendancy but its laying of constitutional foundations that have withstood the test of time and have proved sufficiently adept to facilitate the development of a modern, rational British state. The foundations of the sovereignty of the Crown in parliament, the rule of law, civil and religious liberties, and the principle of toleration are rightly to be celebrated. The Act of Union is also worthy of acclamation since it ensured that the Williamite foundations provided the basis of political life throughout the United Kingdom and not only in England. The importance of Ulster's Solemn League and Covenant lies not in the idea of covenant *per se* or in the view that God is on Ulster's side; it consists, rather, in the crucial phrase that pledges defence of unionists' 'cherished position of equal citizenship in the United Kingdom'.[2] And it is via the concept of equal citizenship that the true significance of unionist opposition to the Anglo-Irish Agreement may be gleaned. An agreement that appeared to sound the death knell of the concept of equal citizenship for the people of Northern Ireland unwittingly released powers for its resurrection. It created conditions that not only underscored the futility of clinging to a concept of Northern Ireland defined by Protestant particularism, but also, in making Irish unity a real prospect, helped to expose the latter's unpalatability, by focusing on the social, economic and political disadvantages it would entail.[3] In doing so, ironically the agreement and its aftermath opened up fresh space for a wholehearted recovery of liberal unionism. And this space was quickly occupied in a spirit of evangelical zeal. As Arthur Aughey, echoing Robert McCartney, says of the idea of equal citizenship: in the words of Victor Hugo 'nothing can stop the march of an idea whose time has come'.[4] Hyperbole, it seems, is not the exclusive preserve of cultural unionism.

Hyperbole aside for the moment, a striking feature emerges from these fleeting references to events that provide historical and more recent cues for liberal unionism: how meanings are attributed to the events that signal a distancing from an Ulster unionist way of life. This is striking because liberal and cultural unionists are frequently resorting to the same events as sources of inspiration only to draw very different conclusions. Inasmuch as liberal unionism is sustained by historical memories of such events, then, they are taken to shape a way of life that differs markedly from that associated with cultural unionism in three crucial respects. First, the historical events are interpreted to highlight a political sense of 'Britishness' shared in common with other citizens in the United Kingdom, rather than to reinforce a sense of Britishness mediated through peculiarly Ulster experiences. This interpretative move is of the utmost importance since it allows liberal unionists to avoid entanglement in the cultural Protestant web that is hard to escape once Britishness is qualified by an Ulster dimension. Second, and quite consistently, the memories are taken to focus political attention on Westminster rather than on Stormont or on any envisaged devolved assembly of the future. To be sure, certain liberal unionists are keen to stress that there was more to the old Stormont than simply unconstrained cultural unionist supremacy, that liberal influences tempered potential Protestant excesses, and that life for Catholics was not as bad as is often made out.[5] But even so, there is broad agreement with Aughey's judgement that 'the outcome of the Home Rule debate was not a victory for unionism at all and only a partial victory for Ulster unionists'.[6] Third, in keeping with the emphases on political Britishness and the centrality of Westminster, the memories underpin a corresponding stress on the contractual obligations of the British government to its citizens *as* citizens rather than to any special group. This stress is given a particular twist which is a hallmark of the liberal unionist argument: Westminster's primary obligation is to maintain the Union and from this derive its specific obligations to citizens in Northern Ireland, the majority of whom happen to be pro-Union.

If in the foregoing respects liberal unionists distinguish the way of life to which they are committed from that typical of cultural unionists, it should be noted that the interests of both on occasions coincide. As I pointed out in Chapter 2, Paisley and McCartney have been the two politicians pressing most enthusiastically for a united unionist stance against *Frameworks for the Future*. Cultural and liberal unionists alike reckon that their respective ways of life are endangered by potential violations of British sovereignty in Northern Ireland and by attempts to dilute Northern Ireland's British identity. In responding to these dangers, moreover, liberals are as inclined as culturalists to employ a language of siege. Writing shortly after the republican and loyalist paramilitaries' ceasefires, for instance, McCartney asserted that unionists continue to 'fear that their British identity and way of life will be subsumed in nationalist triumphalism'.[7] And the publication of *Frameworks for the Future* prompted him to reflect that the threat to unionism, already evident in the Anglo-Irish Agreement of 1985, was now reinforced and made more acute by the British government and its 'Fifth Column'.[8]

So if it is true to say that cultural unionism is sometimes kitted out in liberal gear – when emphasising the contractarian strand of its thought, for example – it is equally true to say that, through its appropriation of the language of siege, liberal unionism sometimes borrows freely from the wardrobe of its cultural cousin. Such acts of reciprocity, of course, should not blind us to the substantive differences inherent in their respective ways of life. And in turning to tease out ramifications of those distinctive features of the British political way of life depicted above, we may become clearer still on what precisely liberal unionism stands for and why it is frequently at odds with both the British government and Irish nationalism.

THE UNION AND THE STATE

The essence of liberal unionism's way of life resides in its attachment to the interlocking realities of the Union and the British state. According to Aughey, 'the idea of the union is the willing community of citizens united not by creed, colour or ethnicity but by a recognition of the authority of the union'.[9] And it is precisely such an idea that the British state embodies. It does so, moreover, in a way that the Irish state never could. Thus McCartney contends that the British state is based on a principle of liberty which facilitates a pluralist society whereas the Irish Republic is based on a principle of authority which is inimical to pluralism.[10] Or, as Aughey explains, we are dealing here with two contrasting notions of the state. One notion thinks of the state as the structure that holds together the nation which in turn is typically described in the cultural terms of race, language or religion. Another notion, first articulated in Hegel's political philosophy, conceives of the state primarily as an institution grounded in right and the rule of law. With the first notion it is common to define membership using the cultural term of identity, whereas with the second membership is more appropriately defined through the legal term of citizenship.[11] In Aughey's opinion, the Republic of Ireland is a state in the first sense and the United Kingdom is a state in the second. With regard to the latter he claims: 'the United Kingdom is a state which, being multi-national and multi-ethnic, can be understood in terms of citizenship and not substantive identity ... all are equal citizens under one government'. Furthermore, he continues, 'it is to this notion that intelligent unionism, which embraces both protestants and catholics, owes allegiance. It was from this notion that the Republic of Ireland seceded in order to construct a state on the principle of national unity'.[12]

Being true to the Union that the British state embodies requires wholehearted affirmation of the concept of citizenship at its heart. Accordingly, the political agenda of a thoroughgoing liberal unionism has as its goal the full integration of Northern Ireland within the United Kingdom. This goal was pursued vigorously in the aftermath of the Anglo-Irish Agreement through the Campaign for Equal Citizenship in which McCartney was a leading player and about which Aughey commented sympathetically.[13] Besides its particular plea for citizens in Northern Ireland to be granted the same political rights as those enjoyed by citizens elsewhere in the United Kingdom, a central thesis of the campaign was that integration offered the only effective way of overcoming the sectarian politics that have haunted Northern Ireland since partition, that it afforded easily the best prospects for the flourishing of an inclusive, liberal unionism. Echoes of this thesis continue to be heard even in the wake of *Frameworks for the Future*. McCartney, for example, urges all pro-Union people to campaign for 'the parity of value of British citizenship throughout Great Britain and Northern Ireland'. If successful, the result 'would not be a Union of Protestant or any other ascendancy but a Union which, while accepting a British political identity, fully acknowledged the diverse and different cultural heritage of the entire Northern Ireland community'.[14]

According to liberal unionists, one of the greatest obstacles to the realisation of equal British citizenship for those living in Northern Ireland lies in the widespread acceptance of analytical categories that effectively marginalise its significance. From the Anglo-Irish Agreement to the Downing Street Declaration through to *Frameworks for the Future*, the British government has been complicit in privileging these categories and thereby in according primacy to a nationalist agenda for the future of Northern Ireland. Foster, for example, complains of the language of the Downing Street Declaration: ' "Self-determination by the people of Ireland"; "democratically national and political aspirations"; "both traditions in Ireland": these key phrases in the Declaration are from the lexicon of Irish nationalism, not unionism.'[15] Or take the concept of parity of esteem that appears at frequent junctures throughout *Frameworks for the Future* and has been almost elevated to a first principle in British and Irish government circles. The demand it entails for recognition of an Irish identity in public institutions is deeply discomfiting to liberal unionists. The demand is not a right, we are told, even if the vocabulary of rights is drawn upon, but an illegitimate political claim which subverts unionists' quite legitimate entitlement to equal British citizenship. It is,

McCartney says, merely 'Humespeak'[16] for recognition of the legitimacy of the aspiration for a united Ireland. And, as such, parity of esteem is not something given to people, as is the case with genuine rights, but something given to an aspiration 'which is contrary to the will of the democratic majority' in Northern Ireland.[17] Moreover, attempts to implement parity of esteem between the North's different identities are examples not of liberal neutrality at work but of official capitulation to nationalist propaganda.

The strength of opposition to talk of institutionalising parity of esteem between unionist and nationalist identities becomes properly intelligible against the backdrop of the different senses of the state and of membership that Aughey thinks pertain in Britain and Ireland. In short, such talk only appears reasonable if we accept the terms of Irish nationalism. It is these terms – and the senses of the state and membership they entail – that make parity of esteem between different identities the issue it has become in Northern Ireland. For example, the terms of nationalism require us to conceptualise the clash of interests at play on the island of Ireland as being between two politico-cultural traditions each of which enjoys the right of self-determination. Since this clash is located in the North it follows that new political structures – giving both Westminster and Dublin a role in the government of Northern Ireland – should be created to accord institutional expression to the two traditional identities and thus effect their political reconciliation.[18]

This line of argument loses its force, however, if we do not accept the terms of Irish nationalism. If, on the contrary, Aughey argues, we consider British conceptions of the state and membership to be politically enlightened then it is more appropriate to conceptualise the conflict of interests on the island of Ireland as being between two states. And such a conceptualisation yields a different set of requirements for government in Northern Ireland. This set includes the provision of structures that facilitate the interests of both states in a way that makes possible good-neighbourly relations and mutually beneficial cross-border co-operation. It also includes, within Northern Ireland, a guarantee of the rights of all citizens and tolerance of cultural diversity. What it does not include, Aughey reasons, is recognition that a concept of parity of esteem legitimately extends to a *political* accommodation of different identities within the North. Such recognition is impermissible because it would diminish the sovereignty of the British state of which Northern Ireland is an integral part. It would involve a form of 'joint sovereignty' which would mean 'nothing other than the dissolution of the Union'.[19]

So liberal unionism denies that the right of self-determination properly applies to a nationalist tradition in Northern Ireland, rejects the 'two traditions analysis' underpinning the idea that there should be political parity of esteem between unionists and nationalists, and refuses to equate 'cultural identity with statehood'.[20] From its perspective, the idea of parity of esteem applied to different identities must quite simply be a non-starter. The trick is to purge state institutions of any trace of cultural identities, unionist or nationalist. Intelligent, liberal unionism has a different rationale, one that is fully realisable through Northern Ireland's integration within the United Kingdom and the achievement of equal British citizenship.

The task is to convince the British government. In pursuit of the task, two arguments are typically used: one highlighting the incoherence of the government's position and the other showing that that incoherence is a by-product of a deeper failure of duty. The first is neatly captured by Richard English's exposure of what he regards as the sheer incoherence of the British state's predilection 'to accord equal legitimacy on the one hand to a tradition whose instinct and drive is to support and maintain the state and, on the other, to a tradition aiming at some form of dismemberment of the state'.[21] The oscillating ambiguities that result from such incoherence point to the British government's dereliction of duty in Northern Ireland, and specifically its failure to honour its obligation to maintain the Union. This obligation is compromised consistently: by the government acknowledging that Northern Ireland is an integral part of the Union but treating it as though it is not; by the government acknowledging that the United Kingdom is a sovereign state but being willing to share that sovereignty in Northern Ireland alone. Not only does such incoherence and compromise contribute enormously to political instability in the North, it also reveals a slender grasp of what having an obligation to maintain the Union entails. Quite simply, the Union is not at the disposal of any particular British government but, rather, it belongs to all citizens included within its borders. All citizens therefore have an equal share in it and are entitled to equal rights under its jurisdiction. If when denied their entitlements unionists appear conditionally loyal to the government, it is because the government is conditionally loyal to the Union and, as a consequence, to them.[22] Otherwise put, instances of unionist disloyalty to the government derive from an unconditional loyalty to the Union. The fact of the matter is that the British government incurs contractual obligations to the Union and to citizens within the Union, but persistently breaks them in the case of Northern Ireland.

For liberal unionists, the requirements of sovereignty and rationality dictate that the government be reminded of this apparently ridiculous state of affairs; that it be brought to account for breaching its most basic *raison d'être*; and that it be persuaded to move beyond its deeply contradictory position by assuming its proper responsibilities to the pro-Union majority in Northern Ireland. It is only when Westminster accedes to the force of good arguments based on the implications of its sovereignty that the British political way of life to which liberal unionists are committed will be unambiguously theirs.

DIFFICULTIES

The likelihood of the British government doing anything of the sort seems very remote, however, and as a consequence the way of life liberal unionists covet seems destined to elude their reach.

The twin aspirations of equal citizenship and political integration are not, and never have been, on the government's agenda for Northern Ireland. On the surface, liberal unionism's reluctance to admit this is close to astonishing as it flies in the face of what has been known about British policy in Northern Ireland since partition, and especially since 1985. As the Anglo-Irish Agreement and, more recently, *Frameworks for the Future* have made abundantly clear, integration is not considered an option by either the British or Irish governments. It is not that liberal unionists are unaware of this fact, but more that they are unmoved by it. As Aughey explains, the 'thrust of the integrationist case is that Ulster does not have to submit to those "realities" imposed upon it by the British and Irish governments'.[23] This explanation reflects the tenacity of liberal unionists' determination not to relinquish an idea of the Union to which they think reason commits them, but it scarcely makes their position more practically tenable. Perhaps, as an interim measure, a fallback position is that apparently favoured by David Trimble in which the procedural rules of Westminster's government of Northern Ireland are strengthened in an integrationist direction and an administrative, rather than a legislative, form of devolution is advocated.[24] Of course, there are doubts about the chances of this position gaining acceptance, but at least they are not as slim as those of a purely integrationist line.

British lack of receptiveness to calls for equal citizenship and integration creates a practical difficulty for liberal unionism inasmuch as it denies them full access to the way of life they want. So too does nationalist imperviousness to the liberal unionists' rational case for the Union inasmuch as it blocks the impact of their arguments on government policies in both Britain and Ireland. If liberal unionists seem relatively undeterred by the first difficulty, they are positively cavalier about the second. The simple key to removing the obstacle of nationalist obduracy, Patrick Roche tells us, 'lies in a radical but not precipitate reversal of policy by the Republic and the British government'.[25] It is not to be overcome by any dialogical engagement with nationalists on the prevailing terms of peace and reconciliation. These reflect a nationalist script and need replacing not encouraging. The 'banal but corrosive jargon of the peace process', Aughey says, has to be transformed.[26] Liberal unionism is nothing if not confident of its possession of the intellectual means to effect such a transformation. And there is a barely concealed smugness about the manner in which nationalist claims are disposed of.[27] The point is not to allow one's head to be turned by the difficulty of nationalism's current success in impeding the progress of rational, liberal arguments for the Union. To expose the shallowness of the nationalist position remains the best response.

UNIONISM AND NATIONALISM

Whatever its putative intellectual virtues, liberal unionism's handling of its practical difficulties promises in the immediate term only prolonged political stalemate. But this, seemingly, is a small price to pay given the alternatives. It is also deeply perplexing. Such a manner of thinking betrays, I now wish to suggest, serious occlusions in the horizon of meaning within which liberal unionists operate, acute blind spots which preclude the legitimacy of other ways of seeing the politics of Northern Ireland. The categories through which political Britishness is interpreted, far from having the warrant of pure reason, entail highly contentious, and I think some quite implausible, suppositions. Or so I want to argue by attending to three theses on certainty, sovereignty and a liberal society which are encouraged by liberal unionism's horizon of meaning.

CERTAINTY AND HISTORY

Liberal unionism's thesis on certainty may be put as follows: whatever the pitfalls, we can be assured that rational unionism will eventually be vindicated. But in the current shambles that is Northern Irish politics, it may be wondered where such assurance comes from. From a resolute historical hope seems to be the answer. At any rate, this is what seems to be communicated through much liberal unionist language. As we have noted, Aughey, for example, announces that equal citizenship is an idea whose time has arrived and cannot be prevented from winning out. Presumably this is partly why the integrationist case insists that 'Ulster does not have to submit to those "realities" imposed upon it by the British and Irish governments'. Right and history are on its side not theirs. Furthermore McCartney, the one prominent unionist politician to have grasped the nettle on equal citizenship and integration, is seen by Aughey as bringing to politics 'a special mood – the mood of his being the advocate of a noble purpose, of articulating a new conception of politics which transcends the predictable'. In doing so, McCartney apparently passes the Hegelian test of 'political genius'.[28] Given that the idea for which McCartney stands has already been declared irrepressible, this Hegelian casting of his role virtually invites us to perceive the MP for North Down as a special vehicle of *Geist*'s cunning in history.[29] And if this is the case, clearly neither the British government nor Irish nationalism stand a chance in the long run and the practical problems they pose for liberal unionism are dismissable as mere trifles.

Is this all just hyperbole? To me it is, but I am not so sure it is to Aughey. Perhaps, given its Hegelian resonances, the certainty thesis is analogous to Francis Fukuyama's thesis on the 'end of history' and should be read in the latter's light. According to Fukuyama, liberal democracy has proved itself superior to its major ideological rivals from the left and the right in the twentieth century and will continue to exert its superiority over potential rivals – such as nationalism and religious fundamentalism – in the foreseeable future. In its strong form, this thesis is conveyed through claims like these: we are witnessing 'the end of history as such, that is, the end point of mankind's ideological evolution and the universalisation of Western liberal democracy as the final form of human government';[30] although the universal victory of liberal democracy awaits definitive material expression, 'there are powerful reasons for believing that it is the ideal that will govern the material world in the long run'.[31] Now claims like these could easily be taken to fit with liberal unionist claims in the particular circumstances of Northern Ireland: the liberal-democratic ideal is embodied in the British state, it is opposed by irrational ideals of religious fundamentalism and Irish nationalism, but, in aspiring to realise it through a rational emphasis on political Britishness, liberal unionists may be confident of the final victory.

But, again, what is the basis of such confidence? If tied to Fukuyama's thesis, the basis is more than a little shaky. Fukuyama, perhaps like Aughey, derives confidence from an appropriation of Hegel's historical teleology: liberal democracy is the definitive outcome of a long but purposeful historical struggle, and maybe by extension unionism may be seen as such too. The trouble is that Fukuyama's use of Hegel is selective and controversial, his defence of historical teleology is conducted with little of Hegel's intellectual depth and sophistication, and, perhaps most telling, Hegel's own, much more impressive, case for standing at the 'end of history' is viewed as considerably less than compelling even by his most sympathetic commentators.[32] For Fukuyama to succeed where Hegel is widely acknowledged to have failed demands arguments of a sort he does not even attempt to provide. He fails to attend to philosophical problems, not least those of contingency and relativity, that confront talk of the 'end of history' or of definitive political outcomes. Hegel, in contrast, was alert to such problems and tried to resolve them through his distinctive 'philosophy of identity'.[33] Hegel, in other words, recognised that pointing to the unique political achievements of modernity was not enough to clinch an argument for the arrival of history's end; that such an argument required in addition a set of metaphysical and ontological demonstrations. That Hegel failed to deliver the necessary demonstrations is now commonly accepted. That Fukuyama supposes he can avoid attempting philosophical demonstrations of any sort, even as he expects his version of history's ineluctable goals to be taken seriously, is nothing short of astonishing.

The foregoing is a possible interpretation of the certainty thesis which links the fate of liberal unionism in Northern Ireland to the global fate of liberal democracy. It is one that suggests that whatever may be profitably said about their respective fates, it is difficult to be certain of their ultimate triumph. And in a Northern Irish context, this leaves liberal unionism's certainty thesis in a peculiarly awkward situation. As it stands, and whether it should be linked to Fukuyama's thesis or not, it is probably no more or less hyperbolic than the thesis that Paisley is God's unique man in Ulster appointed to play a quasi-messianic role in its hour of need, that Ulster is special because it contains 'more born again people ... to the square-mile than anywhere else in the world',[34] and that Ulster's destiny is assured because it enjoys a privileged place in the scheme of divine providence. Or, indeed, no more or less hyperbolic than Sinn Féin's thesis that Irish unity is historically inevitable. I do not happen to believe any of these stories that anticipate with apparently comparable certainty the vindication of a British, or an Ulster or an Irish way of life. But it seems their advocates do. And because they all believe history is uniquely on their side they each reduce politics to a zero-sum game.

The irony here is that liberal unionism is as culpable as its culturalist opponents, whether unionist or nationalist. For all of its vaunted boasts to rationality it too encourages an intransigent approach to politics, even if it claims that its content distinguishes itself by its appeal to our intellects alone. And in doing so, it contributes to a deepening of its own practical difficulties. For if it is true to say, as Foster does, that 'aggressive nationalism strengthens unionism',[35] it is equally true to say that patronising, liberal unionist certainty hardens nationalists' resolve. Perhaps only a liberal eschatological faith, that is, a faith in a 'final outcome' of history, could render liberal unionists incapable of seeing that this hardening of nationalist resolve actually makes more distant yet the realisation of liberal unionist aspirations and, far more important, the achievement of a decent social and political life in Northern Ireland.

SOVEREIGNTY AND EQUAL CITIZENSHIP

In addition to the problems just canvassed, the certainty thesis contains in embryonic form two other theses which are also problematic, although for different reasons. One of these is a thesis about sovereignty which may be put thus: right is exclusively on unionism's side since Britain alone has legitimate claim to sovereignty in Northern Ireland. As a legal statement of the legitimacy of Northern Ireland's constitutional status within the United Kingdom, this thesis is entirely correct. As Kevin Boyle and Tom Hadden explain:

> ... legitimacy can properly be claimed for the current constitutional status of Northern Ireland on two internationally recognised grounds: first, in that a substantial majority of its citizens have consistently expressed their support, in free and fair elections, for union with Britain; and secondly, in that in the event of an armed conflict within its boundaries it is almost certain that the unionist community would be able to maintain an effective system of government. The first of these is the universally accepted principle of self-determination. The second is tacitly accepted in the international community in that the victors of an internal conflict or of a revolutionary *coup d'état* are entitled to be granted first *de facto* and ultimately *de jure* recognition.[36]

For liberal unionists such international legal recognition of Northern Ireland's legitimacy and of Britain's entitlement to sole sovereignty in Northern Ireland is the beginning and the end of the matter. The point is to persuade the British government to stand resolute on the sovereignty issue by facing up to its obligation to maintain the Union. The point is not to entertain nationalist counter-claims to sovereignty in Northern Ireland. If legal positivism were all that counted, that is, the sheer legal fact of Northern Ireland's current constitutional status, there would be nothing to quibble about here. But it is not all that counts precisely because historical and moral considerations also come into play in a divided society that is a site of contested sovereignty. These wider considerations cannot be successfully ignored by liberal unionism not only because of their intrinsic worthiness of attention, but also because the government to whom exclusive sovereignty is attributed seems to be swayed by them to some degree. Of course, if it suited Westminster's interests, or even if there were deeply felt common bonds between Britain and Northern Ireland, the strictly legal card favoured by liberal unionists would probably be played without compunction. We do not have to suppose that an altruistic attitude to nationalists underlies the British government's willingness to soften its line on sovereignty in Northern Ireland, at least to the extent of allowing Dublin the consultative role it presently enjoys under the terms of the Anglo-Irish Agreement. But the question is whether liberal unionism has a convincing line on sovereignty in addition to the legal line.

The short answer is not really. Inasmuch as it has another line it curiously inverts the principle of self-determination that Boyle and Hadden use to justify unionists' position. Aughey, especially, cautions against resorting to such a principle on the grounds that it belongs to a nationalist lexicon which is inappropriate to unionism. Or, as he argues, the principle applies to unionists only in the inverted, negative sense that 'British citizens ought not to be compelled against their will to become part of an economically backward, politically authoritarian and religiously exclusive Irish state'.[37] And this is a sense that is better conveyed by sticking to the concept of equal citizenship. This concept enables unionists to claim that all British citizens own the Union and cannot be removed from it without their consent. Since that consent was not forthcoming earlier in the century, unionists were entirely justified in holding out against Home Rule. And since it is not forthcoming now, they remain equally justified in holding out against a united Ireland and against incursions of British sovereignty in Northern Ireland. The idea of equal citizenship entails Northern

Ireland's right not only to be British but to be fully British.

On these terms, there is no space for alternative sovereignty claims, or for the wider historical and moral considerations non-unionists might draw upon to suggest that the rigorous logic adopted by Aughey begins from too restricted a base. That unionists were only able to get their way by defying the will of Westminster and the will of the greater number of Irish people does not give pause to liberal unionist insistence that right is exclusively on their side. Such defiance is precisely what the concept of equal citizenship allows them to justify without blushing. That non-unionists, who consented to Home Rule and thus as it were to be fully Irish, might have a comparable case in reverse, albeit one expressed in the different language of self-determination, does not compute. Legal positivism combined with the concept of equal citizenship permits no compromise here. Northern nationalists' counter-entitlements are simply screened out.

Three comments are in order. First, one thing that can be said with confidence is that such reasoning, much like that involved in the claim to certainty, is a recipe for more lousy politics in Northern Ireland. It is one thing to think that nationalist arguments are not up to scratch, but another entirely to treat them with disdain. Nationalists, it seems, are to be persuaded to accept the integrity of Northern Ireland either by having their fundamental objections ignored or by being (intellectually or politically) bludgeoned into submission. It is hard not to conclude that liberal unionists, with their gaze fixed unwaveringly on the goal of unsullied political Britishness, seem oddly oblivious to the political responsibilities of living in a deeply divided society.

Second, I am not sure that there is a principle of justice that equips us to decide precisely all the rights and wrongs about partition and its aftermath, but I am sure that in so far as the concept of equal citizenship poses as one, it does not qualify. In the situation of historical, political and moral conflict and complexity that was Ireland in the second and third decades of the century and that is Northern Ireland today, the concept discounts itself by virtue of its partiality and narrowness. Its terms decree that unionists alone can be right, that conflict must be resolved by declaring one winner only and an untouchable one at that, and that whole slices of complexity should be cut out and discarded. This makes equal citizenship no doubt an appealing concept for its beneficiaries: it affords a clever device by which they can insulate themselves from the cantankerous complaints of the losers, and from the vicissitudes that tinge many of our moral and political choices with an inescapable tragedy, while still proclaiming indignantly that right belongs to them. But it also makes the concept of equal citizenship a feeble parody of the even-handed approach that justice requires.

Third, the argument that equal citizenship justifies single sovereignty in Northern Ireland is also tied to a substantive claim about the benefits of political Britishness and the costs of politico-cultural Irishness. As the last-cited argument of Aughey put it in terms of those costs, unionists want no part of 'an economically backward, politically authoritarian and religiously exclusive Irish state'. Exactly what would happen to the argument if it could be shown that most non-unionists want no such thing either and that the Irish state does not fit this description anyway raises interesting possibilities. It also leads to a third thesis which focuses on the link between unionism and a liberal society and which I now want to take up. But I should emphasise that my reservations about the plausibility of using the concept of equal citizenship to settle the sovereignty issue are not intended to warrant concluding unambiguously in favour of joint sovereignty in Northern Ireland. They simply suggest that the concept of equal citizenship is deployed to deliver an untimely pre-emptive strike which tries to obliterate too many of the factors that have to be weighed up before a fair conclusion of any sort is reached.

UNIONISM AND A LIBERAL SOCIETY

The third thesis encouraged by liberal unionism's horizon of meaning may be characterised as follows: unionism is a necessary condition of a liberal society in Ireland. There are two major parts to this thesis. One part draws upon a contrast between the British and Irish states and the other reinforces opposition to political parity of esteem in Northern Ireland. Both may be fruitfully explored by taking as a point of departure McCartney's argument in *Liberty and Authority in Ireland*.

McCartney explicates the thesis by drawing on the conceptual framework provided by Isaiah Berlin's famous essay 'Two Concepts of Liberty'.[38] He accepts unreservedly the validity of Berlin's depiction of the 'negative' and 'positive' senses of freedom and, like Berlin, regards the positive sense pejoratively as a bogus justification of political authoritarianism. In doing so, he reiterates a number of Berlin's familiar contrasts between the two senses of liberty. On one side stand advocates of the positive sense seeking to answer the question of who should govern us by emphasising the importance of the notion of self-mastery. Unfortunately, the political translation of such a notion issues in an idea of a collective self who, all too readily, displays a preparedness to override the rights of individuals and minorities for the sake of supposedly 'higher' collective goals. On another side stand advocates of the negative sense endeavouring to answer the question of what a person is free to do and be. They stress, quite properly, that an individual is entitled to choose to live as he/she desires, as free as possible from state interference, and having his/her rights protected. As McCartney puts it:

> Negative freedom is, in essence, the rules for the control or curbing of power. The positive freedom of those who seek the recognition and dominance of their group is the acquisition and use of power and ... the suppression in some degree of the individual's liberty.[39]

The clash between these different senses of freedom is taken to illuminate the issues at stake in contemporary Irish politics. Liberal unionism nails its colours to the mast of negative freedom because it realises that the achievement and maintenance of a pluralist society is a precarious business which is threatened by positive freedom. This means, politically, remaining steadfast in defence of the Union since it is the British state, and not the Irish, that facilitates pluralism and protects individual rights. Nationalist thinking, by contrast, is in a dreadful muddle as a result of its failure to perceive the deep divisions separating the two senses of freedom: this 'is nowhere more evident than in confusion between the desire of Northern Ireland's minority for civil liberties and individual rights and its aspiration for Irish unity'.[40] There is confusion here because realisation of the aspiration would leave the desire unsatiated, while wholehearted pursuit of the desire would radically erode the strength of the aspiration. To explain, the desire for individual rights is in line with the basic thrust of negative freedom and is best satisfied by membership of the United Kingdom. The aspiration for Irish unity, by contrast, follows the star of positive freedom by conceiving of Irish unity in terms of a nationalist ideal. And, under the guise of fulfilling a higher freedom, this ideal warrants a political authoritarianism that entails sacrificing many individual rights and liberties, as much legislation in the Irish Republic testifies.[41] In its extreme form, as manifest in the activities of the IRA, the aspiration for Irish unity exhibits the worst traits of the positive sense of freedom and the virtual eclipse of the negative sense: where a self-appointed elite operating on the 'assumption that they alone know what people really want ... justify murder, oppression, torture and extortion in the name of and on behalf of the real self, the spirit of the Irish people'.[42]

As we can see, then, McCartney's use of Berlin's conceptual distinctions in relation to Irish politics enables him to underpin the thesis that unionism is a necessary condition of a liberal society in Ireland. To be liberal is simultaneously to be unionist and therefore any threat to the Union is also a threat to liberalism. But is this a compelling argument in terms of how we may plausibly interpret the British and Irish states? Is one the undisputed site of negative liberty and the other the site of its enemy?

It is unlikely that anyone without a specific ideological axe to grind would currently think of Britain as a pluralist dream world and Ireland as an authoritarian nightmare. Yet this is seemingly what McCartney and other liberal unionists invite us to believe. In a straightforward sense it is unbelievable. That the British state embodies a principle of negative liberty alone or that it represents a space free from clashing cultural or national interests is a barely credible proposition. As McGarry and O'Leary comment, 'the proposition that the UK state is a model of civic citizenship devoid of national or ethnic cultural content, or that the UK's institutions are ethnically neutral, would produce a hollow laugh amongst "visible minorities" in Britain, as well as audiences of potential immigrants from India, Pakistan, Bangladesh and the West Indies'.[43] That the Irish state embodies the principle of positive freedom (as pejoratively defined by Berlin and McCartney) to such an extent that it overrides the claims of negative freedom and pluralism is barely credible too. I have already made a similar point in Chapter 3 when trying to counteract cultural unionist misconceptions about Ireland. It is enough to say with McGarry and O'Leary again that 'the idea that the United Kingdom is superior to the Republic as a liberal democracy which protects secular rights, individual rights and minority-rights is ... not as obvious as it might seem to a reader of secular disposition'.[44]

To the extent that current political realities count in assessing its validity, the thesis that unionism is a necessary condition of a liberal society in Ireland is hard to maintain. But a recent, and much more subtle and nuanced, essay by Aughey seems to suggest that the thesis might allow of a milder reformulation in the context of Irish politics.[45] Aughey concedes that in some intelligible sense the Republic does qualify as liberal and is becoming more pluralist. And on the strength of this concession, the thesis may be modified to say something like this: one route to a liberal society leads out of Irish nationalist experience, but this route is different in kind from, and in important respects foreign to, the route that leads from unionism. Here those unionist charges against the illiberality of the Republic that have most trouble meeting any empirical test may be dispensed with. But what then is the point?

For liberal unionists the sticking point remains, as McCartney's argument underscores, a difference over authority. And it remains a difference in that the authoritative sources from which Irish nationalism has drawn – the Catholic Church and a particular cultural–historical narrative – are decidedly unauthoritative for unionists. The rub is that it is against the backdrop of these sources that the Irish state tries to define its sense of liberal pluralism. Precisely because the Republic cannot simply deny its Catholic ethos and its founding myths, its route to a liberal society necessarily involves engagement with them: dislodging their claims to exclusive authority certainly, modifying their influence here and diluting their strength there, but never setting them aside altogether. The result is an understanding of liberalism from which most unionists still recoil, since it is mediated through sources that they typically perceive as threats to their way(s) of life. Nationalism with a liberal face is taken to be nationalist first and liberal a poor second.

Accordingly, the salience of McCartney's linking of unionism to a principle of negative liberty retains its force. It is by way of this principle, or its equivalent, that unionists have articulated their opposition to the authoritative sources of nationalism and have worked out their way of being liberal – a way, incidentally, that ties in with broader liberal experience in the history of the West, as McCartney's drawing on Berlin illustrates. So a crucial core of the thesis is still intact and may even facilitate another relatively strong reformulation: inasmuch as it is irrecusably tied to a principle of negative freedom, unionism is in touch with the liberal mainstream and offers a surer route to a liberal society. This could be said to hold even if political realities in Britain generally, not to mention in Northern Ireland particularly, are imperfect approximations of what the principle requires. For the point is to think of negative liberty as a regulative ideal for unionism in a way it could never fully be for nationalism.

Accepting negative liberty as a regulative ideal that is definitive for unionism permits us to see how McCartney's play on the negative/positive liberty distinction also provides an additional rationale for opposing political parity of esteem in Northern Ireland. It amounts to this. Within the context of Northern Ireland, the positive sense of liberty as characterised by Berlin necessarily poses a danger to the pluralism cultivated by liberty's negative sense. The concessions to the positive sense that might apply in the South – where moves to pluralise society in the direction of the negative sense have to defer on occasions to the authoritative sources of Church and tradition – do not obtain in the North where the principle of negative liberty is constitutive of the state. Irish nationalism, with or without a 'liberal' face, therefore continues to threaten the sort of liberty unionists enjoy by virtue of their political Britishness. Accordingly, any diminution of Northern Ireland's Britishness qualifies as an assault not only on unionism but also on a liberal society that reflects the negative principle of freedom. And so demands for political parity of esteem must be rejected for the sake of the liberty the Union guarantees.

The grounds for rejecting such demands are even more com- pelling when we realise that acceding to them is tantamount to taking a fateful step on the road to a united Ireland. That is to say, demands for political parity of esteem project a final destination entailing not just a diminution of political Britishness but its death, not just a pegging back of unionism but its extinction, and not just an incursion into negative liberty but its demise (at least in that form of a liberal society that is canonical for unionists). Thus such demands cannot be dissociated from the positive sense of freedom implicit in the authoritative sources of Irish nationalism in reference to which the IRA justifies its actions. And that is why, at the last, they convince only if interpreted through the categories of positive freedom – categories that sig- nify the end of everything unionism stands for.

One problem with this rationale is that it occludes the fact that unionism too has its authoritative sources – such as those drawn on by cultural unionists – which compromise the claim that negative liberty is its sole guiding regulative ideal. And these are sources that are as unauthoritative for nationalists as nationalist sources are for unionists. In this sense unionism is as inescapably mired in positive freedom as is nationalism. If liberal nationalists have to engage with their sources in order to subvert their ultimate authority, liberal unionists have to do likewise with theirs. And if such engagement by liberal nationalists is not sufficient to vindicate nationalism's liberal credentials in unionist eyes, it is hard to see why comparable engagement by liberal unionists would be sufficient proof of unionism's liberal commitments in nationalist eyes. Or, more pointedly, nationalists might retort that on the issue of illiberality they have most grounds for complaint: what unionists perceive as a threat (from nationalism) does not quite match what nationalists have experienced as a reality (under unionism). In short, liberal unionists are implicated in the 'Ulster' dimension of unionism however much they wish to transcend it. And a rationale that hides this fact wears a bit thin. No doubt unionism and nationalism do offer alternative routes to a liberal society, but whether they represent two different senses of liberty in the manner supposed by liberal unionists is open to serious doubt.

But what happens if we overlook these sorts of complications by simply accepting that for liberal unionists negative liberty is *the* regulative ideal? Is their rationale against political parity of esteem then compelling? Perhaps it is if, with them, we buy Berlin's distinction between the two senses of liberty. But if we do not, and if we think that it is mistaken to define unionism solely in relation to the negative sense, matters alter considerably. It is an argument along such lines that I want to begin to make.

Berlin's distinction admittedly has some force in extreme cases where the rights and liberties of individuals are ignored and an idea of positive freedom is invoked to justify gross coercion. Much of what went on during the Reign of Terror at the end of the French Revolution is a case in point, as is much perpetrated for the sake of 'Ireland's liberation' by the IRA. But to concede that an idea may appear in distorted form is not to agree that it is without insight, or that it is incapable of moderate expression. Indeed there are reasons to maintain, as a number of Berlin's critics have done, that the two senses of freedom are often interconnected, that a purely negative sense is insufficient, and that a positive sense is open to conceptualisations other than the one Berlin offers and is not necessarily saddled with the pejorative connotations he ascribes to it.[46] I hint at some of these reasons later in the chapter when discussing the concept of citizenship, and I develop them at more length in the next. For the moment, let me just intimate the sort of position on freedom they may be taken to support. I have in mind a position that hinges upon three claims: (1) that an important – 'positive' – meaning of freedom is bound up with a notion of citizen self-rule; (2) that a 'negative' emphasis on the fundamental rights and liberties of individuals is indispensable; and (3) that these positive and negative aspects are not incompatible but contribute to a conception of political life that combines civic and protective functions.[47]

The possibility of such a position is blocked out on Berlin's (and McCartney's) terms principally because mention of positive freedom is prejudged as harbouring a dark tendency to collective domination. Thus the prospect of positive freedom referring to a democratic mode of self-government is reduced to a dangerous illusion. And thus the protective function of politics is always given precedence and the civic function is left acutely underdeveloped. The contractarian rejection of an Aristotelian/civic republican conception of politics mentioned in the previous chapter (a rejection that my alternative gloss on positive freedom is intended to oppose) is reiterated and made essential to unionism.

Now such a shutting out of a 'civic republican' construal of positive freedom, and an insistence on the sole adequacy of negative freedom, unduly constrains what may be allowed to a concept of political parity of esteem. In particular, it is culpable in encouraging an interpretation of this concept that I think is perverse in two ways. It is perverse, first, to project a worst-case scenario of possible political outcomes of a concept and then make them constitutive of its meaning. This is what proponents of negative freedom ('liberal minimalists') do with the concept of positive freedom and it is what liberal unionists do with the concept of political parity of esteem. But there is no necessary connection between political parity of esteem within Northern Ireland and (unionists' worst-case scenario of) a united Ireland, any more than there is a necessary connection between positive freedom and (liberal minimalists' worst-case scenario of) collectivist repression of individuals. To superimpose these two scenarios, which is what McCartney effectively does, and to carry on as though necessary connections do exist is to betray a perversity that obscures the issues at hand and that traces back to an excessive reliance on the liberal minimalism of negative freedom. Besides, even if we were to accept that a projection of possible outcomes is a key interpretive tool, I would submit that McCartney's is wide of the mark. A more plausible conjecture might be that unionism's best hopes of staving off a united Ireland lie in welcoming political parity of esteem: its implementation would give nationalists an unprecedented stake in the institutional life of Northern Ireland which would meet their complaints against institutional alienation and might even, with time, diminish their aspiration for an all-embracing Irish unity.

However likely or unlikely such a conjecture may be, it points to a second way in which the influence of a politics of negative liberty is evident in a perverse treatment of political parity of esteem: liberal unionists' sheer inability, or unwillingness, to recognise the legitimacy of non-unionists' wish to identify with Northern Ireland's political institutions on terms other than theirs. Ulterior motives have to be attributed to the wish because rational liberals, it is assumed, require only equal rights and liberties and if these are best provided under a British administration then only those with illiberal intentions will cavil against the sufficiency of a British political identity in Northern Ireland. Here McCartney and others reflect the conceptual blindness of liberal minimalism, namely its incapacity to understand why citizens' identification with their political institutions may be important for more than protective reasons. It balks at this no doubt because such institutional identification features as an essential condition of the notion of citizen self-rule that liberal minimalists are so wary of. The unfortunate upshot of liberal minimalist reasoning in Northern Ireland is that McCartney, and others like him, cannot but advance a perverse account of why nationalists have difficulty accepting the adequacy of a unionist political identity and why they press for political parity of esteem.

To summarise, the thesis that unionism is essential to a liberal society in Ireland fails to impress in either of its two main parts. Based on Berlin's distinction between negative and positive liberty, the thesis does not succeed in capturing the differences between the Irish and British states, since it strains credibility to claim that one state fits one definition of liberty and the other state another. Admittedly, a reformulation of the thesis that takes negative liberty as a regulative ideal for unionism yields *prima facie* a strong case against political parity of esteem in Northern Ireland. But this case is weakened once we factor in the role that 'authoritative sources' – which are closer to Berlin's notion of positive liberty – have played in unionist as well as nationalist discourse. It is weakened further once we call into question the adequacy of Berlin's definition of positive freedom and the wisdom of tying unionism to an ideal of negative freedom alone. Here we witness how a version of liberal minimalism contributes to unionist misperceptions of what talk of political parity of esteem necessarily entails. Beyond that, I have given some anticipations of an alternative theory of unionism. These relate to a wider argument I began to articulate which aims to bring unionism more into line with civic republican, and not just classical liberal, ideals. It is this argument I now want to push further through a critical examination of liberal unionism's concept of citizenship. And this in turn sets a scene for its full elaboration in Chapter 5.

CITIZENSHIP AND IDENTITY

Liberal unionism's reliance on an idea of equal citizenship has already come under fire. I have contended that it is fanciful to suppose that it is an idea 'whose time has come', that it is an inadequate principle of political justice in the context of Northern Irish politics, and that it serves to reinforce political stalemate. Moreover, inasmuch as it is related to a principle of negative liberty, which I think it is, it has come under indirect attack through the criticisms I levelled at that principle. In a nutshell, I have suggested that the idea of equal citizenship does not suf-ficiently equip liberal unionists to argue effectively against na-tionalists' demand for political parity of esteem.

In spite of all this, the core notion of citizenship at work in the idea, as articulated by Aughey, is arguably unscathed by my arguments so far. More than that, it may even be thought to sub-vert at least those arguments that display an openness to the case for political parity of esteem. Aughey might say, for example, that a distinction between citizenship and substantive identity lies at the heart of a liberal unionist position and that it is precisely this distinction that I have blurred. Such blurring, it might be added, is hardly innocent since the terms in which my arguments are couched reveal nationalist predispositions. Accordingly, favour-able noises about political parity of esteem appear reasonable only if nationalist categories are accepted, wittingly or not.

We have seen earlier that Aughey does reason along such lines. And the challenge posed by his reasoning to the position I have been gesturing at is obvious. I propose to meet this challenge by: (1) specifying the senses in which Aughey's distinction between citizenship and substantive identity has a point; (2) showing that it is nevertheless very misleading when pressed too far, not least because it implies too thin a conception of citizenship; and (3) suggesting that a concern with citizenship in Northern Ireland creates openness to requests for political parity of esteem. This suggestion is taken further in the next chapter where I hope to demonstrate that such openness does not presuppose a commitment to nationalism, and that it is misleading of Aughey to infer otherwise.

PROCEDURAL CITIZENSHIP

The clearest sense in which Aughey's distinction between citizenship and substantive identity is valid is when the former is understood inclusively and the latter exclusively. To restrict political membership and its benefits, including the application of civil liberties and individual rights, to those sharing the identity of one's class, gender, ethnicity, religion or language group is anathema to the rationale of the modern liberal-democratic state. A concept of citizenship that breaks with such parochial and restrictive conditions and 'universalises' the notion of membership of a polity captures an idea of political equality that has become indispensable to our modern Western sense of who we are.[48] There can be no going back on this concept, which is integral to the modern state. Considering it in an Irish context, Aughey is right to argue that both the irredentist nationalism enshrined in de Valera's 1937 Irish constitution and the discriminatory practices of successive unionist governments at Stormont violated the requirements of a modern concept of citizenship and traded on exclusive notions of substantive identity.[49]

There is, then, a point to the drawing of a contrast between a modern concept of citizenship and a concept of substantive identity when the latter is defined, say, in terms of nationalist exclusivism. This point is probably sharpened by a realisation that the contrast is prone to a degree of fuzziness given that citizenship now largely finds its locus within the parameters of a nation-state, even if it is true to say that this peculiarly modern political phenomenon is currently undergoing significant transformation.[50] Here Jürgen Habermas provides a salutary reminder of how the sort of emphasis on citizenship Aughey is at pains to underscore should be conceived. 'A nation of citizens', he writes, 'does not derive its identity from some common ethnic and cultural properties, but rather from the *praxis* of citizens who actively exercise their civil rights.'[51] Accordingly, the legitimacy of a polity constituted by such citizens hangs on a notion of popular sovereignty that 'does not refer to some substantive collective will which would owe its identity to a prior homogeneity of descent or form of life', but that reflects a consensus achieved among 'free and equal citizens' whose relations are based on 'mutual recognition', that is, where everyone receives 'equal protection and respect in his/her integrity as a unique individual, as a member of an ethnic or cultural group and as a citizen'.[52]

If considerations of this kind vindicate Aughey's distinction between citizenship and substantive identity then considerations of another kind caution against pushing it too far; or, more forcefully, they undercut it in important ways. I want to highlight three considerations that suggest that a form of citizenship that finds no place for substantive identities is seriously deficient.

BEYOND PROCEDURAL CITIZENSHIP

The first of these three considerations clarifies the limited nature and scope of a liberal unionist concept of citizenship and queries its adequacy. This concept is limited in nature by virtue of being purely legal or procedural, and also in scope by virtue of being confined to lifting restrictions on citizenship's entry requirements and to ensuring that its benefits are enjoyed indiscriminately. The purely procedural nature of the concept is problematic because it implies a weak bond between citizens and the particular state to which they belong. Such an implication seems irresistible given Aughey's contrast between the political identity of citizenship and a substantive identity: attachment to the public institutions and practices of society is of a different order from, and cannot match the depth and strength of, attachment to cultural and religious institutions and practices. An upshot of Aughey's rationale, in other words, is that the latter sorts of attachment provide horizons of meaning and significance within which we make sense of our lives, whereas the former sort does not. But with this upshot there is a hovering suspicion that transfer of membership to another state that afforded similar conditions of citizenship could be undertaken without any transformation of what matters to us, whereas the same could not be said of a transfer of our allegiance from one culture to another or from one religion to another. On Aughey's terms, political identities are, in principle, more easily changed without loss than are substantive identities. Thus the bonds between citizen and state are weakly felt; perhaps so weakly that affairs of state are typically matters of indifference to citizens, or even that the loyalty the state can expect of citizens remains inherently unstable.

These concerns are reinforced by attending to the limited scope of a liberal unionist concept of citizenship. What counts here is making citizenship as accessible as possible – by showing that there are no grounds for exclusion on the basis of class, gender, ethnicity, religion and so on – and guaranteeing that the same procedural entitlements apply to all. Such matters are of course of considerable consequence. But they do not exhaust citizenship's scope. What is lacking, in particular, is any notion that citizenship in itself is intrinsically valuable or that it implies specific forms of political activity with internal goods of their own. There is no suggestion of what, beyond living in a law-abiding fashion, makes for a good citizen, and no sense of what we ought to do as citizens. Politics as such does not rate very highly here and thus being an active or a passive citizen is merely a matter of inclination. Citizenship, in short, is valued only for the external goods it provides or makes available to us, whether these are individual entitlements and a redress of social inequalities, or opportunities to pursue a relatively unhindered life of conspicuous consumption, or whatever. There is, I suggest, something worrying about all of this. A concept of citizenship so limited in scope that it is exclusively concerned with external goods and that makes political engagement itself an optional extra seems scarcely equipped to provide the resources needed to sustain the cohesion of any democratic polity. Aughey's concept of citizenship, much like McCartney's concept of negative liberty to which it is closely related, offers invaluable guarantees to individuals, but barely anything to the quality of civic affairs.

A second consideration is that what may be called the 'circumstances' of citizenship make implausible a strict divorce between a political identity and a substantive identity. Otherwise expressed, a political identity is not formed in a cultural vacuum but relies, like the state itself, on a range of commitments and attachments to the particular polity in which it is shaped. Flying in the face of a consideration of this type, as Aughey appears to do, opens up the possibility of the somewhat ridiculous situation I hinted at above, where a citizen's bonds to the state are so loose that they may be broken effortlessly at any moment. But the truth of the matter is that citizen–state relations are rarely like this, for if they were liberal polities would simply stagger along under the perpetual threat of radical disintegration or atrophy. And a crucial reason why they tend not to do this is that citizen loyalty invariably cuts deeper than Aughey's liberal theory allows. Curiously, Aughey at times seems to realise something of the sort such as when, echoing McCartney again, he observes that 'unionists have willed the state not in the feeble sense of "wishing" to be British. They have willed it by their contributions in treasure, talent and sacrifice in both war and peace.'[53] Now I think that it is through such contributions as these that various unionist traditions and memories have evolved and created a 'culture' of unionism that Aughey's liberal unionist arguments presuppose. Put bluntly, most unionists value, and would not dispose lightly of, their membership of a British state not simply because they are good liberals in the mould of Aughey and McCartney but also, and probably more strongly, because their substantive 'cultural' identities are implicated in such membership. Yet this is what is obscured by liberal unionism's thin concept of citizenship.

I need to clarify what I am arguing here to avoid possible confusion. I agreed earlier that there is an important point to distinguishing citizenship from a substantive identity, but now I seem to be saying that we cannot think of the former independently of the latter. When suitably qualified, I think it is crucial to affirm both emphases and that it can be done without contradiction. A 'nation of citizens' may not, as Habermas notes, locate its identity in common 'cultural properties', but neither may it suppose that such properties are issues of indifference to citizenship. The insight in Habermas's note, to reiterate, is that citizenship should not be denied to those not sharing such properties and therefore that citizenship has, in terms of its entry requirements and procedural entitlements, a different locus. In this sense I maintain with Aughey that a distinction is profitably drawn between citizenship and substantive identities.

Cultural properties cannot, however, be ignored, and thus the above distinction cannot be held too rigidly, for at least two reasons. The first is the reason I have been trying to uncover above and which I will re-express as follows: a polity cannot make do with purely procedural citizens, but requires for its cohesion and stability members who are culturally attached to its institutions and practices as uniquely *theirs*. I would also add here that issues of public concern, affecting the well-being and functioning of a state, often arise from its members' cultural attachments and predispositions. In other words, various debates citizens may engage in and perhaps need to have resolved at a policy level derive much of their content from 'cultural' disputes. To screen out such content in the name, say, of liberal neutrality on substantive issues is not very convincing.[54]

A second, and rather different, reason why the cultural dimension cannot simply be left aside is because even 'procedural citizenship' is not in fact an acultural product; it derives, rather, from an Enlightenment-inspired cultural package that seeks to dislodge the particular and parochial and replace them with the 'universal'. That is to say, we are dealing with a historically specific concept of citizenship which is bound up with a cluster of beliefs, dispositions, orientations and prejudices that issue, in part, in specific notions of rationality, personhood, social and political relations, moral practices and so forth.[55] Although differentiated from exclusive, parochial identities, this historically specific concept of citizenship carries with it substantive baggage of another sort. In short, a concept of procedural citizenship strikes a chord with those of us living in the late modern West only because we stand in a cultural space opened up by the Enlightenment. Civilisations lacking this space make little sense of such a concept of citizenship. Thus we may see from another angle why citizenship cannot be understood in a cultural vacuum, and why Aughey's attempt to banish culture from the politics of the state is too stretched to work.

To press further yet, if we bring together these different reasons why it is important to recognise an interrelation of citizenship and cultural identities, it becomes possible to reformulate one of my central objections to Aughey: he tacitly accepts the sufficiency of a modern, enlightened 'cosmopolitan' identity (even if he employs it to argue for a very parochial cause), whereas I do not. Although I do not go as far as some in saying that such an identity should be abandoned altogether,[56] I do think that we need to find a balance between the 'universal' and the 'particular', and between procedure and substance. This is a theme I want to return to from a slightly different perspective in the next chapter. But I want to suggest now that there are cultural pulls in both directions: towards a set of 'universal–cosmopolitan' predispositions and towards 'particular–local' attachments. An adequate theory of citizenship needs to reflect both these pulls and therefore to be open to much more than Aughey is prepared to admit.

A third consideration is that inclusive citizenship should not be restricted to its procedural functions but warrants a distinctive substantive identity of its own. Attempts to balance the universal and the particular, the procedural and the substantive, or cosmopolitan and local identities are misconceived if it is assumed that *inclusiveness* attaches solely to the universal, procedural and cosmopolitan and *exclusiveness* attaches solely to the particular, substantive and local. This assumption occludes the possibility I now want to advocate of conceiving of inclusiveness in relation to the particular, substantive and local. And it makes sense to do so, I believe, when the procedural entry requirements and entitlements of citizenship are acknowledged and forged with an active understanding of what it is to be a citizen. Here I envisage a situation where citizens *as* citizens identify with particular institutions and practices that define crucial elements of their polity's way of life and are regarded as the common possession of all rather than the exclusive preserve of one group, tribe or tradition.

Central to the achievement of this sort of situation is, as I have intimated, a rehabilitation of the active meaning of citizenship which Aughey, in common with contractarianism, classical liberalism and what we call Augustinian Protestantism, glosses over. This meaning, which is central to a civic republican tradition, is foreshadowed in Habermas's claim that the identity of a 'nation of citizens' stems from 'the *praxis* of citizens'. There are a number of ways of explicating this active meaning of citizenship or of articulating the entailments of the *praxis* in question, though I cannot examine them in any detail here. There is, for example, the classical way represented by Aristotle's distinction between *poiesis* and *praxis* and his account of the administrative, judicial and deliberative roles performed by citizens of ancient Athens.[57] Or, more recently, there is the way advocated by Hannah Arendt's attempt to distinguish 'action' from both 'work' and 'labour' and her account of how a properly *political* community is attainable only through citizens' words and deeds.[58] Or, again, there are the ways suggested by Habermas's distinction between technical and communicative forms of action and his account of how a species of the latter alone captures the democratic spirit to which we all pay lip service; and by Taylor's distinction between instrumental and deliberative modes of action and his account of why a type of citizen self-rule is necessary to avert crises of legitimation and alienation which imply a malaise at the heart of contemporary social and political life.[59]

Extrapolating from these different ways of understanding the active meaning of citizenship, with their respective distinctions and accounts, we can say that they point to the following conclusions: (1) that the participation of citizens in public life is crucial to the health of a polity; (2) that the core of political participation consists in some notion of public dialogue which is taken to create a unique space for citizenship, that is, one that cannot be substituted by non-dialogical forms of action; (3) that various institutions and practices, and the way of life they embody, are sustained by citizen participation and cannot be replaced by bureaucratic modes of organisation, except at great loss; and (4) that citizens' identities as citizens of a particular state are strengthened and shaped through their dialogical encounters and participation and are inseparable from the institutions and practices that make these possible.

Given the above considerations, the relationship between citizenship and identity appears richer and more complex than Aughey's liberal unionist argument supposes. Once we recognise the limited nature and scope of his concept of citizenship, it is possible to articulate three senses in which there is a relationship between citizenship and identity. It holds, first, in the sense he allows where citizenship is associated with an inclusive, procedural identity, albeit one implying substantive, 'cultural' commitments of a cosmopolitan sort that Aughey leaves unexplored. Second, the relationship holds in a sense he expressly denies where citizenship presupposes the presence of often exclusive, substantive ('cultural') identities which bind members to a particular state. And the relationship may hold in a third sense that Aughey, reflecting the blindness of liberal minimalism, discounts where citizenship entails an inclusive, substantive ('political') identity that is a product of citizens' actions and involvement in the institutions and practices of their polity.

ON PARITY OF ESTEEM AGAIN

Appropriating these three senses of relationship between citizenship and identity generates a very different approach from Aughey's to the concept of parity of esteem in Northern Ireland. This is an approach that, I think, accommodates the spirit of liberal tolerance characterising Aughey's position at its best, even as it avoids the blindness and stereotyping typical of it at its worst, and offers a broad, analytical framework conducive to the conduct of substantive and creative politics. It is an approach that I hint makes it possible to welcome political parity of esteem without thereby revealing nationalist predilections.

To elucidate, it is evident that the procedural identity approved of in Aughey's concept of citizenship entails a positive response to requests for parity of esteem in two respects. First, such parity is integral to this procedural identity inasmuch as it speaks of the procedural entitlements of every member of society which are secured by guaranteeing the equal rights and liberties of all citizens. Second, Aughey's concept of citizenship facilitates talk of cultural parity of esteem by advocating a set of social arrangements that tolerate difference and encourage pluralism. The tolerance and pluralism in question pertain to the life of civil society where unionists and nationalists, say, are equally at liberty to carve out a space within which they may express their respective cultural identities. Presumably, the only constraints on these expressions are that they do not involve a violation of the rights and liberties of other groups or individuals. Now, as far as it goes, I have no quibble with this vision of a culturally diverse, flourishing civil society backed up by the state's respect of the dignity of individuals.

Quibbles begin, however, with the distortions Aughey's vision encourages on the topic of political parity of esteem in Northern Ireland. These distortions fall into two categories. One concerns the *blindness* of his position which prevents him from acknowledging the degree to which 'British' institutions in the North are mired by the cultural connotations of unionism. This is another way of putting my earlier point that liberal unionism is implicated in the 'Ulster' dimension of unionism. Aughey denies this point by supposing that a procedural identity obtaining at the level of the state is hermetically sealed, as it were, from the substantive, cultural identities at play in civil society. In doing so, he thinks that a sufficient rejoinder to the claims of nationalists lies in laying out the liberal benefits of union with Britain. But here he ignores the significance of how, within Northern Ireland, symbols of Britishness, rather than automatically expressing impartial, procedural, liberal values, have often acquired partial, substantive overtones of sectarian-unionist triumphalism. He also appears oblivious of the extent to which British symbols and institutions are perceived as exclusive and biased towards cultural unionism in the minds of many nationalists.[60] Aughey no doubt regrets that nationalists' acceptance of the even-handedness of his liberal unionist vision is handicapped by such perceptions, just as he regrets that an exclusive unionist particularism chooses to communicate itself through various media of 'Britishness' such as the Crown and the flag. It remains, nevertheless, altogether glib to imagine that these uncomfortable facts can be overcome by a kind of procedural fiat whereby, at the level of the state, Britishness and unionism are seen unambiguously to connote inclusiveness alone and the voices clamouring for political parity of esteem are thus put to silence.

If blindness to the political impact of cultural unionism constitutes one distortion, a tendency to stereotype cultural nationalism constitutes another. Admittedly, as we saw previously, Aughey has now corrected that tendency. But he certainly capitulated to it until fairly recently and it continues to play a role in the analyses of other liberal unionists. This is the tendency to seize upon an old notion of Irish nationalism – couched in terms of Gaelic and Catholic exclusiveness and plotting the realisation of a unitary Irish state – and to make it paradigmatic of nationalist aspirations. The advantage of this ploy is that it provides an easy target for liberal criticism. The disadvantage is that it concentrates attack on a notion that increasingly raises barely a flicker in many nationalist imaginations. A nationalist identity, even within Northern Ireland, seems more open and fluid than most liberal unionists are willing to concede.[61] And that is another reason why granting it political recognition within the North scarcely signals the first step on a road that leads inevitably to a united Ireland.

These distortions, which highlight practical limitations of Aughey's 'thin' understanding of citizenship in the circumstances of Northern Ireland, are avoidable by embracing a more expansive, 'thicker' understanding which in turn invokes a broader analytical framework. As I have indicated, this is an understanding that incorporates a procedural political identity, finds room for cultural identities, and values the development of a substantive political identity. Within the wide parameters of the analytical framework such an understanding makes available, there appears a solid basis for responding positively, in principle, to requests for political parity of esteem and fresh possibilities of political movement in Northern Ireland. Or so I want to argue in my next and final chapter. There I develop an alternative way of conceptualising talk of parity of esteem, build upon the alternative way of thinking about citizenship laid out above, offer an alternative way of articulating a unionist position which reflects more closely political realities in Northern Ireland and links unionism to civic republicanism, and, in sum, submit an alternative political vision for Northern Ireland.

CONCLUSION

Liberal unionism is as closed to political movement in Northern Ireland, on terms other than its own, as is cultural unionism. It too subscribes to a notion of unionism that can admit of no compromise. But the hardening of political arteries it promotes is not just a product of its subscription to a particular notion of unionism. It is reinforced by an association of unionism with a

narrowly conceived liberal political theory. I have tried to expose
weaknesses in this theory and to encourage scepticism of liberal
unionism's immodest boast to having reason exclusively on its
side. A politics of constitutional standoff can only be overcome by
dissociating unionism from constrained liberal, as well as exclusivist Protestant, attachments. It is only when unionism is released from its cultural and liberal straitjackets that proper
dialogue with non-unionists will be possible. It is only then that
concessions to certain nationalist arguments will be seen as
something other than selling out the Union and capitulating to
nationalist discourse. As it stands, the horizon of political meaning within which liberal unionist orientations are shaped is too
restrictive to accommodate new political or dialogical possibilities
in Northern Ireland.

5

CIVIC UNIONISM

If cultural unionists or their liberal counterparts are to be believed, there is nothing to be said for unionism beyond the horizons of their visions. Each group, of course, thinks its particular vision of unionism is the best possible. But, whatever their disagreements, each finds sufficient space within its visual range to concede that the other belongs within the unionist fold. This is principally because each regards the Union as an end in itself; or, better, as *the* end to which all other ends are subservient. The basis of unionist unity under the peculiar political circumstances of Northern Ireland consists in agreement on this fundamental point. Common cause can be found in defence of the Union, since its maintenance guarantees the respective ways of life to which culturalists and liberals are committed. Accordingly, upholding the primacy of the Union is what matters most in unionist politics.

This is unfortunate. The civic unionist alternative I now wish to propose does not share the priorities of cultural and liberal unionists and, as a consequence, risks falling outside their visual range. It does not start from the conviction that 'the Union, the whole Union and nothing but the Union' is what matters most; it does not regard the Union as a sufficient end in itself but as one among other ends. And if working with some hierarchy of ends is inevitable, which I think it is, then the ultimate end for civic unionism is not the Union *per se* but the quality of social and political life in Northern Ireland – a Northern Ireland that includes not just unionists but also nationalists and non-unionists of other descriptions. This is a shocking inversion of unionist priorities. And that is why civic unionism lies beyond the horizons of most unionists. Put another way, in so far as it poses as a unionist position at all – which it does – it must seem to jar with typical unionist sensibilities, for it comes perilously close to committing the most unpardonable of all sins: compromising the Union in the name of unionism.

Two comments are in order. First, the all-or-nothing thinking that judges any rearrangement of unionist priorities unpardonable has been the bane of politics since the formation of Northern Ireland. And it is a type of thinking that is deprived of any legitimate claim to the moral or intellectual high ground. Or so I have been trying to argue over the last two chapters. Second, to lay out just what is involved in my seemingly off-beat version of unionism is, none the less, important. It is to this task that I turn immediately by locating civic unionism in what I refer to as a Northern Irish way of life. I then delineate and defend the larger political and philosophical implications of such a way of life in a way that enables me to draw together threads that have run throughout the book, and especially through Chapter 4. This requires taking up again from a different angle those questions of parity of esteem, citizenship and freedom that I have suggested other unionist positions do not treat adequately.

I recast talk of parity of esteem in terms of a theory of recognition which I think illuminates the important issues such talk throws up and equips us to decide some of the knottier problems it presents. Substituting the term 'due recognition' for that of 'parity of esteem' also makes easier the acceptance of the political meaning of parity of esteem that I have been edging towards. And this in turn sets up a return to the themes of citizenship and freedom that builds both on the criticisms I made of the views of McCartney and Aughey and on the counter-claims I began to articulate. Here I argue specifically for a civic republican theory that also brings into play notions of reason and dialogue, of civil society and the state, and of justice and the good. Thinking of unionism in broadly conceived civic republican categories, I shall argue, opens unionism up to new possibilities from which it is closed off when defined only in Protestant or liberal categories. And, more significant, doing so gives added substance to the prospect – hinted at towards the end of Chapter 4 – of discovering fresh opportunities for political movement in Northern Ireland.

A NORTHERN IRISH WAY OF LIFE

I mentioned in Chapter 2 that it was easier to be clear about the respective ways of life of cultural and liberal unionism than about the way of life of civic unionism. This is because the way of life that civic unionism tries to articulate is more diffuse and inchoate, based more on signposts than on settled destinations, more on possibilities than on definitive forms. It is a way of life struggling for adequate expression because its potential is invariably stifled by its powerful rivals and their simple, but reassuring, myths of Protestant heritage, undiluted Britishness and Irish destiny. That Northern Ireland, in all its complexities and contradictions, might be the site of a way of life that is peculiarly its own is a disturbing thought to those whose sights remain firmly set on Westminster or Dublin, and one distorted beyond recognition by those who claim 'Ulster' as the exclusive home of their tribe or tradition. Under the circumstances, it is not difficult to see how possibilities of an emerging Northern Irish way of life have frequently been choked in their infancy and remain today acutely underdeveloped. This does not make them any the less real, however, or make the way of life to which they point a mere chimera. On the contrary, it is the ways of life of their powerful rivals – none of which enjoy complete expression either, it should be added – that are closer to being chimerical, since each in its own fashion projects a mode of being and a vision of the future that, crucially, involve denying too much of the reality that is Northern Ireland. The point is to refuse their denials, to make explicit that which for too long has been forced to remain implicit, to bring the obvious out of the background and into the foreground.

DIFFERENCE AND OPENNESS

One way of doing so is to think of Northern Ireland as 'a place apart'. An advantage of this metaphor is that it draws attention to the fact that the North is neither 'as British as Finchley' nor 'as Irish as Cork', and that those who like to suppose otherwise are indulging first-class fictions. A disadvantage is that it encourages a narrow parochialism too easily latched upon by advocates of an 'independent Ulster'. A corrective perhaps lies in invoking Edna Longley's alternative metaphor of Northern Ireland as a 'cultural corridor' open at both ends to the flow of British and Irish traffic.[1] Holding both these metaphors in mind simultaneously – and re-casting them for convenience through the terms 'difference' and 'openness' – sheds considerable light on our Northern Irish con-dition. And it does so especially if we think of their relation in terms of what I want to call a 'difference through openness' thesis. That is to say, Northern Ireland is different by virtue of be-ing the site where British and Irish influences peculiarly converge and conflict and in the process get reworked in distinctive ways – ways that may yield senses of Britishness and Irishness un-recognisable in other parts of Britain and Ireland.

Irish and British influences intermingle and run through or-dinary life in the North and admit of any number of expressions. An Irish language enthusiast, for example, may equally be a Liverpool or Manchester United enthusiast. More generally, these influences no doubt percolate through society, subtly shaping all of us in manners we are scarcely aware of. This suggests that an intermix of British and Irish factors provide a vastly under-appreciated stock of common background meanings which many of our practices presuppose and bear at least implicit traces of. Although this suggestion would repay exploration, it is not one I intend pushing any further here. I wish, rather, to consider explicit handlings of what I am calling the 'difference through openness' thesis.

Its most prevalent handling is one that exhibits variations of a mode of cultural and/or political refusal of its implications. It is such a mode that has characterised the major Ulster Protestant, British political and Irish nationalist attempts to reduce Northern Ireland's complexities in line with their self-images. To clarify, what cannot be denied is the presence of British and Irish influences in Northern society, but what can be denied is that these should be appropriated culturally or politically. As we know only too well, the cultural–political denials of Ulster Protestantism and Irish nationalism have issued not only in competing sovereignty claims over the North, but also in exclusive conceptions of cultural Britishness and cultural Irishness. They both amount to forlorn, insular endeavours to live as though one end of the 'cultural corridor' has been closed off and unwanted British or Irish traffic has been banned from entry.

Liberal unionism's stress on political Britishness of course places it in a different situation since it is open to cultural traffic from both directions. Thus Aughey regards Longley's metaphor as entirely apposite. He is quick to add, however, that 'the complexity of intellectual and cultural experience is not the political issue'.[2] Cultural openness does not translate into political openness and Northern Ireland's cultural difference does not imply its political difference. Accordingly, on matters political the corridor is closed off at one end; politically speaking, Ulster is presumed to be as British as Finchley. But as I have tried to show, this reasoning is too facile. Much of the cultural complexity ingrained in Northern society is politically charged through and through and cannot be depoliticised by the wave of a procedural wand.

It might have been otherwise. Perhaps cultural diversity in the North might have lacked its sharp political edge if the Stormont experiment had been handled better, or if full integration rather than devolution had immediately followed partition. Or, then again, perhaps things would have turned out differently if Gladstone's first Home Rule Bill had been passed, or if there had not been an Act of Union, or if French support for the United Irishmen had not taken such a farcical turn.[3] 'If only' is a constant refrain in Irish history, but it offers slender consolation in our present plight. Perhaps, in the future, cultural differences in the North will lose their current political bite through some integrated British or Irish political arrangement that satisfies everyone. But that is impossible to envisage now. The point remains that political conditions prevailing in Northern Ireland today cannot be divested of their cultural complexity and intensity just because liberal unionists prefer their politics untarnished by culture.

In their various ways, then, liberal unionists, cultural unionists and cultural nationalists refuse to entertain the 'difference through openness' thesis because it clashes with their notions of the Union or of a united Ireland. The problem is not merely that their refusals have helped disguise the truth about our peculiar situation in the North, but also that they have exacted a terrible price. Political stalemate, undemocratic government, violence, segregated housing and education, sharpening division and unremitting sectarianism have been among the notable costs paid by citizens in Northern Ireland for the sake of the Union or for the sake of an all-Ireland dream. The grand promises that in an Ulster back under unionist control, or in an integrated Britain, or in a united Ireland such costs would no longer have to be incurred ring hollow because we know two things: that any one of these 'solutions' disregards too much of the truth about who we collectively are and is likely to pitch Northern Ireland into even bleaker conditions than those experienced during the last quarter of a century; and that it is prudent to be sceptical of politicians who tacitly regard these costs as an acceptable price to pay in the short term for the sake of their ultimate goals. That a plague be visited on all their houses seems a decent enough response under the circumstances.

Decent but not adequate. For such decency to become adequate an alternative mode of response is required to the 'difference through openness' thesis, one replacing refusal with appropriation. Appropriating the metaphors of 'a place apart' and a 'cultural corridor' entails allocating proper space to cultural diversity and allowing the possibility that we are all shaped in various ways by the interweaving of British and Irish influences. It also implies political arrangements facilitating such diversity and reflecting Northern Ireland's difference even as they remain open at both ends to Westminster and Dublin. Two crucial questions therefore become pressing. What sort of political vision should inform how such arrangements are devised? And what form should these arrangements take?

A WAY OF LIFE WORTH HAVING

A political vision capable of informing arrangements suited to the complex reality that is Northern Ireland must satisfy the requirements of inclusiveness and flexibility. It must be sufficiently broad to enable the totality of our relationships to be addressed and the range of our social, cultural and political concerns to be captured. And it must be sufficiently pliable to facilitate redefinitions of our collective purposes. Such a vision will include two basic dimensions: one aimed at accommodating the insight that the North's difference does not signify enclosure but openness, since it is the product of its having an open-ended corridor; and another directed at breathing political life back into Northern society by intimating institutions and practices with the capacity to deliver a set of common goods that appeal to us citizens *as* citizens. A vision encompassing these dimensions articulates a way of life worth having for all of us in Northern Ireland.

An immediate complication arises in relation to the first

dimension as soon as we ask about the political significance attributable to British and Irish factors. To admit that both ends of the Northern Irish corridor must be kept open is not to say that these factors must be given strictly equivalent treatment. The 'difference through openness' thesis indicates a framework within which a political vision for Northern Ireland should be conceived, but other considerations then have to be slotted in if any vision is not to appear ultimately vacuous.

One crucial consideration is that British factors carry most weight. Three interlocking points explain why. First, the legitimacy of Northern Ireland's status as an integral part of the United Kingdom is recognised in international law. Second, according to basic democratic standards, the views of a majority of citizens in a polity must count when its constitutional future is at stake, and they cannot be legitimately overridden. And, third, given that a conspicuous majority in Northern Ireland expressly wish to remain part of the United Kingdom that wish must be respected. Similar points cannot be marshalled to warrant either prioritising or granting equal weight to Irish factors. And these points are not convincingly refuted by invoking an abstract criterion of justice to subvert the legitimacy of partition, as any such criterion is too abstract to admit of an unambiguous application to the circumstances prevailing in Ireland in the first quarter of the century. Nor are they undermined by citing a one-off election result in 1918, since its status is not sufficiently privileged to trump subsequent elections and government agreements.[4] Northern Ireland's place within the United Kingdom cannot be altered without the consent of her people, as every political party in Ireland, with the exception of Sinn Féin, now acknowledges. And the reasons that make this position unassailable also tell against any proposal for strict joint sovereignty in the North.

Another important consideration cautions against pressing this line of reasoning to the point of sealing off the Irish end of the corridor on political matters. Denial of strict equivalence for Irish factors does not have to mean denial of any input whatsoever.

And there are good grounds for thinking it should mean nothing of the sort. In addition to riding roughshod over nationalist claims and snubbing its nose at the drift of recent Anglo-Irish policy, denial of input seems to me wrong in principle. If there is no criterion of justice to demonstrate the illegitimacy of partition, neither is there one to demonstrate its legitimacy. Perhaps the best we can say is that, as A.T.Q. Stewart puts it, 'partition is not a line drawn on the map; it exists in the hearts and minds of Irish people'.[5] But in saying this we also have to concede that not everyone's heart and mind ended up on its preferred side of the border and that it was a messy solution to a messy set of circumstances with which we have all had to live.

To be sure, I have suggested above that international legal recognition of Northern Ireland's status has to count and is something nationalists have to accept. I also argued in Chapter 4, however, that it is not enough simply to expect a resort to legal positivism to settle all that needs settling here (see pages 143–6). Attention has to be paid to wider moral and historical issues pertaining to the nationalist minority who lost most through Ireland's division and the drawing of the border, whose identity has been marginalised and who continue to struggle for its recognition, and whose alienation from the Northern state was reinforced under the Stormont administration. By allowing these kinds of issues to figure in our deliberations about the best route forward for Northern Ireland, room may be found for welcoming some low-level involvement of Dublin in Northern affairs and for a recognition of an Irish identity in public institutions. Only by discovering such room can the Northern corridor be kept politically open at both ends; only to the extent that it is can we forge a political understanding that adequately reflects our collective condition; and only then can we anticipate a recovery of political life in Northern Ireland. In short, a vision aimed at shaping arrangements the purposes of which are to enhance political recovery cannot permit one end of the Northern corridor to be blocked off. Otherwise a necessary condition of our enjoyment of a way of life worth having will remain unsatisfied.

If acknowledgement of the political importance of British and Irish factors in Northern Ireland is a necessary condition of such a life, it is certainly not a sufficient condition. A vision aspiring to direct the sort of arrangements appropriate to a way of life worth having has to include more. This brings us to the vision's other dimension, which focuses on what matters to citizens *as* citizens. Its underlying premises are that the quality of social and political life in Northern Ireland is what matters most to her citizens, and that they are entitled to have a say in its shape. Working from these premises, what is required is a vision that does not place its faith in unduly procedural or bureaucratic modes of government and that entertains a maximalist rather than a minimalist view of politics, that is, one recognising that there is more to politics than merely offering citizens protection. Put polemically, what is being invoked is a vision that is the antithesis of the sort of masterful inactivity Aughey thinks served unionism so well in the past by preventing political life in Northern Ireland from acquiring too much vibrancy of its own and developing too much autonomy from Westminster.[6]

Expressed positively, what is needed is a vision designed to inspire the creation, protection and maintenance of a way of life worth having for all citizens. At a minimum, this is to envisage certain types of political, legal and socio-economic institutions and practices. At an overtly political level, for example, it must comprise institutions and practices with which citizens identify and that command their allegiance. This means, ideally, institutions and practices that define the polity's way of life through being sustained by citizens' actions, that is, their words, deeds and deliberations. Here a particularly important role is being granted to political institutions by encouraging forms of political activity that are open to all citizens and by having on centre-stage public representatives who have real power to implement policies beneficial to society and who are subject to usual forms of democratic accountability. A crucial part of the *raison d'être* of political institutions, in other words, is to safeguard a public space that is constituted by inclusiveness and dialogue. And this extends to the life of civil society, where scope should be given to institutions and practices that express the diversity of individuals, associations and groups – except those entailing a victimisation of others – and where the toleration of difference is made central.

The vision also advocates the institutionalisation of legislation guaranteeing the protection of the rights of individuals and groups against discrimination. Beyond that, it imagines legal and security institutions that are open to applicants of sufficient merit, whatever their background, that are widely recognised as impartial and that, through their inclusive symbolic emblems and uniforms, are seen as representative of all citizens and not merely of one group.

On socio-economic matters, the vision projects the presence of institutions geared to providing conditions conducive to the flourishing of all members of society; that is, institutions not left to the mercy of market forces alone but based upon acceptable principles of social justice. This is to conceive of a way of life defined by structures suited to permit space and scope for the mix of individual, group, company and government initiatives and investments, especially in areas of acute deprivation, that are crucial to a thriving economy. It is also to conceive of a way that is characterised by the development of specific policies, in such areas as health, education, employment, social benefits and so on, that are aimed to ensure that no persons or groups are systematically discriminated against or forced, through unfortunate circumstances, to fall below certain acceptable standards of living, and to provide for all persons fair access to, and an equitable share of, society's resources and opportunities.

A way of life defined by the sort of political, legal and socio-economic institutions tersely outlined above captures in broad terms what I think politics should principally be aiming to achieve. And it gives some indication of how the quality of social and political life in Northern Ireland may be enhanced. It suggests a vision that is intended to be equally acceptable to those of any persuasion, unionist, nationalist or neither. Within the context of Northern Ireland its point is this: if efforts were concentrated on creating, protecting and sustaining such a way of life or vision new possibilities would open up and old hostilities would be put under severe pressure. Common ground would be discovered by citizens devoted to making Northern Ireland work; new forms of citizen attachment and identity might appear alongside traditional ones. New divisions would also undoubtedly surface, but at least they would not necessarily cut along predictable sectarian lines.

CONSTRAINTS AND ARRANGEMENTS

Some vision of a way of life worth having has to guide arrangements capable of breaking the deadlock that has turned Northern Ireland into a political desert. For the vision I have quickly sketched to assume such a guiding role, three constraints have to be reckoned with.

The first constraint, which alludes to our current political circumstances, is potentially the most devastating. These circumstances seem to militate against the realisation of anything approximating the vision I have articulated and threaten to reduce it to the status of a millenarian wish. But to defer to these circumstances is to lapse into the sterile politics of constitutional standoff. The point is to pierce through them by relinquishing the grip of constitutional polarities on our imaginations, by refusing to let our sense of the politically possible be hemmed in by zero-sum prognoses. This constraint matters, of course, to the extent that it has the capacity to make any proposed arrangements unworkable. But it is hard to know what sort of concessions can be made to it, since to try to accommodate its various, and conflicting, concerns is tantamount to giving up on the vision and falling back on outmoded and unhelpful shibboleths. The most that can be done here is to try to convince recalcitrant unionists or nationalists that the kind of arrangements envisaged for Northern

Ireland will not amount to the sale of their respective birthrights, whatever the scaremongering claims to the contrary.

A second constraint is one imposed by the 'Westminster–Dublin' dimension of the vision on the 'citizenship within Northern Ireland' dimension. Westminster's ultimate control of Northern Ireland and the need to facilitate a role for Dublin, probably through some modification of existing Anglo-Irish structures, limit the extent of power citizens in the North can expect to exercise over their own affairs. This has to be the case if the Northern corridor is to be kept politically open at both ends. It makes a nonsense of our collective Northern Irish condition to suppose that our political affairs can be conducted autonomously from either the rest of Britain or the rest of Ireland, or, for that matter, the rest of Europe. Ideals of, say, citizenship and freedom and of legal and social justice intended to energise political life cannot be pursued as though Northern Ireland were an in-dependent state. This does not make the ideals redundant, how-ever, for at least three reasons. First, they have as much applicability to political life in the United Kingdom at large and in the Republic of Ireland as they have to that in Northern Ireland. Second, through representation at Westminster, citizens in Northern Ireland have some input into policies bearing on the character of their society, though it would be silly to exaggerate how much, and, ideally, their interests should be represented at Anglo-Irish negotiations which impinge on politics in Northern Ireland. Third, a devolution of certain powers would bring to Northern Irish citizens a measure of control over their own affairs and enable them as a concerted body to pressurise Westminster, Dublin or Brussels for a better social and economic deal.

At a minimum, then, arrangements mirroring the need to bal-ance the 'citizenship within Northern Ireland' dimension in the light of the Anglo-Irish dimension might include continuing rep-resentation at Westminster, maintenance of the British subvention in addition to European or international funding for specific pro-jects, the introduction of a devolved assembly in Northern Ireland

and of a bill of rights protecting individuals and groups against discrimination. They might also entail public institutions exhibiting British and Irish symbols, or even new symbols of Northern Irishness, to reflect our complex condition and to help purge these symbols of their exclusive, sectarian connotations. And they might involve, further, an extension of North–South bodies to facilitate matters of mutual concern, advantage and harmony and a development of East–West or Anglo-Irish relationships and structures through which Dublin might have the degree of input into Northern affairs that nationalists currently see as a guarantee of their position and interests.

A third constraint is one that the second dimension of the vision (focusing on what matters to citizens *as* citizens) puts on the first (the need to recognise the importance of both British and Irish factors in Northern Ireland). It has already been hinted at above. On the premise that citizens of a society are entitled to a say on matters affecting their collective life, any arrangements have to be devised in that premise's light. Thus tendencies notable in *Frameworks for the Future*, for example, to develop complicated levels of bureaucratic administration as a way of solving the conundrum of Northern politics are as misguided and undemocratic as present rule by unaccountable quangos and the Anglo-Irish Secretariat.[7] The ideal of citizen self-rule, whatever its limitations, has to count for something. And what it minimally counts for here is preventing an exacerbation of the soft despotic rule Northern Ireland has been subject to for much too long.

Arrangements reflecting some notion of citizen self-rule might be expected to include the establishment of a legislative, rather than merely an administrative, assembly in the North. This is to envisage an assembly that embodies principles of proportionality and weighted majorities in its decision-making structures, and that (eventually) enjoys comparable powers to the old Stormont. Such arrangements might also be expected to make the conduct of North–South bodies partly answerable to a devolved assembly and to give the latter's voice a role in Anglo-Irish processes bearing on life in Northern Ireland. A similar principle of collective responsibility underlies each of these proposed arrangements. Only once Northern Ireland's citizens are allowed, and prepared, to assume responsibility for those affairs that have divided us for too long, can we realistically hope to build a society free of sectarianism, one in which we all have a sense of belonging.

This explication of possible entailments of what I have called a Northern Irish way of life offers a much wider horizon of political meaning than that which emerges from either 'Ulster unionist' or 'British political' ways. This becomes particularly evident when we consider what it tells us about the sort of position a civic unionist position is. Its 'civic' component includes the 'liberal' strain that is present in cultural unionism and that comes into its own in liberal unionism. But it adds to this strain an active and 'thicker' idea of citizenship which derives from a stronger emphasis on the importance of politics. And here it draws heavily from a civic republican tradition in Western thought and practice (see pages 107–8). Its 'unionist' component consists in a defence of the integrity of Northern Ireland's status which it shares with the other unionist positions. It differs from them, however, in seeing the North not merely as a site of the Union but as the site of a co-mingling and clash of British and Irish factors all of which have to be accommodated and reconciled. This is what I have tried to capture in the 'difference through openness' thesis.

Any arrangements for Northern Ireland, in my view, have to do justice to these entailments, and I have suggested a few that might fit the bill. No doubt many of these are controversial and need teasing out, and no doubt, too, many more need to be canvassed. But attending to the details of such arrangements is not the purpose of this book. I am more concerned to explore patterns of thought that make various arrangements possible (or impossible) to conceive of. And here I want to develop further and defend two of the central claims of a civic unionist outlook: that British and Irish identities should be accommodated within

Northern Ireland, and that we need a 'thick' conception of citizenship and its correspondingly strong or maximalist notion of politics. These claims are distinct and yet, in my scheme, interrelated. In defending them, I hope to show that, even if a civic unionist vision of Northern Ireland remains a long way off realisation, thinking in civic unionist terms provides an illuminating orientation to many of our immediate dilemmas – one that stresses the need for reconciliation without implying an abandonment of our critical faculties.

DUE RECOGNITION

The case for accommodating British and Irish identities within Northern Ireland is frequently made through the language of 'parity of esteem', and it is just as frequently rejected (by unionists) when it is seen to have political ramifications. I have been arguing against the reasons unionists typically employ to justify their rejection of any political embodiment of the concept of parity of esteem. But there is a possible liberal unionist rejoinder to my arguments which I consider shortly. First, however, I want to recapitulate and tidy up what is being claimed, counter-claimed and claimed again (at least by me) in the name of parity of esteem, and to provide a sharper focus on the important issues at stake.

RECAPITULATION

In Chapter 2, I suggested that the concept of parity of esteem carries three principal meanings referring in turn to the entitlements of individuals, of cultural groups or traditions, and of political identities. Its introduction into political discourse in Northern Ireland has to be understood against the backdrop of a denial of these various entitlements to nationalists and others which was said to have occurred under the Stormont administration. And the sense of many is that, however much matters have improved for non-unionists under direct rule, there is yet more progress to be made. Thus at the level of individual entitlements, for instance, there is claimed to be a need for 'reverse' discrimination policies to redress an imbalance in employment patterns and opportunities that has developed over decades.

On the surface, many unionists should have little problem conceding the appropriateness of the spirit of the individual and cultural senses of parity of esteem, even if they unsettle certain wistful recollections of the Stormont years. On closer inspection, however, a slightly different story emerges. There is a widespread perception in unionist circles, for example, that too much is being given to Catholics as a consequence of reverse discrimination tendencies, that Protestants are now receiving unfair treatment under fair employment and equal opportunity legislation. None the less, it would be unwise to make too much of this perception. Whatever its substance, it is capable of being dealt with in terms of the individual sense of parity of esteem. Here, in other words, the difficulties are not so much with the principle as with its application in specific instances. Matters are trickier in relation to the cultural sense of parity of esteem. What is unclear is whether a disagreement in principle or merely in application is at work in, say, Orangemen's objections to being prevented from marching along traditional routes. Is it simply that nationalists are, as they say, denying parity of esteem to their cultural expression and so a quibble over application? Or is it a deeper objection in principle to the idea that their cultural form, which is presumed to embody Ulster's Protestant heritage, is no more privileged than any other? For some it is probably the former, for others the latter, and for yet others a bit of both.

There is no equivocation, however, over the implacable opposition in principle shared by culturalists and liberals to the political sense of parity of esteem. I have considered the grounds of this opposition mostly in reference to arguments developed by liberals. I have maintained that the argument based on negative liberty, which recognises only the entitlements of individuals, is unconvincing because it either projects possible, but not necessary, consequences as decisive or distorts the nature of political allegiance. And, I have averred, much the same can be said about the argument deriving from a procedural conception of citizenship: it too is blind to the importance of substantive identities to political allegiance. I have also contended that the idea of equal citizenship does not provide a sufficient basis to support claims about the undiluted political Britishness of Northern Ireland. In sum, I have submitted that the conceptual weapons unionists rely upon to destroy a political interpretation of parity of esteem are too blunt to perform the tasks asked of them.

So what am I proposing instead? I have implicitly or explicitly revealed a willingness to entertain all three senses of parity of esteem. On its most controversial, political sense, I have suggested that it is easier to welcome it in principle if we situate unionist discourse within a broad civic republican, rather than narrow Protestant or liberal, framework, and if we accept the 'difference through openness' thesis. At any rate, antipathy towards this sense is considerably tempered, for example, by subscribing to a political theory that attaches significance to citizens' identification with the institutions and practices of their society. And once Northern Ireland is conceptualised via the 'place apart' and 'cultural corridor' metaphors, it becomes hard to resist the impulse towards political parity of esteem already generated from a commitment to basic civic republican tenets.

What is at stake here, of course, is a dispute about the sort of unionist vision that is appropriate for Northern Ireland. And in relation to the specific issues raised by talk of parity of esteem, what is specifically at stake is how questions of identity – whether individual, cultural or political – should be treated and resolved. The position on these questions that I have been laying out requires more explicit articulation in order to reinforce its basis and to make clearer my intellectual and practical disagreements with other unionist positions. And I want to begin this articulation process by suggesting that the phrase 'parity of esteem', which I have been using up till now, obscures as much as it illuminates questions of identity and, for my purposes at least, needs replacing.

LIMITATIONS OF PARITY OF ESTEEM

Taken in its cultural and political senses, the phrase 'parity of esteem' is used by the British and Irish governments to signal the even-handedness of their approach to Northern Irish politics, to indicate that the North's two major traditional identities are equally deserving of accommodation or equally undeserving of privileged treatment. Beyond its currency in government circles, the phrase is intended to apply to the thinking of all of us. Any desire to seek advantages for our own tradition should be curbed by respect for the integrity and entitlements of the other. Here the term 'esteem' is, I suspect, employed to convey an important insight that is in keeping with the hermeneutic approach I have been adopting, and that I shall describe as follows. It is vital to be opened up beyond one's own tradition of meaning and value to the claims of other traditions, since: (1) none of us have an exclusive grasp of meaning and value; (2) others' traditions engage their identities and so deserve our respect; and (3) we may be enriched by what we can learn about and from these other traditions. If this is an insight of general relevance, it is particularly relevant in a divided society such as Northern Ireland where intense traditional parochialism and caricatural typecasting of the 'other' tradition is altogether too familiar. It is an insight I wish to retain.

An appropriation of the insight is perhaps made harder than it need be, however, by other connotations of the phrase 'parity of esteem'. One awkward connotation, for instance, is the presumption that esteem can be unproblematically accorded to another traditional identity simply by virtue of its significance to those who bear it. But what is it that we are being expected to accord? Is it acknowledgement of others' entitlement to an expression of their identity? Or is it also an affirmation of the intrinsic worthiness of the identity in question and of the way of life with which it is associated? Even allowing for the ambiguities of the English language, it is difficult not to suppose it is the latter since some affirmation of worthiness is implied by the term 'esteem'. And it is this that proves a stumbling block. To expect Catholics to esteem an Orange culture that they perceive as inherently anti-Catholic and triumphalist is as far-fetched as expecting unionists to admire a nationalist culture that expresses itself through such slogans as 'Brits Out'. Moreover, it is precisely the lack of esteem unionists and nationalists often show towards the content of each other's identity that inhibits the extent to which they are willing to tolerate each other's right to expression. It is because nationalists find Orangeism offensive that they object to its expression in their areas.

The phrase 'parity of esteem', then, seems to obstruct as much as aid the requirement of reciprocal openness to others' traditions by imposing conditions that are practically impossible to meet. And these conditions imply another connotation which I find intellectually impossible to agree with too. The idea that traditional identities are equally worthy because it is in terms of them that unionists and nationalists make sense of themselves and their world implies a relativism that renders them invulnerable to serious critical scrutiny. To accept this idea is to leave what is generally known as the peace and reconciliation process open to the typical unionist charge of a woolly-mindedness that invites bad politics.[8] More particularly, it is to blur two crucial distinctions upon which my argument has been based: between taking others' self-understandings seriously and endorsing them, and between accommodating different identities and accommodating them equally.

The first distinction is vital because only by holding to it are we able to insist that claims made in the name of unionist (or nationalist) identities are susceptible to rational evaluation. To surrender this hold is to admit, for example, that although we may not approve of the sectarian features of certain of these identities, their adherents' self-interpretations are bound up with them and so our criticisms must be severely muted. And this is tantamount to conceding that although sectarianism may not be 'true' for us it may be 'true' for others. Of course nobody quite puts it like this, but the point is that the kind of criticism permitted on these terms is deprived of any force since it amounts to saying 'as we do not approve of sectarianism we do not think you should either'. This, I submit, is feeble. But unless we allow that the content of claims made about identities is available to critical inspection it is all we are left with. And if this is what full subscription to the concept of parity of esteem entails, there is something very troubling about the thinking that informs it.

The second distinction is also important. The concept of parity of esteem worries many unionists because it seems to them manifestly unjust that a nationalist identity should be regarded as equal to a unionist identity when devising political arrangements for Northern Ireland. Here the question is not merely whether both identities are worthy, but whether the term 'parity' connotes the requirement of strictly equivalent treatment. I think that at times it properly does – when considering, say, the entitlements of individuals *as* individuals – and at other times it properly does not. I have already argued that in relation to political arrangements strict equivalence is inappropriate and that, given the current circumstances in Northern Ireland, more is due politically to a British identity than to an Irish one. This qualification is crucial to allay familiar unionist fears that political parity of esteem necessarily means strict joint sovereignty. Accordingly, it is important to maintain a distinction between accommodating identities and treating them equally in every instance. But it is a distinction that is too easily lost when 'parity' is construed to mean simple equality.

The problem now becomes how to retain the insight entailed in the language of 'parity of esteem' while overcoming the language's limitations. The answer I propose is to substitute the term 'due' for that of 'parity' and the term 'recognition' for that of 'esteem'. Put together the phrase 'due recognition' captures more closely the arguments I have been developing and now wish to strengthen than does that of 'parity of esteem'. To give identities their due, for example, is a reasonable request which encourages deliberation and informed judgements about what individual, cultural and political identities are entitled to given the different types of claims they imply and the historical context in which they are made. And 'recognition' is a less loaded term than 'esteem', one that is capable of facilitating the affirmative dimension conveyed by the latter without leaving us hamstrung in the face of obnoxious facets of certain identities. More than that, as I now try to show, it is a far more appropriate term inasmuch as it is bound up with what it means to have an identity. Drawing on it thus yields a deeper understanding of what identity claims consist in than mere reliance on the term 'esteem' possibly could.

RECOGNITION AND IDENTITY

Meaningful talk of identity cannot progress far without resorting to talk of recognition. The two are interrelated not least because a lack of recognition by others leaves us with a radically diminished and precarious sense of who we are. This point is tellingly illustrated in probably the most famous section of Hegel's *Phenomenology of Spirit*, 'Of Lordship and Bondage', where identity recognition is depicted as a quest, as a struggle involving many unsatisfactory outcomes *en route*.[9] One such outcome is a master–slave situation where characteristic relations of domination and subservience make it impossible for either party to recognise the personhood of the other, with the result that both master and slave are forced to cope with acutely impoverished and frustrating self-understandings. The quest for recognition of our identities as persons cannot stop here. Or, as Charles Taylor puts the point:

> Our identity is partly shaped by recognition or its absence, often by the *mis*recognition of others, and so a person or a group of people

can suffer real damage, real distortion, if the people or society around them mirror back to them a confining or demeaning or contemptible picture of themselves.[10]

The insight that misrecognition of 'who' we are inflicts serious wounds on our sense of ourselves implies, as Taylor remarks, that 'due recognition is not just a courtesy we owe to people. It is a vital human need.'[11] And due recognition, in turn, implies an absence of relations of domination and subservience and the presence, rather, of relations of reciprocity. Accordingly, talk of identity is severely truncated without talk of recognition: due recognition is constitutive of a healthy identity just as misrecognition is constitutive of a warped identity.

Something like this understanding of the identity–recognition nexus, even if not always explicitly acknowledged, is present in many spheres of human concern, from the intimate to the public. Restricting attention to its public manifestations, I am concerned to ask what light it throws on issues of individual and cultural–political identity. I leave aside here its bearing on a political identity based upon a life of common citizenship. In relation to those issues I do consider, a similar emphasis emerges but in distinctive, and potentially conflicting, forms.

One of the most important public presences of the identity–recognition nexus appears in claims that individuals possess fundamental rights and liberties and that these warrant institutional and legal guarantee by the state. Underlying these claims, that is to say, is an affirmation that our identities as persons are bound up with our having rights and liberties and with having them publicly recognised. Thus to deny the rights of any individuals is tantamount to misrecognising who they are as persons; it is to traduce their identities, to impair their sense of themselves.

This point is made in a good deal of contemporary liberal theory, especially among theorists who trace their liberalism back to Immanuel Kant. It is evident, for instance, in Ronald Dworkin's argument that particular rights and liberties to which we typically lay claim derive from a fundamental right of equality of respect which is due to all persons.[12] It is also entailed in John Rawls's claim that 'each person possesses an inviolability founded on justice that even the welfare of society as a whole cannot override'.[13] For Rawls and Dworkin, the 'inviolability' of individuals or the right to equality of respect, upon which so much else depends, attests to a status of personhood we enjoy by virtue of being rational agents who are capable of directing our lives through principles. As Taylor explains, what is 'of worth here is a *universal human potential*, a capacity that all humans share. This potential, rather than anything a person may have made of it, is what ensures that each person deserves respect.'[14]

So due recognition of our identities as persons underpins the rights and liberties liberal unionists and others properly take to be the entitlements of individuals. And the claim to such entitlements carries such undeniable force for most of us because it refers to an unconditional core of our personhood that cannot be legitimately discriminated against. Accordingly, a society that institutionalises the rights and liberties of individuals, that treats us as 'free and equal citizens', to use Rawls's phrase,[15] reflects back to us an image of ourselves that affirms our identities as persons. It provides formal recognition of the reciprocity necessary for the development of healthy as opposed to warped identities.

Appeals for due recognition of our identities extend beyond the realm of individual entitlements into that of traditional or cultural entitlements. Given that many of us define ourselves through our cultural attachments, and do not see ourselves as purely autonomous individuals, not to have our cultural traditions properly recognised is to have damage inflicted on our identities. If respect for our individual identities issues in entitlements to which we are due, then respect for our cultural identities should issue in comparable entitlements. But what is a comparable entitlement? What does it mean to give cultural identities the recognition that is their due? Three lines of response, which either extend or reinforce answers I have already offered, give some clue.

First, we need to distinguish between individual and cultural claims for recognition and to discern how they stand in relation to one another. Both appeal for respect but do so on a different basis. With individual claims, we are asked to respect something that is the same in all of us, that is, a dignity we share by virtue of being persons. With cultural claims, we are asked to respect something that separates us from each other, that is, a distinctiveness that makes us the particular people we are. With individual claims, recognition means granting entitlements that treat people in a difference-blind fashion; whereas with cultural claims, recognition means conferring entitlements precisely because of our difference. It is easy to see how the two may conflict. To insist that a principle of non-discrimination is sufficient to work out people's entitlements invites the accusation that this forces us into a homogeneous mould which is untrue to us, and one that is not neutral but a reflection of a dominant culture.[16] This is to say that much advocated in the name, say, of liberal proceduralism amounts to a misrecognition of who we are as cultural beings. If we are to recognise that our identities involve elements of sameness and difference, liberal proceduralism cannot be enough, and some balance must be struck between individual and cultural claims.

Striking such a balance is a complicated business which I can scarcely hope to explore fully here. But as a working formulation of what shape it might take I propose the following: accommodating cultural difference cannot justifiably entail violating basic rights crucial to individuals' status as persons, since this is to deny recognition of a dignity that we all share, but not all invocations of individual rights should be permitted to override cultural entitlements, since this is to deny due recognition of a difference without which we would not understand ourselves to be the particular persons we are. What is of the essence in such a formulation is to keep the focus firmly on the centrality of the identity–recognition nexus. By prioritising it, we may sometimes judge that the entitlements due to cultures cannot be granted to the exclusion of those due to individuals; equally, at other times we may judge that entitlements due to individuals cannot be insisted upon to the detriment of those due to cultures.

A second line of response expands upon this formulation by noting certain of the entitlements and judgements it implies. The major entitlement that is owing to a cultural tradition is adequate space for its expression and flourishing in civil society. Recognition here entails enabling people freely to engage in those religious, linguistic, historical and other practices with which their identities are bound up. But it does so within limits, such as respecting others' basic rights and cultural identities. There is a *prima facie* case for tolerating – some even say fostering – cultural diversity,[17] but since toleration has boundaries the case is overstated if it presumes immunity from evaluation. The *fatwah* issued against the writer Salmon Rushdie, for instance, was deemed intolerable because it violated his most fundamental rights which Britain is pledged to protect. And, in its being so deemed, the sort of recognition due to a Muslim identity was necessarily judged to be restricted. Similarly in Northern Ireland restrictions apply to the degree of recognition that specific expressions of British and Irish identities are entitled to. Expressions engendering sectarian practices that range from various acts of violence through to various types of discrimination manifestly disqualify themselves by virtue of their contempt of human dignity.

Restrictions may also be warranted where an unhampered expression of one cultural identity entails misrecognition of another through, say, a triumphalist denigration of the other's religion and historical memories. Unlike cultural expressions that offend against basic individual rights, restriction here does not mean banning altogether the cultural expression in question but circumscribing its space. In other words, respect of people's entitlement publicly to bear their identity is still being maintained, even if others do not think this identity is particularly worthy. And in judging that its expression should be circumscribed in specific instances, contextual considerations are also being relied upon to decide whether such a judgement is warranted. For instance, in a particular historical situation would unrestricted cultural expression amount to a serious and not merely a trivial misrecognition of another cultural identity?

Relating this question to the controversial issue of Orange marches passing along 'traditional routes' now inhabited by a nationalist majority that does not want them, the answer seems to me unambiguously yes. The content of Orangeism does amount to a denigration of a nationalist identity and this is the fundamental matter at stake, although Orangemen disagree. To place restrictions on their access to areas where they are not wanted, especially given a context where the mutual mistrust of nationalists and unionists remains very deep, is not a serious infringement of Orangemen's civil and religious liberties since these can be exercised at leisure elsewhere. It is simply to say that claiming a right to march through certain areas is neither an absolute entitlement nor a claim that is spared evaluation of what its exercise means. And a crucial part of what it means is a serious misrecognition of another cultural identity and this, I think, is what must count against it.

Mention of contextual considerations leads to a third line of response to the question of what entitlements are owing to cultural identities. Under certain circumstances it is possible to conceive of allowing more than one identity to be reflected in public institutions. I have already argued that the circumstances currently existing in Northern Ireland justify the representation of British and Irish identities, even if not in a strictly equivalent measure. Now I would simply add that my argument is bolstered by an appreciation of the recognition–identity nexus. To deny political recognition to an Irish identity is to misrecognise it; it is to distort what it consists in, since it cannot simply be privatised without having its nature travestied. It is also to allow that only those who define themselves as British will have their identity reflected back to them through the major institutions of society.

RECOGNITION AND RIGHTS

This, of course, is something that unionists typically suppose is utterly allowable. And part of the reason why they do is because they think that a consistent application of a theory of rights leads to no other conclusion. There are arguments here, developed especially by liberal unionists, that ostensibly tell against my position and to which I need to respond.

According to Robert McCartney, unionists, by virtue of being a majority, have a right to insist that Northern Ireland remain exclusively British, whereas nationalists, by virtue of being a minority, have no right to a political expression of their identity. Here a crucial distinction is drawn between rights and political claims.[18] Now I do not doubt that there is a legitimate distinction to be drawn between rights and political claims, but I do doubt whether McCartney's drawing of it is as effective as he supposes: if not downright incoherent it is certainly too strained to inform good political judgement in Northern Ireland.

On one reading, McCartney's use of the distinction seems incoherent, indeed self-defeating, because the terms of his opposition to political recognition of an Irish identity appear equally to undermine his own position. Consider here three of his central propositions: (1) rights apply equally to all citizens; (2) nationalists have valid claims to rights but as a minority have no valid claim to public-institutional recognition of their identity, since this latter claim is political and not a right; (3) unionists too have valid claims to rights but as they are a majority it is also quite acceptable that public institutions reflect their identity. Given the terms of (1) and the logic of (2) how does (3) follow? A majority's claim to public recognition of its identity must be 'political' in kind since, unlike claims to rights, it does not apply equally to all citizens. So, on these terms, what legitimate basis is there for claiming that a majority is entitled to have its identity recognised whereas a minority, however substantial, is not? Granted his premises, the basis cannot be found in rights unless he subscribes to some theory of transubstantiation according to which political claims to identity-recognition are mysteriously transformed into rights claims through a sacramental head count. But on balance this seems unlikely. And in the absence of some such improbable theory his pitch for the recognition of the unionist majority's identity appears arbitrary.

I suspect, however, that not too much should be made of this reading. The contrast McCartney is drawing attention to is not so much one between rights and political claims as between two sorts of political claims, one that purportedly is entitled to invoke the language of rights and the other which is not. The basis of the distinction is located more in democratic theory than in a liberal theory of the universal rights of individuals. It is from democratic theory that a political claim concerning a British identity can appear in the form of majority rights whereas there is no comparable form in which a political claim concerning an Irish identity can appear. Thus a sufficient rejoinder to the latter is presumed to be that it 'is contrary to the wishes of the democratic majority' in Northern Ireland.[19] The possibility remains, then, that liberal unionists do possess the wherewithal to deliver a knockout blow to the idea of political recognition of an Irish identity.

In considering this possibility, it is not simply a matter of setting aside the liberal aspect of McCartney's theory and concentrating entirely on the democratic aspect. The two are interrelated: the democratic emphasis on majority rights is always qualified by the liberal emphasis on the inviolability of individual rights. The right of a majority is never absolute, since, as John Stuart Mill stressed, majorities may behave tyrannically toward minorities.[20] Accordingly, liberal unionists insist that a unionist majority is never entitled to override the rights of a nationalist minority. But the rights that can never be legitimately overridden are those recognised on the terms of negative liberty, that is, those pertaining to nationalists as individuals and not those pertaining to them as a political identity, since rights cannot be ascribed to the political identities of minorities. I think there is a huge oversight here: just as the terms of the liberal unionist argument render unintelligible demands for political identification on grounds other than protection of individual rights, so they obscure from view the damage done when such demands are repeatedly ignored. My point is not that the language of rights should necessarily be stretched to include political recognition of an Irish identity, as I think this language is already overburdened and not strictly necessary here,[21] but that the sovereignty of a majority's right should be limited for reasons besides violations of individual rights. As I have tried to show, misrecognition of who we are as persons occurs not only when our individual rights are denied, but also when our cultural–political identities are not given their due. And it is this point that the liberal unionist argument cannot quite grasp.

Put another way the point is that, in this instance, prioritisation of the right of the majority strains the political judgement necessary in a divided society such as Northern Ireland. The 'priority' of such a right cannot be convincingly invoked as an abstract first principle obtaining whatever the circumstances and thus applicable in a historically blind manner. Privileging a majority's right, much like accepting a norm of majority rule, may be relatively uncontroversial in societies with settled constitutions and undisputed boundaries. But in a society troubled by constitutional and boundary questions matters are much less straightforward. Many unionists admit as much at one level when they concede that devolved government in Northern Ireland can no longer be envisaged in terms of majority rule, but has to entail power-sharing between unionists and nationalists. And yet they recoil from admitting it at another level – which would see power-sharing complemented by political recognition of British and Irish identities – because the principle of a majority's right is treated as a trump card. But why should a majority's right be thought to trump considerations of political reconciliation? Is the 'good' achieved through denying due political recognition and maintaining the undiluted Britishness of Northern Ireland – and thus leaving unbridged the society's most serious divisions – higher, nobler, or even more democratic than the 'good' that might be achieved by creating institutions that reflect British and Irish identities? It is hard to see why in the circumstances of Northern Ireland a majority's right is trumps or how the 'good' it realises is at all superior given that, besides appeasing unionist pride, it reflects a distorted picture of our collective condition, involves a serious case of misrecognition, yields little more than political stalemate, and risks a lot worse.

This does not mean, of course, that the wishes of the majority should count for nothing. When not exaggerated, the principle of majority right is important for what it safeguards and guarantees: the integrity of a unionist identity which is reflected in the institutions and practices of society, and the impossibility of Northern Ireland being shunted out of the United Kingdom in the absence of majority consent. But admitting this leaves open the question of the manner in which Northern Ireland remains within the British fold, a question that cannot be answered satisfactorily by denying an Irish dimension or by refusing to engage in substantive dialogue with nationalists. Overrating the importance of majority right impedes a proper exploration of this question and unduly circumscribes dialogical possibilities, and all at a price that seems exorbitant.

EXPANSIVE CITIZENSHIP

Conclusions reached through this discussion of due recognition fit with those gestured at during the discussion of Aughey's view of citizenship in Chapter 4. There I hinted at the possibility of a broad analytical framework capable of finding political room for a procedural identity, cultural identities and what I called a substantive political identity, that is, one deriving from a 'thick' conception of citizenship. The case for accommodating the first two of these identities is fortified by the arguments developed on due recognition. A procedural political identity is indispensable, for example, because it grants legal recognition of entitlements due to all citizens by virtue of their common status as persons. Cultural identities should be permitted to flourish within set limits in civil society because it is only as they are that adequate recognition is given to many people's self-definitions. Under specific circumstances, such as those prevailing in a Northern Ireland understood in terms of the 'difference through openness' thesis, due recognition also involves entitling certain identities – namely, British and Irish – to representation in public institutions.

The discussion on due recognition, however, is silent about the third kind of identity I referred to in Chapter 4 and sketched broadly earlier in this chapter. How does a substantive political identity stand in relation to the other two? With regard to the re-cognition of a shared individual identity embedded in procedural citizenship the answer is straightforward: proceduralism is a necessary but not sufficient condition of an identity bound up with citizen self-rule. With regard to political recognition of cul-tural identities the answer is trickier. In one sense the two are quite independent. For instance, arguments for due recognition of cultural identities do not rely on an argument for a substantive political identity, and it does not rely on them. The two sorts of argument are irreducible to each other.[22] But that does not mean there is no relation between them. In another sense they are in-terrelated: in the circumstances of Northern Ireland at least, the possibility of achieving a substantive political identity presup-poses political recognition of British and Irish identities.

Political recognition of British and Irish identities is presup-posed for this reason: the prospect of developing a common life of citizenship with which all members identify assumes commit-ment to the polity in which they live. In classical republics, of course, this commitment was inseparable from the common life sustained through concerted citizen action. But in the peculiar conditions of Northern Ireland concerted action is difficult to im-agine without some prior measures to reconcile divided people. And these measures include political recognition of the two major identities, since without it Northern society will continue to want for the cohesion and stability it has always lacked. It is only as nationalists as well as unionists are persuaded fully to invest in political life in Northern Ireland that an identity based on concerted citizen action becomes conceivable.

CIVIL SOCIETY AND THE STATE

The intelligibility of talk of concerted citizen action is constrained by conditions peculiar to Northern Ireland, namely, the present absence of a common commitment to the state and the fact that Northern Ireland is not an independent state anyway. It is also constrained, or at least complicated, by conditions peculiar to the modern West, namely, the demise of small city-republics in which ideas of citizen self-rule flourished and the development of what we now know as civil society and the state as two distinct realms of social and political life. In other words, citizenship now has to be worked out in the context of how we understand the relationship between these two realms.

The distinction between the two indicates that the proper business of the state has boundaries; that a good deal of social life should be lived independently of state or government interference. Or, put another way, at the heart of the distinction lies the basic idea that we inhabit a society satisfying conditions of civility that are independent of political organisation by the state. Michael Walzer captures the gist of this idea when he says that the term 'civil society' names 'the space of uncoerced human association and also the set of relational networks – formed for the sake of family, faith, interest, and ideology – that fill this space'.[23] But of all the ideas that are associated with a modern concept of civil society, two in particular were integral to its development in the eighteenth and nineteenth centuries and remain crucial to us today.

The first concerns the depiction of society as an economy, that is, as a whole of interrelated acts of production, exchange and consumption which has its own internal dynamic, its own autonomous laws. This depiction is developed initially by Adam Smith.[24] Its upshot is that it defines a dimension of social life potentially outside the ambit of politics. Hegel picks up this upshot when he makes central to the operation of civil society the self-regulating, entrepreneurial economy that emerges through the development of the capitalist market.[25]

A second idea concerns the transformation of the concept of 'public space'. Previously, this concept had been defined in relation to the political organisation of society. For Aristotle, for example, public space was the arena of political debate where citizens deliberated together to reach a common view of some matter that was recognised by them all. During the eighteenth century a new sense of public space emerged with the circulation of newspapers, reviews, books, and so on. And with it came a different notion of public opinion as that which is elaborated entirely outside the channels and public spaces of the political structure, as that which is independent of political authority.[26]

Civil society develops, then, through modern ideas of a self-regulating economy and a media-driven public opinion. Through these it lays claim to a unity of its own and thus to an identity free from co-ordination by the state.

One response to the development of the realm of modern civil society is to relocate civic republicanism's understanding of citizenship, placing it here rather than in the state. If citizenship is about participation and not just about representation and if politics is creative and not merely protective, then occupying the public space that civil society makes available is the best antidote to citizen alienation from the bureaucratic state and to growing political apathy. This response has a particular salience in Northern Ireland where 'politics of the state' has remained gripped in a constitutional gridlock that has drained politics of much of its meaning to the life of citizens. As I observed in Chapter 2, a 'politics of civil society' to which the concerns of standard unionism are largely irrelevant is in many respects blossoming. At any rate, the sphere of civil society in Northern Ireland is comprised of large and active voluntary associations and agencies, community organisations and activists with concerns that are pursued independently of political parties. Moreover, in the wake of the Opsahl Commission and the development of new ventures such as Democratic Dialogue, increased attempts have been made to define a new plural space in civil society to which all citizens have access.[27] Expectations here sometimes run so high as to project that the way around constitutional gridlock at the level of the state lies in co-ordinating disaffected voices through citizens' forums and perhaps even 'a Northern Ireland-wide, popular Constitutional Convention'[28] autonomous from those dominated by political parties and the British and Irish governments. The rationale of these proposals is that they may provide ordinary citizens with an opportunity to articulate opinions to which unionist and nationalist parties will have to pay heed. And they anticipate a certain understanding of the relationship between civil society and the state.

Now there is little doubt that the foregoing examples point to endeavours to re-energise political life in Northern Ireland in ways that bear resemblance to the emphases of civic republicanism. But for their impact to make a difference, and to amount to more than frustrated pleas from disparate voices, a specific understanding of civil society and the state is required. And I think this is one that does not simply say that civic republicanism is relevant only to civil society, but, rather, maintains that ideals of deliberative action and creative politics apply to the state as well.

To hold such a view is at once to oppose a dominant, classical liberal, way of viewing the relationship between civil society and the state. Stated roughly it runs like this. Civil society is the arena in which voluntary associations, organisations, and private interests find their niche. It is also where individual tastes are satisfied, rights are asserted, liberties are enjoyed, diversity is permitted, and a spirit of tolerance prevails. Civil society, in short, is the realm in which matters and activities of utmost significance to human beings find their proper contours. And it is possible for this to be the case mainly because the institutions and practices of the market economy play a central role in this realm. In such a classical liberal picture, the state's function is restricted to drawing up, administering and enforcing rules to protect the life of civil society. Its authority to do so is generally recognised because it is based on popular consent, because those vested with political power have been elected according to the principles and procedures of representative democracy, and because those administering and enforcing the rules are themselves subject to the rule of law. But political power is legitimately exercised only in a circumscribed sense: when directed at protecting, rather than interfering in, the affairs of civil society.

A modification of this view is one proposed by welfare liberals who think that the state has business interfering in civil society when issues of social justice are at stake. Here we also witness an amendment of what it means to have our individual identities recognised through a series of procedural entitlements. Formal political recognition of individual rights and liberties may not be enough because entrenched and acute social inequalities remain undisturbed. The 'worst-off' members of society, to use Rawls's term,[29] may still be left wrestling with debilitating self-images that mere procedural recognition of their intrinsic worth as persons is scarcely able to assuage. Rawls and Dworkin are aware of this problem and develop from their respective theories of justice and rights redistributive principles aimed at redressing the worst effects of unfortunate social and natural causes of inequality. And both do so in the belief that social justice ramifications are entailed in respect of the integrity of individual identities.

This modification of a classical liberal view of the state and civil society goes some way to addressing concerns of those actors within civil society who are anxious to see 'politics of the state' systematically tackle matters of social deprivation and inequality. However welcome it is in this regard, it is not adequate to provide the type of understanding of the two realms that is required on civic republican terms. Political participation remains inconsequential in itself, and what is lost from sight is any idea that political organisation is related to a common good.

An alternative and, I think, a more adequate view of the relationship between civil society and the state, with roots in the political theories of Hegel and Alexis de Tocqueville, may be briefly characterised as follows.[30] The classical liberal view is right to insist upon the state's role in protecting the life of civil society by respecting the negative liberties and cultural expressions enjoyed there. But its depiction of relations between the two realms, central to which is its indifference to any active dimension of citizenship, is in other respects deficient. Not enough emphasis is given, for example, to the scope of politics within civil society and the bearing of this upon affairs of the state. Hegel tries to capture this emphasis by stressing that it is a feature of life in civil society for citizens to organise themselves into classes and corporations which represent the interests of civil society within institutions of the state. Tocqueville goes further, and in a direction that is more in line with the opinions of current advocates of a politics of civil society, by recommending a proliferation of voluntary associations and a pluralisation of power. Through power's decentralisation the state's despotic potential is curbed and citizens are given meaningful experience of self-rule at various levels in civil society.

The classical liberal view, even in its modified version, also fails to grant enough recognition to the state's bearing on civil society. This is a failing shared by those advocates of a politics of civil society who suppose that something like a Tocquevillian pluralisation of power is sufficient. It is a failing that a more Hegelian line on the state's unity goes some way to correcting, even if we demur from the larger metaphysical claims associated with it. A metaphysically pruned Hegelian line permits us to say at least this. A modern state worth its salt is more than a 'grand protection agency', to use Robert Nozick's provocative description,[31] and more than the site where the plural tendencies in civil society converge. It is also the site of the institutions, practices and symbols that express the unity of the collective life of society. Through these it articulates a common good with which citizens can identify, a political way of life they can value. What matters to citizens, on this view, is not exhausted by what they do in their private lives or through their voluntary associations in civil society, but also encompasses what goes on through the public life of the state. And the assumption at work here is that the life of the state consists of considerably more than a form of bureaucratic rule to which citizens have little access and from which they are alienated. This assumption conceives of bureaucratic functions serving ends not of their own devising but of the devising of the body politic.

Three further comments about the state, which take us beyond Hegel, are in order. First, the unity the state represents is wrongly thought of as an imposed homogeneity, with or without metaphysical warrant, which flies in the face of society's diversity. On the other hand, it should be added, proponents of sheer diversity are prone to overplay their hand, since denial of any principle of unity in the state is an invitation to fragmentation and loss of any political direction. But unity and diversity are false dichotomies. In the type of limited state I have suggested is possible in Northern Ireland, for example, unity is inconceivable unless it incorporates the diversity of society's Britishness and Irishness. And the achievement of such unity, far from being envisaged as a heavy-handed imposition, is anticipated more as the product of a delicate balancing act. More generally, unity should not be considered as a constant, as a once-and-for-all achievement. Through the state's receptivity to the diversity of civil society, rather, the form of unity remains open to reformulation and revision. Perhaps a notion of unity through diversity, as opposed to a notion of unity as homogeneity, comes closest to capturing what I am suggesting the state represents.

Second, what holds true for the idea of unity also holds true for the idea of the common good represented by the state. It is not metaphysically underwritten, but is articulated and rearticulated in the course of public debate. This is a debate to which voices from civil society should contribute, but it is one carried out primarily at the level of state institutions, in particular through parliament. Advocacy of more participatory forms of democracy, which I endorse, is not made at the expense of political representation in parliament. By the same token, accountable representation should mean more than periodic elections – it also demands an interchange with citizens through the public spaces of civil society. The point is that ideas of the common good are the fruit of debate and dialogue at many levels, but ultimately they are articulated through political institutions of the state, and thus become the possession of all citizens.

Third, the necessity for the state to have a conception of the common good, that is, one that represents the interests of all citizens and not just a select or privileged few, is important when considering the role the state should play in socio-economic affairs. I said earlier in the chapter that provision of a way of life worth having implies providing conditions under which all citizens can flourish, and that that means not leaving the fate of individuals to the mercy of market forces. Welfare liberals agree that our fates should not be left to such precarious winds of fortune, but for them intervention in the market is based on neutral principles of justice consistent with treating citizens as free and equal agents, and not on notions of human flourishing that imply an attachment to notions of the good. I am not convinced, however, that treating citizens as free and equal by virtue of a dignity that they all share is a strictly neutral position. It certainly comes suspiciously close to an affirmation of a good that liberals value. I am rather more convinced that some conception of human flourishing is indispensable to a life of citizenship, and that it shapes the sort of arrangements the state makes available in the name of social justice and the common good.

The conception of human flourishing I have in mind here is consistent with respect for the diversity of civil society. It is one that says that there are numerous ways in which humans may flourish, that a 'good life' comes in a plurality of forms, but that a common good consists in the provision of conditions available to all citizens that make possible our flourishing. Or, put another way, it is because it is considered a good thing that citizens are enabled to flourish that the state provides for the possibility of such a flourishing for all citizens. This means that a primary task of the state is to ensure that no citizens are deprived of sustenance or of the institutional, material and educational support required for their flourishing. Thus, for example, there is an onus on governments to promote what Martha Nussbaum calls 'institutional' rather than 'residual' welfare.[32] That is to say, it is not a matter of waiting to see who suffers in the marketplace, who fails to cope in the absence of state support, and then stepping in to bail them out with a bit of state aid. It is, rather, more a matter of implementing a comprehensive scheme of state health care, for instance, or a complete plan of education for all citizens over a complete life. It is only through provisions such as these that all citizens are given equal opportunities to flourish and are not forced to rely on state handouts because they cannot afford private health care or private education. And it is through such provisions that a common good is articulated and society is made more just.

To summarise, civil society has a certain autonomy from the state, especially through the operations of a capitalist economy and the carving out of a public space not under the control of political organisation. The state, for its part, is not simply subsumed under the life of civil society but maintains its independence through affording principles of unity, the common good and justice that would otherwise be unavailable. These are not, however, entirely separate realms, with entirely separate tasks. Neither civil society's autonomy from the state nor the state's independence from civil society is absolute. Both are relative, and I have depicted their interrelation in terms of a to-and-fro movement that facilitates a politics of civil society without abandoning the centrality of a politics of the state. Crucial to the politics of both and to the movement between them are the activities of citizens. It is these activities that prevent the state from lapsing into despotism and civil society from fragmenting. And it is through these activities that the old republican ideal of citizen self-rule proves its vitality in new forms. In doing so, it offers a richer, more expansive and stronger conception of politics and its possibilities, not least for Northern Ireland, than an emphasis on citizenship's procedural entitlements alone ever could.

CITIZENSHIP AND FREEDOM

The fear that citizen self-rule might disguise a dark desire for collective domination should be barely credible in view of the above discussion. That this citizen self-rule is anticipated in a political context that advocates protection of individuals' basic rights and liberties, and that balances unity with diversity, centralisation with pluralisation, participation with representation, and so on, should be enough to put it to rest. Pointing this out is a sufficient rejoinder to those who think that relating citizenship to more than negative liberty is a dangerous step on the road to a closed society. But it is not a rejoinder I am content to settle with. It is still worth drawing out what is involved in the version of positive freedom that I associate with citizen self-rule. It allows me to bring into the open the role played by reason and dialogue in the type of political activity that I think is necessary to sustain the political vision I have been elaborating. Let me try to spell this out by taking my cue from a crucial part of Isaiah Berlin's critique of positive freedom.

Berlin contends that advocates of positive freedom work with these assumptions: (1) that humans have only one true purpose – self-directed rationality; (2) that there is a single, universal pattern of rational ends which some see more clearly than others; (3) that conflict in human affairs is the result of a clash between rational and irrational forces and is therefore eliminable through us all becoming rational; and (4) that when we are all rational we will obey the rational laws of our own natures and in doing so be fully free. Translated politically, these assumptions are dangerous because they enable an 'enlightened' few who claim to grasp what is truly rational to justify forcing the unenlightened many into social and political patterns that are good for them. And all of this can be done in the name of rationality and freedom. Thus we get the idea that people can be forced to be free and with it the notion of collective domination that rides roughshod over individual rights for the sake of a 'higher', rational freedom.[33]

None of these rationality assumptions pertain to the civic republican thesis that freedom involves us having a say in the collective formula under which we live in society. This thesis does not assume that humans have only one true purpose, although it does allow that a broadly defined ideal of self-directed rationality may be a good thing. But it is certainly opposed to the assumption that there is a single universal set of rational ends. On the contrary, it is more disposed to take Berlin's own view that there are plural ends not all of which may be realisable simultaneously, and which on occasions therefore face us with hard, if not tragic, choices. The assumption that conflict is eliminable by rationality's victory over irrationality is also inimical here. Rationality in human affairs in general and in political affairs in particular is not seen in terms of final victories. It is viewed more as a mode of deliberation and judgement, of evaluating options and sifting through alternatives, of arriving at provisional conclusions which are always open to revision. And thus the fourth assumption, linking freedom to a notion of 'true' rationality which may be fully available only to an 'enlightened' elite, does not hold at all.

Indeed, the idea that a free society can be secured by an elite is more objectionable on civic republican terms than on those of liberal minimalism. Despotic rule doubtless would infringe many negative liberties but it could grant many too, whereas it is a contradiction of the very ideal of a self-rule in which all citizens participate. As indicated in reference to Berlin's second assumption, the concept of rationality that is appropriate here is utterly unlike the one he identifies. It is a concept of practical reason more illuminatingly related to a notion of 'insight', which permits us to discern what is best for our society given our particular circumstances and given the sort of beings humans are. Such insight, crucially, is something we win through to together and is not fully available outside the spaces of public dialogue. It is as 'we' collectively attend to social and political issues of import to the life of society that what is best, or most appropriate, or most advisable, becomes clearer. This is to say that dialogue, or dialogical rationality, is central to the ideal of citizen self-rule that is at the heart of the civic republican view of politics I have been advocating. In its absence, in fact, it is hard to say that we have politics at all; or, at any rate, what we have is a grossly degenerate form of politics. And such a loss of politics is simultaneously a loss of political, or positive, freedom; which is why despotic rule, even in the soft bureaucratic form in which it currently appears in Northern Ireland, is ultimately intolerable from this point of view.

So it is only as we exercise control over our affairs through our common deliberations about what course we should take, what goals we should pursue and which should be prioritised, about what policies we should adopt, and so on, that we are free in the positive sense of the term. And, since such freedom is something we realise together, it requires inclusive public spaces open to the disparate voices in society. It is by arguing with and listening to one another, by proposing and counter-proposing, agreeing and disagreeing, evaluating and judging together, that we may hope to reach decisions about our collective life with which we can all live and to which we can be committed.

Here there is an overlap with the hermeneutical emphasis that I signalled at the start of the book and that has shaped the orientation I have adopted throughout. Dialogue is indispensable because the human condition, not least in its political manifestations, is opaque and something we strive to become clearer about by engaging one another. That is why there is such a need to be open beyond the confines of our particular traditions or horizons: not only to avoid hubris, but to be freed from a political intransigence that cuts out the voice of the 'other'. If this is an orientation that is hermeneutically driven, it is also one that tallies with the kind of positive freedom I think is involved in citizen self-rule, a freedom that is unachievable without the inclusive dialogue and practical reason we rely upon if we are to be free together.

CONCLUSION

Various of the arguments I have presented under the rubric of civic unionism, like many of the suggested political arrangements I said were conceivable on its terms, need to be unpacked further. But if, in their current incomplete state, they help to open up fresh debate on some well-worn topics they will have served their purpose. In a sense, the civic unionist vision I have been articulating is appropriately understood as offering a possible way forward once we leave behind the visions of cultural and liberal unionism. And, quite clearly, these are visions that I think we should leave behind, even if we take with us certain of their insights.

It is not at all that I expect something like a civic unionist vision to be quickly adopted in Northern Ireland, though I would hardly complain if it were. It is more that I think that this vision gives us a better angle from which to approach our political problems and opens up new possibilities for doing politics, possibilities that remain forever closed within the horizons of other unionist visions. The seemingly unthinkable becomes quite thinkable upon close inspection and it does so not simply because it is prudent to be pragmatic. In arguing that due political recognition should be given to an Irish identity, for example, I am not saying that this is advisable because it is the only way to contain nationalist violence. I am saying, rather, that such an identity should be recognised because it deserves to be. Here I depart most obviously from other unionist positions which tolerate no tinkering with the Union. I disagree with them principally because I think they misread our collective Northern Irish condition. But I also think that their misreading is compounded by their reliance on conceptual tools that are radically deficient. These tools create narrow political theories which, when joined to unionism, leave little room for manoeuvre and make concessions to political opponents difficult to give in principle and, in practice, certainly impossible to give except grudgingly. Such tightness derives, of course, from a commitment to 'the Union, the whole Union and nothing but the Union', but it also traces back to a minimalist view of politics encouraged by the political theories to which cultural and liberal unionists resort. As a consequence, culturalists and liberals move within horizons that screen out too much about politics generally and about Northern Irish politics in particular. I have tried to move beyond these horizons not only by conceptualising Northern Ireland in more embracive terms, but also by employing a political theory that is as broad as other unionists' theories are narrow.

Put most generally, I am arguing that breadth of vision is what is required most and that without it there is little prospect of us sorting out our acute difficulties. This is not to propose some grand 'solution' to the problem of Northern Ireland, but to clear space for another path of thinking that can accommodate questions of identity and recognition as well as those of justice and democracy. To rethink unionism is also to rethink what counts as politics in Northern Ireland. And both sorts of rethinking seem to me inescapable unless we are simply to despair of our lot and allow the scene to be dominated by the constrained visions that seem capable of producing nothing more than a politics of constitutional standoff. To hold out against despair, constrained visions and stalemate is to insist, in the rich language of civic republicanism, that politics matters.

AFTERWORD

In the opening chapter I mentioned that I aimed to achieve specific personal, political and philosophical purposes through writing this book. I now want to bring to a close my discussion of unionism by reflecting on how the arguments I have been developing relate to these purposes. Doing so also enables me to present my major claims from a slightly different, and, I hope, an illuminating, angle.

The personal purpose of writing the book, namely to deal with my frustration with the paltry political conduct of unionism, needs little additional comment. The book as a whole stands as a fulfilment of that purpose. This does not mean, however, that there are no longer reasons to be frustrated. It is not that in the period between starting and finishing the book unionist conduct has been so transformed that frustration has given way to hope. Quite the contrary. To take the two most significant events that have occurred since the bulk of the book was completed – the commencement of new political talks and the worst week of violence in recent Northern Irish history – the grounds for frustration are even deeper. In the name of conducting talks about the future of Northern Ireland, we have so far witnessed unionist leaders jockey for position, haggle endlessly over procedural rules and guidelines, and avoid any discussion of substantive matters. And in the name of defending Orangemen's alleged right to parade where local residents object to their presence, we have witnessed a united show of unionist defiance which constituted a serious disruption of civic life and provoked countless acts of violence and sectarian intimidation. Protecting narrowly construed unionist interests in a spirit of impeccable self-righteousness continues to be more important to unionist politicians than making conciliatory gestures aimed at reconciling divided people. Not only is the source of frustration that prompted this excursion into unionism left intact but the main negative message the excursion conveys is confirmed: in the absence of a serious rethink unionism offers a grim future for the citizens of Northern Ireland.

The prospect of such a future ought to give pause to unionist belligerence and intransigence and, in my view, to prompt self-inspection. It underlies the political purposes of this book. The first of these was to show *why* unionism's standard visions of politics are inadequate generally, and in Northern Ireland particularly. This inadequacy stems from unionists' attachment to exclusivist conceptions of the character of Northern Irish society. For cultural unionists, the North is primarily the site of a Protestant-British way of life which alone warrants public institutional recognition. For liberal unionists, it is the site of a British political way of life shared in common with the rest of the United Kingdom. In neither case are unionists sufficiently equipped to take seriously the political presence and claims of non-unionists within Northern Ireland. As a consequence, they have little to offer to the resolution of society's most pressing political problems. Cultural and liberal unionists also have difficulty dealing with such problems and in initiating creative political solutions because they work with very restricted notions of what politics is about – both accord politics a minimal role in human affairs by reducing it to a protective instrument. When linked to exlusivist conceptions of the political entitlements of unionists, this minimalism exacerbates unionism's inability to cope with non-unionist requests for parity of esteem and the like. In short, the horizons of unionism cramp the sort of political possibilities unionists can entertain.

A second political purpose of this book was to show *how* it is possible to move beyond such horizons by appropriating an inclusive vision of Northern Ireland and a broader notion of politics. This is what I tried to accomplish in Chapter 5 especially, by depicting Northern Ireland in terms of a 'difference through openness' thesis – which acknowledged the cultural and political entitlements of unionists and nationalists – and by relating union-ism to a civic republican theory of politics. These depictions run the risk of placing civic unionism beyond the boundaries of the unionist fold. This is a risk eminently worth taking, since what matters most, in my opinion, is not maintaining anachronistic standards of unionist orthodoxy but achieving a decent social and political life for all citizens in Northern Ireland.

My attempt to achieve these political purposes was closely tied to a purpose of another kind, namely that of showing how a cer-tain philosophical orientation, which I describe as 'hermeneutic', to the study of human affairs hugely enhances the possibility of fruitfully rethinking unionism. The penetrating questions such a philosophical orientation makes primary permitted me to carry out more effectively my 'negative' political purpose of showing why traditional modes of unionist thought and practice are inadequate and open to serious dispute. Both cultural and liberal unionist ways of life were seen to suffer from deep practical strains, if not troubling contradictions. And when conceptually articulated, their respective horizons of meaning were also shown to contain incoherent arguments and to suffer from an acute in-ability to deal with practical and intellectual challenges from other horizons. In short, irreparable flaws were revealed in the positions of cultural and liberal unionism.

My 'positive' political purpose of entertaining a broader vision of unionism was also reinforced by philosophical considerations which underwrite a commitment to a politics celebrating the centrality of dialogue in political affairs and the need to be open to horizons beyond one's own. When this commitment is aligned with considerations that enrich and deepen the conception of citizenship at the heart of a civic republican view of politics, by drawing on insights into what we are as rational and moral beings, a strategy emerges to point the way towards a new civic unionism. Or so I have maintained.

Although separate, all of the purposes at work in my discussion of unionism interconnect. My political and philosophical purposes interweave and are in turn energised by the sense of frustration indicated by my personal purpose. Together they make this endeavour to rethink unionism the kind of exercise that it is. If, as I said at the end of Chapter 5, civic republicanism permits us to see that politics matters, I should now add that a hermeneutic orientation to human affairs permits us to see that philosophy matters too. Showing how and why they matter in the peculiar circumstances of Northern Ireland is what I have been trying to do. Events in the North during the 1996 marching season underscore not only that they matter, but that they matter urgently.

NOTES

CHAPTER 1

1   I borrow this phrase from Paul
    Bew, Peter Gibbon and Henry
    Patterson, *Northern Ireland 1921–
    1994: Political Forces and Social
    Classes* (London: Serif, 1995),
    p. 192.
2   Michael Farrell, *Northern Ireland:
    The Orange State*, 2nd rev. edn
    (London: Pluto Press, 1980),
    p. 347
3   I appropriate this term of self-
    description from a slight
    adaptation of the title of Steve
    Bruce's *The Edge of the Union: The
    Ulster Loyalist Political Vision*
    (Oxford: Oxford University Press,
    1994).
4   At the very least, it is possible to
    claim that for most of the fifty
    years of unionist rule at Stormont
    – during a period when the
    Unionist Party was virtually
    unchallenged, nationalist
    abstentionism and resignation
    were conspicuous, the IRA posed
    little threat, and the constitutional
    status of Northern Ireland was
    rarely a genuine concern – crass
    opportunism motivated
    unionism's refusal to relinquish
    the constitutional card.
5   For an instructive study of this
    phenomenon see Graham Walker,
    *The Politics of Frustration: Harry
    Midgley and the Failure of Labour in*

Northern Ireland (Manchester:
Manchester University Press,
1985).
6   See, for example, William E.
    Connolly, *Identity\Difference:
    Democratic Negotiations of Political
    Paradox* (New York: Cornell
    University Press, 1991)
7   Compare the Opsahl
    Commission's recommendation
    that Northern Ireland's politicians
    should participate in 'an
    expanded programme of
    education and training for
    political leadership'. Andy Pollak
    (ed.), *A Citizens' Inquiry: The
    Opsahl Report on Northern Ireland*
    (Dublin: Lilliput Press, 1993),
    p. 113.
8   The UUP has recently moved to set
    up an office in Washington, for
    example. Reflections on the
    party's need to become more
    'entrepreneurial' in its handling of
    the unionist message are
    contained in the pamphlet
    sponsored by the Ulster Young
    Unionist Council, *Selling Unionism
    Home and Away* (Belfast: Ulster
    Young Unionist Council, 1995).
9   Molyneaux's principal political
    goals consisted in winning 'a
    Select Committee for Northern
    Ireland affairs, upgrading the
    Northern Ireland Committee to
    Grand Committee status, and
    ending the Order in Council

procedure for primary legislation in Ulster'. James Molyneaux, 'Accountable Democracy at Westminster', *Unionist Voice*, no. 12 (October 1994), p. 3.

10 *Frameworks for the Future* (Belfast: Her Majesty's Stationery Office, 1995). These documents are frequently referred to popularly and in these pages as 'the framework documents'.

11 See, for example, contributions by McCartney and others to 'Visions for the Union', *News Letter*, 29 June 1995. See also the critical response by Ian Paisley, 'Flawed Visions for the Union', *News Letter*, 30 June 1995

12 In one sense it is misleading to contrast McCartney's liberal unionism with traditional unionism since he traces his position back to the traditional stance of Edward Carson. But if we allow that traditional unionism as developed after partition has been inextricably associated with cultural Protestantism, then the above contrast has some salience.

13 They are indebted to the 'philosophical hermeneutics' developed most thoroughly in recent times by Hans Georg Gadamer. See, especially, his *Truth and Method*, trans. G. Barden and J. Cumming (London: Sheed and Ward, 1975). See also Charles Taylor, *Philosophical Papers*, vol. 1, *Human Agency and Language* (Cambridge: Cambridge University Press, 1985).

14 The phrase is Thomas Nagel's. See Thomas Nagel, *The View From Nowhere* (Oxford: Oxford University Press, 1986).

15 I am breaking with a tendency to treat as synonyms the terms 'civic' and 'liberal' unionism. For an example of this tendency see John McGarry and Brendan O'Leary, *Explaining Northern Ireland: Broken Images* (Oxford: Blackwell, 1995), pp. 92–137. At the heart of the distinction I draw between the two lies a substantive difference between what I call 'thick' and 'thin' conceptions of citizenship.

CHAPTER 2

1 The term 'masterful inactivity' is originally Brendan Clifford's. See his *The Road to Nowhere* (Belfast: Athol Books, 1987), pp. 1–2. For Aughey's appropriation of it see, for example, Arthur Aughey, 'Unionism and Self-determination', in Patrick Roche and Brian Barton (eds.), *The Northern Ireland Question: Myth and Reality* (Aldershot: Avebury, 1991), pp. 10–11.

2 Arthur Aughey, 'In Search of a New Vision for Unionism', *Belfast Telegraph*, 10 August 1995

3 See Aughey's dismissal of the idea that unionism is suffering an identity crisis in his *Under Siege: Ulster Unionism and the Anglo-Irish Agreement* (London: Hurst and Company; Belfast: Blackstaff Press, 1989), pp. 13–18. The plausibility of Aughey's argument hangs on his claim that cultural identities are irrelevant to the political stance of unionism. As I intimate later in the chapter, I find this claim problematic. I argue against it in chapters 4 and 5.

4 The six parties are the Ulster Unionist Party (UUP), Democratic Unionist Party (DUP), Alliance Party of Northern Ireland (Alliance), Ulster Democratic Party (UDP), Progressive Unionist Party (PUP) and United Kingdom Unionist Party.

5 Perhaps this judgement is a little unfair on the Alliance Party, since

it can claim the distinctions of having cross-communal membership and having engaged in talks with all other parties without preconditions being satisfied. The PUP and UDP have made favourable noises about participating in such talks, but as yet have failed to engage with Sinn Féin. Whatever their intentions, they suffer from a handicap from which the Alliance Party is free: as things stand at the time of writing, the UUP and DUP are unwilling to enter formal talks with either of them.

6   The DUP has consistently opposed the Downing Street Declaration and has attacked what it regards as the acute gullibility of the UUP for taking too 'soft' a line on it.

7   In the absence of UUP support, the proposed vehicle of unity – a Unionist Convention – has been set aside for the time being.

8   See Steven Livingstone and John Morison, *An Audit of Democracy in Northern Ireland*, supplement to *Fortnight*, no. 337 (April 1995).

9   John McGarry and Brendan O'Leary, *Explaining Northern Ireland: Broken Images* (Oxford: Blackwell, 1995), pp. 94–5

10   *Ibid.*, p. 94

11   There is an irony here that, if not qualified, may appear as a stark contradiction. Earlier I suggested that there is no convincing rationale for the presence of so many unionist parties, since a number of them lack a distinctive stance that differentiates them from others. Now I am saying that unionists are divided by matters of substance. So is there a contradiction? I do not think so: the substantive differences among unionists to which I am alluding are not differences that separate one unionist party from another

but, rather, differences that are often found within parties. This is particularly the case with the UUP, the largest and most important unionist party. Its minimalist creed and explicit 'broad-church' appeal allow for the appearance of any number of political disagreements among its members.

12   Unionists may object to the British government being considered an 'external' force in Northern Ireland, just as some nationalists may object to the Irish government being so described. Such a unionist objection in particular has a valid point: since Northern Ireland is constitutionally part of the United Kingdom the government of that United Kingdom can hardly be described as 'external'. But it is external in the sense that Northern Ireland's membership is not treated as equivalent to the membership enjoyed by England, Scotland or Wales. I discuss what I mean by this non-equivalence in the text below.

13   Commenting on Article 1(c) of the Anglo-Irish Agreement, Hume reasoned that it 'is an implicit declaration by the British that they have no interest of their own in staying in Ireland ... In short, the British government is neutral in that it is no longer pro-Union. There is nothing, therefore, to stop the British government from becoming pro-Irish unity in their policies.' Quoted in Padraig O'Malley, *Northern Ireland: Questions of Nuance* (Belfast: Blackstaff Press, 1990), p. 18.

14   Anthony Kenny, *The Road to Hillsborough* (Oxford: Pergamon Press, 1986), pp. 135–6

15   David Lloyd George, quoted in Padraig O'Malley, *The Uncivil*

Wars: Ireland Today (Belfast: Blackstaff Press, 1983), p. 205

16 'Joint Declaration: Downing Street', 15 December 1993, p. 3

17 See, for example, paragraphs 2, 5 and 10 of 'A New Framework for Agreement', in *Frameworks for the Future* (Belfast: Her Majesty's Stationery Office, 1995)

18 For an analysis of recent British policy in Northern Ireland see Michael J. Cunningham, *British Government Policy in Northern Ireland 1969–89: Its Nature and Execution* (Manchester: Manchester University Press, 1991).

19 As a consequence it evoked furious unionist reactions. One of the most powerful was delivered by the late Harold McCusker, former UUP MP for Upper Bann, when during a speech in the House of Commons he remarked: 'I shall carry to my grave with ignominy the sense of injustice that I have shown to my constituents down the years when in their darkest hours I exhorted them to put their trust in this House of Commons, which one day would honour its fundamental obligation to treat them as equal British citizens.' Quoted in Antony Alcock, *Understanding Ulster* (Lurgan: Ulster Society Publications, 1994), p. 76.

20 The paragraph reads as follows: 'In the event that devolved institutions in Northern Ireland ceased to operate, and direct rule from Westminster was reintroduced, *the British Government agree that other arrangements would be made to implement the commitment to promote co-operation at all levels between the people, North and South,* representing both traditions in

Ireland, as agreed by the two Governments in the Joint Declaration, and to ensure that the co-operation that had been developed through the North/South body be maintained' (emphasis added). 'A New Framework for Agreement', p. 34.

21 For different appraisals of the Anglo-Irish Agreement see, for example, Arthur Aughey, *Under Siege*; Michael Connolly and John Loughlin, 'Reflections on the Anglo-Irish Agreement', *Government and Opposition*, 21, (1986), pp. 146–60; Brendan O'Leary and John McGarry, *The Politics of Antagonism: Understanding Northern Ireland* (London: Athlone Press, 1993), pp. 220–76.

22 The UUP and the DUP in particular remain implacably opposed to entertaining the prospect of entering negotiations with the framework documents on the table.

23 The claim appears in Article 3 of the Irish constitution but has to be understood in the light of Article 2. Article 2 reads as follows: 'The national territory consists of the whole island of Ireland, its islands and the territorial seas.' Article 3 then adds the twist so offensive to unionists: 'pending the re-integration of the national territory, and without prejudice to the right of the parliament and government established by this constitution to exercise jurisdiction over the whole of that territory, the laws enacted by that parliament shall have the like area and extent of application as the laws of Saorstat Éireann and the like extra-territorial effect.' Bunreacht na hÉireann, Constitution of Ireland, 1937.

24 See, for example, recent

statements by the DUP leader, Ian
Paisley, and the UUP leader, David
Trimble. Paisley refers to the Irish
taoiseach, John Bruton, as 'a
meddling foreign head of state
who still refuses to move on the
illegal Articles 2 and 3 of his
country's constitution', and as 'the
head of a hostile foreign state'. Ian
Paisley, 'Why I Oppose the
Downing Street Deal', *Belfast
Telegraph*, 6 December 1995.
In response to an invitation from
the Irish tánaiste, Dick Spring, to
engage in preparatory talks about
the political process in Northern
Ireland, Trimble replied: 'We are
not prepared to negotiate the
internal affairs of Northern
Ireland with a foreign
government.' *Belfast Telegraph*,
6 December 1995.

25   See Christopher McGimpsey and
Michael McGimpsey, Plaintiffs, *v.*
Ireland, An Taioseach and others,
Defendants, SC NO. 314 of 1988
Supreme Court, 1 March 1990. *The
Irish Reports 1990*, vol. 1,
Incorporated Council of Law
Reporting for Ireland, 1990,
pp. 110–25.

26   For analyses see, for example,
Clare O'Halloran, *Partition and the
Limits of Irish Nationalism* (Dublin:
Gill and Macmillan, 1988); Joseph
J. Lee, *Ireland 1912–1985: Politics
and Society* (Cambridge:
Cambridge University Press, 1989)

27   See the analysis of Brian Girvin,
'Constitutional Nationalism and
Northern Ireland', in *The Northern
Ireland Question: Policies and
Perspectives*, Brian Barton and
Patrick Roche (eds.), (Aldershot:
Avebury, 1994), pp. 5–52

28   See 'A New Framework for
Agreement', paragraph 21

29   Of course, should unionists take
up and respond positively to this
invitation it would send

shockwaves through the Republic.
Most curiously, it would confront
the Irish government with the sort
of quandary that unionists are
being pressured to confront: how
to refashion the institutions of
state in such a way that both
Britishness and Irishness are
permitted expression.

30   This is argued by Richard
Kearney: 'Is it not probable that a
lasting solution to the Ulster
conflict is most likely to be found
in a new Europe where the
borders separating the nation
states of Britain and Ireland
would be transcended in favour of
a federation of equal and
democratic regions? ... It is in this
context of a European federation
of equal regions that we might
begin to talk genuinely about the
re-unification of Ireland. An
Ireland without frontiers is
obviously an Ireland without
borders. This does not however
entail a "united Ireland" in the
traditional sense of the term. For
the nation states of Britain and
Ireland, which constitute the very
basis for the opposing claims of
nationalist and unionist
ideologies, would be superseded
by a European constellation of
regions. An alternative model
would have emerged
transcending both the nationalist
claim to exclusive unity with the
Republic and the unionist claim to
exclusive union with Britain.'
Richard Kearney (ed.), *Across the
Frontiers: Ireland in the 1990s*
(Dublin: Gill and Macmillan,
1988), p. 17.

31   Robin Wilson, quoted in Andy
Pollak (ed.), *A Citizens' Inquiry:
The Opsahl Report On Northern
Ireland* (Dublin: Lilliput Press,
1993), p. 416

32   Indeed, Dennis Kennedy argues

that as the concept of a 'Europe of the regions . . . has been explored and clarified it has emerged as essentially hierarchical, with the regional element contained within the unit of the national state. If regions do play a greater role, it will be within a framework where member states retain a key and powerful role, not where they wither away.' Dennis Kennedy, 'The European Union and the Northern Ireland Question', in Barton and Roche (eds.), *The Northern Ireland Question: Policies and Perspectives*, p. 182.

33 Lionel Shriver, 'An American at the Hearings: An Outsider's View', in Pollak (ed.), *A Citizens' Inquiry* (the Opsahl Report), p. 417

34 See Will Hutton, *The State We're In* (London: Cape, 1995)

35 See Lee, *Ireland 1912–1985*

36 Feargal Cochrane, 'Any Takers? The Isolation of Northern Ireland', *Political Studies*, vol. 42, no. 3 (1994), p. 381

37 See the critical comments on Cochrane's article in Paul Dixon, 'Internationalization and Unionist Isolation: A Response to Feargal Cochrane', *Political Studies*, vol. 43, no. 3 (1995), pp. 407–505; and Cochrane's reply, 'The Isolation of Northern Ireland', *ibid.*, pp. 506–8.

38 In Chapter 5 I suggest that the term 'parity of esteem' is misleading and is illuminatingly substituted by the term 'due recognition'.

39 Unionists could of course point out with some justification that the convergence of such interests reflects the success of nationalists, spearheaded by John Hume, in convincing Ireland, Britain and the world at large of the cause of nationalism. Reduced to its lowest common denominator, unionism

has been beaten hands down by nationalism in the propaganda war. Admitting this does not, however, exhaust all there is to say about nationalism's use of the concept of parity of esteem. It remains an open question whether this use is justifiable. And this is the question that should ultimately matter.

40 For a provocative development of the idea see, for example, Will Kymlicka, *Contemporary Political Philosophy: An Introduction* (Oxford: Clarendon Press, 1990), pp. 50–94.

41 This formulation begs the question of whether the putative rights of groups/traditions are inherent possessions, or whether they are properly ascribed to them in a derivative sense only where they represent the rights of individuals to choose to express themselves through groups/ traditions. For the former view see Will Kymlicka, *Liberalism, Community, and Culture* (Oxford: Clarendon Press, 1989); and for the latter view see Yael Tamir, *Liberal Nationalism* (Princeton: Princeton University Press, 1993).

42 Andy Pollak (ed.), *A Citizens' Inquiry* (the Opsahl Report), p. 113

43 *Ibid.*, p. 112

44 The idea of civil society being invoked here has its origins in Hegel's political philosophy. See G.W.F. Hegel, *Philosophy of Right*, trans. T.M. Knox (Oxford: Oxford University Press, 1967), Part 3, sections 2 and 3, pp. 122–207. For a helpful contemporary discussion of the idea see Michael Walzer, 'The Idea of Civil Society: A Path to Social Reconstruction', *Dissent* (Spring 1991), pp. 293–304.

45 Ken Maginnis of the UUP, for example, referred to the Opsahl Commission as being 'middle-

class', 'naive' and 'simplistic'.
Quoted in Shriver, 'An American
at the Hearings', p. 339. The
McGimpsey brothers made a
submission to the commission, but
otherwise it was ignored by the
UUP.

46   See, for example, Leszek
Kolakowski, 'The Myth of Human
Self-identity: Unity of Civil and
Political Society in Socialist
Thought', in Leszek Kolakowski
and Stuart Hampshire (eds.), The
Socialist Idea: A Reappraisal
(London: Weidenfeld and
Nicolson, 1974), pp. 18–35. But see
also the reply by Stuart
Hampshire in the same volume,
'Unity of Civil and Political
Society: Reply to Leszek
Kolakowski', pp. 36–44.

47   For an account of the origins and
historical development of a
Protestant/unionist 'siege
mentality' see A.T.Q. Stewart, The
Narrow Ground: Patterns of Ulster
History (Belfast: Pretani Press,
1986).

48   John Whyte, Interpreting Northern
Ireland (Oxford: Clarendon Press,
1990), p. 97

49   Ibid., p. 99

50   Ibid., p. 101

51   Philosophical reasons are among
the best here but this is not the
place to rehearse them. For a
sample, see the different attempts
to shift the focus of Western
philosophy away from the
'philosophy of consciousness'
with which it has been
preoccupied since Descartes in
Richard Rorty, Philosophy and the
Mirror of Nature (Princeton:
Princeton University Press, 1979);
and Jürgen Habermas, 'An
Alternative Way Out of the
Philosophy of the Subject:
Communicative versus Subject-
centred Reason', in his The

Philosophical Discourse of
Modernity: Twelve Lectures
(Cambridge, MA: MIT Press, 1988),
pp. 294–326.

52   For surveys of the range of
explanatory theories available see
Whyte, Interpreting Northern
Ireland; and McGarry and
O'Leary, Explaining Northern
Ireland.

53   Not everyone agrees. For excellent
discussions of how our emotional
states are open to the evaluations
of practical reason see the papers
collected in Charles Taylor,
Philosophical Papers, vol. 1, Human
Agency and Language (Cambridge:
Cambridge University Press,
1985).

54   For an illuminating discussion of
how a point such as this emerges
through the philosophies of
Heidegger and Wittgenstein see
Charles Taylor, 'Lichtung or
Lebensform: Parallels between
Heidegger and Wittgenstein', in
his Philosophical Arguments
(Cambridge, MA: Harvard
University Press, 1995), pp. 61–78.

55   I am indebted to Dessie O'Hagan
for this formulation.

CHAPTER 3

1   Robert McCartney, Liberty and
Authority in Ireland, Field Day
Pamphlet No. 9 (Derry: Field Day,
1985), pp. 25–6

2   Arthur Aughey, Under Siege:
Ulster Unionism and the Anglo-Irish
Agreement (London: Hurst and
Company; Belfast: Blackstaff
Press, 1989), p. 200

3   Ibid., p. 202

4   See Padraig O'Malley, Biting at the
Grave: The Irish Hunger Strikes and
the Politics of Despair (Boston:
Beacon Press; Belfast: Blackstaff
Press, 1990). For the criticisms see
John McGarry and Brendan

O'Leary, *Explaining Northern Ireland: Broken Images* (Oxford: Blackwell, 1995), pp. 245–8. I discuss aspects of these criticisms in the text below.

5 This is a reconstruction of points made in McGarry and O'Leary, *Explaining Northern Ireland*, pp. 243–4.
6 *Ibid.*, p. 244
7 *Ibid.*, p. 247
8 *Ibid.*, p. 251
9 *Ibid.*, p. 250
10 *Ibid.*, p. 251
11 *Ibid.*, p. 248
12 For an excellent discussion along these lines see Jean Hampton, 'Rethinking Reason', *American Philosophical Quarterly*, vol. 29, no. 3 (July 1992), pp. 219–36.
13 For a recent statement of an Aristotelian position see Alasdair MacIntyre, *After Virtue: A Study in Moral Theory* (London: Duckworth, 1981). For one in a more Kantian mode, albeit very modified, see Jürgen Habermas, *Justification and Application: Remarks on Discourse Ethics*, trans. Ciaran Cronin (Cambridge, MA: MIT Press, 1993).
14 Informative discussions of the significance of each of these events may be found under one cover in Roy F. Foster, *Modern Ireland 1600–1972* (Harmondsworth: Penguin, 1989).
15 For contrasting accounts of how these powers were used see Michael Farrell, *Northern Ireland: The Orange State*, 2nd rev. edn (London: Pluto Press, 1980); and Tom Wilson, *Ulster: Conflict and Consent* (Oxford: Blackwell, 1989).
16 For different angles see Peter Gibbon, *The Origins of Ulster Unionism* (Manchester: Manchester University Press, 1975); and B.M. Walker, *Ulster Politics: The Formative Years*

1868–1886 (Belfast: Ulster Historical Foundation and Institute of Irish Studies, 1989).
17 That the interests of capital were suited is emphasised in Paul Bew, Peter Gibbon and Henry Patterson, *Northern Ireland 1921–1994: Political Forces and Social Classes* (London: Serif, 1995).
18 The phrase is James Craig's as quoted in Wilson, *Ulster*, p. 73.
19 See the survey evidence presented in Fred Boal, John A. Campbell and David N. Livingstone, 'The Protestant Mosaic: A Majority of Minorities', in Patrick Roche and Brian Barton (eds.), *The Northern Ireland Question: Myth and Reality* (Aldershot: Avebury, 1991), pp. 99–129.
20 On these events in general see Foster, *Modern Ireland*, pp. 79–100, 138–63. And for their significance to Protestant memories see A.T.Q. Stewart, *The Narrow Ground: Patterns of Ulster History* (Belfast: Pretani Press, 1986), pp. 43–76.
21 See A.T.Q. Stewart, *The Ulster Crisis* (London: Faber and Faber, 1967)
22 Accounts of loyalist paramilitaries and their thinking are found in Steve Bruce, *The Red Hand: Protestant Paramilitaries in Northern Ireland* (Oxford: Oxford University Press, 1992), and Sarah Nelson, *Ulster's Uncertain Defenders: Loyalists and the Northern Ireland Conflict* (Belfast: Appletree Press, 1984).
23 Ian Meredith and Brian Kennaway, *The Orange Order: An Evangelical Perspective* (Belfast, 1993)
24 For a survey of different, and conflicting, uses of symbols in Northern Ireland see Lucy Bryson and Clem McCartney, *Clashing Symbols? A Report on the Use of Flags, Anthems and Other National*

Symbols in Northern Ireland (Belfast: Institute of Irish Studies, 1994).

25   Ian Paisley, quoted in Steve Bruce, *God Save Ulster: The Religion and Politics of Paisleyism* (Oxford: Clarendon Press, 1986), pp. 269–70

26   For an informative account of Presbyterian values see John Dunlop, *A Precarious Belonging: Presbyterians and the Conflict in Ireland* (Belfast: Blackstaff Press, 1995).

27   Charles Taylor, *Sources of the Self: The Making of the Modern Identity* (Cambridge: Cambridge University Press, 1989), Part III, especially pp. 211–33

28   On this see Marianne Elliott, *Watchmen in Sion: The Protestant Idea of Liberty*, Field Day Pamphlet No. 8 (Derry: Field Day, 1985), p. 9

29   Ian Adamson, *The Cruithin: A History of the Ulster Land and People* (Belfast: Pretani Press, 1974); and Ian Adamson, *The Identity of Ulster: The Land, the Language and the People* (Belfast: Pretani Press, 1982)

30   As advocated explicitly by the Ulster Independence Movement, for example, and more equivocally hinted at by the Ulster Defence Association and its political associates.

31   Including Ian Paisley and the now extinct Vanguard Party of which the current leader of the UUP – David Trimble – was once a member.

32   Michael Ignatieff, *Blood and Belonging: Journeys into the New Nationalism* (London: Chatto and Windus, 1993), p. 185

33   This recalls Steve Bruce's thesis that evangelical Protestantism is at the core of a unionist identity. See his *God Save Ulster*, pp. 249–73.

This thesis is exaggerated, since it does not capture the identities of either liberal or civic unionists.

34   John Fulton, *The Tragedy of Belief: Division, Politics, and Religion in Ireland* (Oxford: Clarendon Press, 1991), p. 95

35   Padraig O'Malley, *The Uncivil Wars: Ireland Today* (Belfast: Blackstaff Press, 1983), p. 171

36   These other Northern Ireland Protestants are represented, for example, by two pamphlets produced by the Shankill Think Tank: *Ulster's Protestant Working Class*, Island Pamphlets No. 9 (Belfast: Island Publications, 1994); and *A New Beginning*, Island Pamphlets No. 13 (Belfast: Island Publications, 1995).

37   George Graham as quoted in Bruce, *God Save Ulster*, p. 251

38   For a brief discussion see George Sabine, *A History of Political Theory*, 3rd rev. edn (London: George Harrap, 1951), pp. 431–4.

39   Ian Paisley, *Protestant Telegraph*, August 1979, p. 1

40   For a discussion see Martha Abele MacIver, 'Ian Paisley and the Reformed Tradition', *Political Studies*, vol. 35 (1987), pp. 370–1.

41   Professor C.A.M. Noble, 'The Constitutional Significance of Britain's Protestant Heritage', *New Protestant Telegraph*, March 1996, p. 6

42   See Elliott, *Watchmen in Sion*, pp. 13–14

43   Ignatieff, *Blood and Belonging*, p. 169

44   For an illuminating discussion of this route, which picks up its multifaceted dimensions, see Charles Taylor, *Hegel* (Cambridge: Cambridge University Press, 1975), pp. 3–51.

45   For discussions bearing on these points see, for example, Ralph Della Cava, 'Vatican Policy,

1978–90: An Updated Overview', *Social Research* (1993), pp. 169–99; R. Bruce Douglass and David Hollenbach, *Catholicism and Liberalism: Contributions to American Public Philosophy* (Cambridge: Cambridge University Press, 1994).

46 Of relevance here are Dermot Keogh, 'The Role of the Catholic Church in the Republic of Ireland 1922–1995', in *Building Trust in Ireland: Studies Commissioned by the Forum for Peace and Reconciliation* (Belfast: Blackstaff Press, 1996), pp. 85–214; and 'Submission from the Irish Catholic Bishops' Conference' to the Forum for Peace and Reconciliation (19 January 1996).

47 See McGarry and O'Leary, *Explaining Northern Ireland*, pp. 130–3.

48 A good discussion of Calvin's political thought is provided in Sheldon Wolin, *Politics and Vision: Continuity and Innovation in Western Political Thought* (Boston: Little, Brown and Company, 1960), pp. 165–94.

49 John Rawls, *Political Liberalism* (New York: Columbia University Press, 1993), p. xxiv

50 Quentin Skinner, *The Foundations of Modern Political Thought*, vol. 2, *The Age of Reformation* (Cambridge: Cambridge University Press, 1978), p. 352

51 Machiavelli, quoted by Quentin Skinner, 'On Justice, the Common Good and Liberty', in Chantal Mouffe (ed.), *Dimensions of Radical Democracy: Pluralism, Citizenship, Community* (London: Verso, 1992), p. 217

52 Thomas Hobbes, *Leviathan*, edited by C.B. Macpherson (Harmondsworth: Penguin, 1968); John Locke, *Two Treatises of Government*, edited by Peter

Laslett (New York: Cambridge University Press, 1960)

53 For an informed discussion see John Dunn, *The Political Thought of John Locke: An Historical Account of the Argument of the Two Treatises of Government* (Cambridge: Cambridge University Press, 1969).

54 David Miller, *Queen's Rebels: Ulster Loyalism in Historical Perspective* (Dublin: Gill and Macmillan, 1978)

55 Aristotle, *The Politics*, trans. T.A. Sinclair (Harmondsworth: Penguin, 1962)

56 Augustine, *The City of God*, trans. Henry Bettenson (Harmondsworth: Penguin, 1972)

57 See Wolin, *Politics and Vision*, pp. 141–94

58 C.B. Macpherson, *The Political Theory of Possessive Individualism: Hobbes to Locke* (Oxford: Oxford University Press, 1962)

59 Michael Sandel, *Liberalism and the Limits of Justice* (Cambridge: Cambridge University Press, 1983)

60 Thus Paisley says: 'I happen to be a democrat. And I believe in the rule of the majority. And I would say that if the majority of the people in Northern Ireland want to become part of the Republic, well, as far as I'm concerned, that's it.' Quoted in O'Malley, *The Uncivil Wars*, p. 196.

61 For a fuller account see MacIver, 'Ian Paisley and the Reformed Tradition', pp. 359–78.

62 But sufficiently openly to enable Paisley to put his particular gloss on it.

63 Miller, *Queen's Rebels*, p. 132

64 This is made clear, for instance, in 'Paths to a Political Settlement: Realities, Principles and Requirements', Final Paper of the Drafting Committee of the Forum for Peace and Reconciliation.

65 Miller, *Queen's Rebels*, p. 131.
Admittedly, I am making the
contrast between 'diffuse' and
'contractual' support more acute
than Miller does. Miller's point is
that Stormont enjoyed diffuse
support because it was assumed
to satisfy contractual assumptions.
This may be true. But the fact that
there was a diffuse support for
Stormont that there was not for
Westminster indicates, I think,
that it reflected shared covenantal
understandings which could
obtain at Stormont but not at
Westminster.

66 Peter Robinson, *The Union Under
Fire: United Ireland Framework
Revealed* (Belfast: Peter Robinson,
1995), p. 4

CHAPTER FOUR

1 John Wilson Foster, 'Introduction',
in John Wilson Foster (ed.), *The
Idea of the Union: Statements and
Critiques in Support of the Union of
Great Britain and Northern Ireland*
(Vancouver: Belcouver Press,
1995), p. 4

2 Quoted in David Miller, *Queen's
Rebels: Ulster Loyalism in Historical
Perspective* (Dublin: Gill and
Macmillan, 1978), p. 97.

3 Arthur Aughey, *Under Siege:
Ulster Unionism and the Anglo-Irish
Agreement* (London: Hurst and
Company; Belfast: Blackstaff
Press, 1989), pp. 146–57

4 *Ibid.*, p. 157

5 See Tom Wilson, *Ulster: Conflict
and Consent* (Oxford: Blackwell,
1989); and Patrick Roche and
Brian Barton (eds.), *The Northern
Ireland Question: Myth and Reality*
(Aldershot: Avebury, 1991)

6 Arthur Aughey, 'The Idea of the
Union', in Foster (ed.), *The Idea of
the Union*, p. 9

7 Robert McCartney, 'Parity of

Esteem Has Got Little to Do with
Civil Rights', *Belfast Telegraph*,
19 January 1995

8 Robert McCartney, 'Time to Face
the Crisis', *News Letter*, 7 March
1995

9 Aughey, 'The Idea of the Union',
p. 12

10 See Robert McCartney, *Liberty and
Authority in Ireland*, Field Day
Pamphlet No. 9 (Derry: Field Day,
1985)

11 Aughey, *Under Siege*, Chapter 1

12 *Ibid.*, p. 19

13 See Campaign for Equal
Citizenship, *Northern Ireland Says
Yes to Equal Citizenship* (Belfast:
Campaign for Equal Citizenship,
1987); Aughey, *Under Siege*,
Chapter 5

14 McCartney, 'Time to Face the
Crisis'

15 John Wilson Foster, 'The
Declaration and the Union', in *The
Idea of the Union*, p. 100

16 'Humespeak' has become a
common term of abuse in unionist
circles, aimed at discrediting what
are regarded as the pious
platitudes – disguising an
uncompromising nationalism – of
the SDLP leader John Hume.

17 McCartney, 'Parity of Esteem'

18 Arthur Aughey, 'Irresistable
Force?', *Fortnight*, 321 (October
1993), pp. 14–17

19 Arthur Aughey, 'The End of
History, the End of the Union', in
Selling Unionism Home and Away
(Belfast: Ulster Young Unionist
Council, 1995), p. 13

20 *Ibid.*

21 Richard English, 'Unionism and
Nationalism', in Foster (ed.), *The
Idea of the Union*, p. 136

22 See Aughey, 'The Idea of the
Union', pp. 8–19

23 Aughey, *Under Siege*, p. 135

24 See David Trimble's 'Foreword' to
Desmond Nesbitt, *Unionism*

Restated: An Analysis of the Ulster Unionist Party's 'Statement of Aims' (Belfast: Ulster Unionist Information Institute, 1995), pp. vii–viii

25 Patrick Roche, 'Northern Ireland and Irish Nationalism', in Foster (ed.), *The Idea of the Union*, p. 133

26 Arthur Aughey, 'McCartney in the Wings', *Fortnight*, 340 (June 1995), p. 12

27 See, for example, the patronising title of Patrick Roche and Esmond Birnie, *An Economics Lesson for Irish Nationalists and Republicans* (Belfast: UUII, 1995)

28 Aughey, 'McCartney in the Wings', p. 12

29 On the cunning of reason or *Geist* in history see G.W.F. Hegel, *The Philosophy of History*, trans. J. Sibree (New York: Dover, 1956).

30 Francis Fukuyama, 'The End of History? After the Battle of Jena', *Quadrant*, vol. 33, no. 258 (August 1989), p. 15

31 *Ibid.*

32 See, for example, Shlomo Avineri, *Hegel's Theory of the Modern State* (Cambridge: Cambridge University Press, 1972); Charles Taylor, *Hegel* (Cambridge: Cambridge University Press, 1975), pp. 389–427

33 See G.W.F. Hegel, *Phenomenology of Spirit*, trans. A.V. Miller (Oxford: Clarendon Press, 1977); G.W.F. Hegel, *Logic*, trans. William Wallace (Oxford: Clarendon Press, 1975)

34 Paisley, quoted in Steve Bruce, *God Save Ulster: The Religion and Politics of Paisleyism* (Oxford: Clarendon Press, 1986), p. 269

35 John Wilson Foster, 'Why I Am a Unionist', in Foster (ed.), *The Idea of the Union*, p. 59

36 Kevin Boyle and Tom Hadden, *Ireland: A Positive Proposal*

(Harmondsworth: Penguin, 1985), p. 27

37 Arthur Aughey, 'Unionism and Self-Determination', in Roche and Barton (eds.), *The Northern Ireland Question*, p. 9

38 Isaiah Berlin, *Four Essays on Liberty* (Oxford: Oxford University Press, 1969), pp. 118–72

39 McCartney, *Freedom and Authority in Ireland*, p. 10

40 *Ibid.*

41 *Ibid.*, pp. 14–18

42 *Ibid.*, p. 19

43 John McGarry and Brendan O'Leary, *Explaining Northern Ireland: Broken Images* (Oxford: Blackwell, 1995) p. 130

44 *Ibid.*

45 Arthur Aughey, 'Obstacles to Reconciliation in the South', in *Building Trust in Ireland: Studies Commissioned by the Forum for Peace and Reconciliation* (Belfast: Blackstaff Press, 1996), pp. 1–52

46 See, for example, C.B. Macpherson, *Democratic Theory: Essays in Retrieval* (Oxford: Clarendon Press, 1973), pp. 95–119; Gary F. Reid, 'Berlin and the Division of Liberty', *Political Theory*, vol. 8, no. 3 (August 1980), pp. 365–80; Charles Taylor, 'What's Wrong with Negative Liberty', in *Philosophical Papers*, vol. 2, *Philosophy and the Human Sciences* (Cambridge: Cambridge University Press, 1985), pp. 211–29.

47 In claiming that the civic and protective functions of political life are not incompatible, I am not claiming that they never clash. Their clashes are not, however, any more difficult (or easy) to resolve in principle than are clashes internal to the protective function where different claims to rights, say, are frequently in conflict.

48 This 'universalisation' of membership only applies, of course, to those already connected to a particular state. Restrictions exist on the conferring of membership on 'outsiders', which often enough are defined in ethnic terms.

49 Aughey, *Under Siege*, pp. 10–12, 100–6

50 See, for example, the informative discussions on the theme of the 'crisis of the nation-state' in *Political Studies*, vol. 42 (special issue) (1994)

51 Jürgen Habermas, 'Citizenship and National Identity: Some Reflections on the Future of Europe', *Praxis International*, vol. 12, no. 1 (1992), p. 3

52 *Ibid.*

53 Aughey, *Under Siege*, p. 26

54 There is by now a vast literature on the topic of liberal neutrality. For a clear defence of such neutrality see Charles Larmore, *Patterns of Moral Complexity* (Cambridge: Cambridge University Press, 1987), pp. 40–68. For, in my view, decisive arguments against it see Ronald Beiner, *What's the Matter with Liberalism?* (Berkeley: University of California Press, 1992), pp. 39–79.

55 See further Charles Taylor, 'Two Theories of Modernity', *Hastings Center Report*, vol. 25, no. 2 (March–April 1995), pp. 24–33

56 See the different arguments to this effect in Alasdair MacIntyre, *After Virtue: A Study in Moral Theory* (London: Duckworth, 1981); and Jean-Francois Lyotard, *The Postmodern Condition* (Minneapolis: University of Minneapolis Press, 1984).

57 Aristotle, *Nicomachean Ethics*, trans. J.A.K. Thomson (Harmondsworth: Penguin, 1966);

Aristotle, *The Politics*, trans. T.A. Sinclair (Harmondsworth: Penguin, 1972). Book III.

58 Hannah Arendt, *The Human Condition* (Chicago: University of Chicago Press, 1958)

59 Jürgen Habermas, *Justification and Application: Remarks on Discourse Ethics*, trans. Ciaran Cronin (Cambridge, MA: MIT Press, 1993), Chapter 5; Charles Taylor, 'Alternative Futures: Legitimacy, Identity and Alienation in Late Twentieth Century Canada', in Alan Cairns and Cynthia Williams (eds.), *Constitutionalism, Citizenship and Society in Canada* (Toronto: University of Toronto Press, 1985), pp. 183–229.

60 See Fionnuala O Connor, *In Search of a State: Catholics in Northern Ireland* (Belfast: Blackstaff Press, 1993), Chapter 3

61 *Ibid.*, Chapter 9

CHAPTER 5

1 Edna Longley, cited in Cultural Traditions Group, *Giving Voices* (Belfast: Institute of Irish Studies, 1995), p. 13

2 Arthur Aughey, 'Obstacles to Reconciliation in the South', in *Building Trust in Ireland: Studies Commissioned by the Forum for Peace and Reconciliation* (Belfast: Blackstaff Press, 1996), p. 19

3 On France's role here see Thomas Pakenham, *The Year of Liberty: The Great Irish Rebellion of 1798* (London: Hodder and Stoughton, 1969); and Marianne Elliott, *Partners in Revolution: The United Irishmen and France* (New Haven: Yale University Press, 1982).

4 See Joseph J. Lee, *Modern Ireland 1912–1985: Politics and Society* (Cambridge: Cambridge University Press, 1989), pp. 38–43

5   A.T.Q. Stewart, *The Narrow Ground: Patterns of Ulster History* (Belfast: Pretani Press, 1986), p. 159

6   Arthur Aughey, *Under Siege: Ulster Unionism and the Anglo-Irish Agreement* (London: Hurst and Company, 1989), pp. 101–3

7   As suggested in 'A Framework for Accountable Government in Northern Ireland', in *Frameworks for the Future* (Belfast: Her Majesty's Stationery Office, 1995), paragraphs 18–22.

8   Compare Steve Bruce, *The Edge of the Union: The Ulster Loyalist Political Vision* (Oxford: Oxford University Press, 1994), pp. 133–42.

9   G.W.F. Hegel, *Phenomenology of Spirit*, trans. A.V. Miller (Oxford: Clarendon Press, 1977), pp. 111–19

10   Charles Taylor, *Multiculturalism and 'The Politics of Recognition'* (New Jersey: Princeton University Press, 1992), p. 25. See also Axel Honneth, 'Integrity and Disrespect: Principles of a Conception of Morality Based on the Theory of Recognition', *Political Theory*, vol. 20, no. 2 (May 1992), pp. 187–201

11   Taylor, *Multiculturalism*, p. 26

12   Ronald Dworkin, *Taking Rights Seriously* (Cambridge, MA: Harvard University Press, 1977)

13   John Rawls, *A Theory of Justice* (Oxford: Oxford University Press, 1972), p. 3

14   Taylor, *Multiculturalism*, p. 41

15   John Rawls, *Political Liberalism* (New York: Columbia University Press, 1993), p. 3

16   See Taylor, *Multiculturalism*, pp. 42–4

17   For an argument for fostering cultural differences see Stephen K. White, *Political Theory and Postmodernism* (Cambridge:

Cambridge University Press, 1991).

18   Robert McCartney, 'Parity of Esteem Has Got Little To Do with Civil Rights', *Belfast Telegraph*, 19 January 1995

19   *Ibid.* See also Dennis Kennedy, 'The Realism of the Union', in *The Idea of the Union: Statements and Critiques in Support of the Union of Great Britain and Northern Ireland* (Vancouver: Belcouver Press, 1995), pp. 28–36.

20   John Stuart Mill, *Utilitarianism, Liberty and Representative Government* (London: Dent, 1910), pp. 256–75

21   For an argument that a vocabulary of rights is not essential to express our fundamental moral and political concerns see Ronald Beiner, *What's the Matter with Liberalism?* (Berkeley: University of California Press, 1969), pp. 80–97.

22   The distinction between the two is close to the distinction Yael Tamir draws between arguments for national self-determination and those for political self-rule. See her *Liberal Nationalism* (Princeton: Princeton University Press, 1993), pp. 57–77.

23   Michael Walzer, 'The Idea of Civil Society: A Path to Social Reconstruction', *Dissent* (Spring 1991), p. 293

24   Adam Smith, *The Wealth of Nations* (Harmondsworth: Penguin, 1986)

25   G.W.F. Hegel, *Philosophy of Right*, trans. T.M. Knox (Oxford: Oxford University Press, 1967), pp. 131–4

26   See further Charles Taylor, 'Invoking Civil Society', in his *Philosophical Arguments* (Cambridge, MA: Harvard University Press, 1995), pp. 204–24.

27   See the contributions in

Democratic Dialogue,
Reconstituting Politics, Report 3
(Belfast, 1996).

28 Elizabeth Meehan, 'Democracy
Unbound', in *Reconstituting
Politics*, p. 38

29 Rawls, *A Theory of Justice*,
Chapter II

30 See Hegel, *Philosophy of Right*,
pp. 126–227; Alexis de
Tocqueville, *Democracy in America*,
edited by Richard D. Heffner
(New York: Mentor Press, 1984),
pp. 301–14.

31 Robert Nozick, *Anarchy, State and
Utopia* (New York: Basic Books,
1974), pp. 88–119

32 Martha Nussbaum, 'Aristotelian
Social Democracy', in
R.B. Douglass *et al*. (eds.),
Liberalism and the Good, (New
York: Routledge, 1990),
pp. 203–52

33 Isaiah Berlin, 'Two Concepts
of Liberty', in his *Four Essays
On Liberty* (Oxford: Oxford
University Press, 1969), especially
pp. 154ff

BIBLIOGRAPHY

Adamson, Ian, *The Cruithin: A History of the Ulster Land and People*
(Belfast: Pretani Press, 1974)
The Identity of Ulster: The Land, the Language and the People
(Belfast: Pretani Press, 1982)
Alcock, Antony, *Understanding Ulster* (Lurgan: Ulster Society
Publications, 1994)
Arendt, Hannah, *The Human Condition* (Chicago: University of
Chicago Press, 1958)
Aristotle, *Nicomachean Ethics*, trans. J.A.K. Thomson
(Harmondsworth: Penguin, 1966)
The Politics, trans. C. Lord (Chicago: University of Chicago
Press, 1984)
Aughey, Arthur, 'The End of History, the End of the Union', in
Selling Unionism Home and Away (Belfast: Ulster Young
Unionist Council, 1995)
'In Search of a New Vision for Unionism', *Belfast Telegraph*,
10 August 1995
'Irresistible Force?' *Fortnight*, no. 321 (October 1993)
'McCartney in the Wings', *Fortnight*, no. 340 (June 1995)
'Obstacles to Reconciliation in the South', *Building Trust
in Ireland: Studies Commissioned by the Forum for
Peace and Reconciliation* (Belfast: Blackstaff Press, 1996)
Under Siege: Ulster Unionism and the Anglo-Irish Agreement
(London: Hurst and Company; Belfast: Blackstaff Press, 1989)

'Unionism and Self-determination', in Patrick Roche and
   Brian Barton (eds.), *The Northern Ireland Question: Myth
   and Reality*, (Aldershot: Avebury, 1991)
Augustine, *The City of God*, trans. Henry Bettenson
   (Harmondsworth: Penguin, 1972)
Avineri, Shlomo, *Hegel's Theory of the Modern State* (Cambridge:
   Cambridge University Press, 1972)
Beiner, Ronald, *What's the Matter with Liberalism?* (Berkeley:
   University of California Press, 1992)
Berlin, Isaiah, *Four Essays on Liberty* (Oxford: Oxford University
   Press, 1969)
Bew, Paul, Gibbon, Peter and Patterson, Henry, *Northern Ireland
   1921–1994: Political Forces and Social Classes* (London: Serif,
   1995)
Boal, Fred, Campbell, John A. and Livingstone, David N., 'The
   Protestant Mosaic: A Majority of Minorities', in Patrick Roche
   and Brian Barton (eds.), *The Northern Ireland Question: Myth and
   Reality* (Aldershot: Avebury, 1991)
Boyle, Kevin and Hadden, Tom, *Ireland: A Positive Proposal*
   (Harmondsworth: Penguin, 1985)
   Northern Ireland: The Choice (Harmondsworth: Penguin, 1994)
Bruce, Steve, *The Edge of the Union: The Ulster Loyalist Political
   Vision* (Oxford: Oxford University Press, 1994)
   God Save Ulster: The Religion and Politics of Paisleyism (Oxford:
   Clarendon Press, 1986)
   The Red Hand: Protestant Paramilitaries in Northern Ireland
   (Oxford: Oxford University Press, 1992)
Bryson, Lucy and McCartney, Clem, *Clashing Symbols? A Report
   on the Use of Flags, Anthems and Other National Symbols in
   Northern Ireland* (Belfast: Institute of Irish Studies, 1994)
*Building Trust in Ireland: Studies Commissioned by the Forum for
   Peace and Reconciliation* (Belfast: Blackstaff Press, 1996)
Bunreacht na hÉireann, Constitution of Ireland, 1937
Campaign for Equal Citizenship, *Northern Ireland Says Yes to Equal
   Citizenship* (Belfast: Campaign for Equal Citizenship, 1987)

Clifford, Brendan, *The Road to Nowhere* (Belfast: Athol Books, 1987)

Cochrane, Feargal, 'Any Takers? The Isolation of Northern Ireland', *Political Studies*, vol. 42, no. 3 (1994)

'The Isolation of Northern Ireland', *Political Studies*, vol. 43, no. 3 (1995)

Connolly, Michael and Loughlin, John, 'Reflections on the Anglo-Irish Agreement', *Government and Opposition*, vol. 21 (1986)

Connolly, William E., *Identity\Difference: Democratic Negotiations of Political Paradox* (New York: Cornell University Press, 1991)

Cultural Traditions Group, *Giving Voices* (Belfast: Institute of Irish Studies, 1995)

Cunningham, Michael J., *British Government Policy in Northern Ireland 1969–89: Its Nature and Execution* (Manchester: Manchester University Press, 1991)

Della Cava, Ralph, 'Vatican Policy, 1978–90: An Updated Overview', *Social Research* (1993)

Democratic Dialogue, *Reconstituting Politics*, Report 3 (Belfast, 1996)

Dixon, Paul, 'Internationalization and Unionist Isolation: A Response to Feargal Cochrane', *Political Studies*, vol. 43, no. 3 (1995)

Douglass, R. Bruce and Hollenbach, David, *Catholicism and Liberalism: Contributions to American Public Philosophy* (Cambridge: Cambridge University Press, 1994)

Drafting Committee of the Forum for Peace and Reconciliation, 'Paths to a Political Settlement: Realities, Principles and Requirements', Final Paper

Dunlop, John, *A Precarious Belonging: Presbyterians and the Conflict in Ireland* (Belfast: Blackstaff Press, 1995)

Dunn, John, *The Political Thought of John Locke: An Historical Account of the Argument of the Two Treatises of Government* (Cambridge: Cambridge University Press, 1969)

Dworkin, Ronald, *Taking Rights Seriously* (Cambridge, MA: Harvard University Press, 1977)

Elliott, Marianne, *Partners in Revolution: The United Irishmen and France* (New Haven: Yale University Press, 1982)

Watchmen in Sion: The Protestant Idea of Liberty, Field Day Pamphlet No. 8 (Derry: Field Day, 1985)

Farrell, Michael, *Northern Ireland: The Orange State*, 2nd rev. edn. (London: Pluto Press, 1980)

Foster, John Wilson (ed.), *The Idea of the Union: Statements and Critiques in Support of the Union of Great Britain and Northern Ireland* (Vancouver: Belcouver Press, 1995)

Foster, Roy F., *Modern Ireland 1600–1972* (Harmondsworth: Penguin, 1989)

Frameworks for the Future (Belfast: Her Majesty's Stationery Office, 1995). Also known as 'the framework documents'.

Fukuyama, Francis, 'The End of History? After the Battle of Jena', *Quadrant*, vol. 33, no. 258 (August 1989)

The End of History and the Last Man (London: Hamish Hamilton, 1992)

Fulton, John, *The Tragedy of Belief: Division, Politics, and Religion in Ireland* (Oxford: Clarendon Press, 1991)

Gadamer, Hans Georg, *Truth and Method*, trans. G. Barden and J. Cumming (London: Sheed and Ward, 1975)

Gibbon, Peter, *The Origins of Ulster Unionism* (Manchester: Manchester University Press, 1975)

Girvin, Brian, 'Constitutional Nationalism and Northern Ireland', in Brian Barton and Patrick Roche (eds.), *The Northern Ireland Question: Policies and Perspectives* (Aldershot: Avebury, 1994)

Habermas, Jürgen, 'Citizenship and National Identity: Some Reflections on the Future of Europe', *Praxis International*, vol. 12, no. 1 (1992)

Justification and Application: Remarks on Discourse Ethics, trans. Ciaran Cronin (Cambridge, MA: MIT Press, 1993)

The Philosophical Discourse of Modernity: Twelve Lectures (Cambridge, MA: MIT Press, 1988)

Hampton, Jean, 'Rethinking Reason', *American Philosophical Quarterly*, vol. 29, no. 3 (July 1992)

Hegel, G.W.F., *Logic*, trans. William Wallace (Oxford: Clarendon Press, 1975)

Phenomenology of Spirit, trans. A.V. Miller (Oxford: Clarendon Press, 1977)

The Philosophy of History, trans. J. Sibree (New York: Dover, 1956)

Philosophy of Right, trans. T.M. Knox (Oxford: Oxford University Press, 1967)

Hobbes, Thomas, *Leviathan*, edited by C.B. Macpherson (Harmondsworth: Penguin, 1968)

Honneth, Axel, 'Integrity and Disrespect: Principles of a Conception of Morality Based on the Theory of Recognition', *Political Theory*, vol. 20, no. 2 (May 1992)

Hutton, Will, *The State We're In* (London: Cape, 1995)

Ignatieff, Michael, *Blood and Belonging: Journeys into the New Nationalism* (London: Chatto and Windus, 1993)

Irish Catholic Bishops, 'Submission from the Irish Catholic Bishops' Conference to the Forum for Peace and Reconciliation' (19 January 1996)

'Joint Declaration: Downing Street' (Belfast: Her Majesty's Stationery Office, 15 December 1993). Also known as the 'Downing Street Declaration'.

Kearney, Richard (ed.), *Across the Frontiers: Ireland in the 1990s* (Dublin: Gill and Macmillan, 1988)

Kennedy, Dennis, 'The European Union and the Northern Ireland Question', in Brian Barton and Patrick Roche (eds.), *The Northern Ireland Question: Policies and Perspectives* (Aldershot: Avebury, 1994)

'The Realism of the Union', in John Wilson Foster (ed.), *The Idea of the Union* (Vancouver: Belcouver Press, 1995)

Kenny, Anthony, *The Road to Hillsborough* (Oxford: Pergamon Press, 1986)

Keogh, Dermot, 'The Role of the Catholic Church in the Republic of Ireland 1922–1995', in *Building Trust in Ireland: Studies Commissioned by the Forum for Peace and Reconciliation* (Belfast: Blackstaff Press, 1996)

Kolakowski, Leszek and Hampshire, Stuart (eds.), *The Socialist Idea: A Reappraisal* (London: Weidenfeld and Nicolson, 1974)

Kymlicka, Will, *Contemporary Political Philosophy: An Introduction* (Oxford: Clarendon Press, 1990)

Liberalism, Community, and Culture (Oxford: Clarendon Press, 1989)

Larmore, Charles, *Patterns of Moral Complexity* (Cambridge: Cambridge University Press, 1987)

Lee, Joseph J., 'Dynamics of Social and Political Change in the Irish Republic', in D. Keogh and M.H. Haltzel (eds.), *Northern Ireland and the Politics of Reconciliation* (Cambridge: Cambridge University Press, 1993)

Ireland 1912–1985: Politics and Society (Cambridge: Cambridge University Press, 1989)

Livingstone, Steven and Morison, John, *An Audit of Democracy in Northern Ireland*, supplement to *Fortnight*, no. 337 (April 1995)

Locke, John, *Two Treatises of Government*, edited by Peter Laslett (New York: Cambridge University Press, 1960)

Lyotard, Jean-Francois, *The Postmodern Condition* (Minneapolis: University of Minnesota Press, 1984)

McCartney, Robert, *Liberty and Authority in Ireland*, Field Day Pamphlet No. 9 (Derry: Field Day, 1985)

'Parity of Esteem Has Got Little To Do with Civil Rights', *Belfast Telegraph*, 19 January 1995

'Time to Face the Crisis', *News Letter*, 7 March 1995

'Vision for the Union', *News Letter*, 29 June 1995

McGarry, John and O'Leary, Brendan, *Explaining Northern Ireland: Broken Images* (Oxford: Blackwell, 1995)

McGimpsey, Christopher and McGimpsey, Michael, Plaintiffs, *v.* Ireland, An Taioseach and Others, Defendants, SC NO. 314 of 1988 Supreme Court, 1 March 1990. *The Irish Reports 1990*, vol. 1, Incorporated Council of Law Reporting for Ireland, 1990

MacIntyre, Alasdair, *After Virtue: A Study in Moral Theory* (London: Duckworth, 1981)

MacIver, Martha Abele, 'Ian Paisley and the Reformed Tradition', *Political Studies,* vol. 35 (1987)

Macpherson, C.B., *Democratic Theory: Essays in Retrieval* (Oxford: Clarendon Press, 1973)

The Political Theory of Possessive Individualism: Hobbes to Locke (Oxford: Oxford University Press, 1962)

Meredith, Ian and Kennaway, Brian, *The Orange Order: An Evangelical Perspective* (Belfast, 1993)

Mill, John Stuart, *Utilitarianism, Liberty and Representative Government* (London: Dent, 1910)

Miller, David, *Queen's Rebels: Ulster Loyalism in Historical Perspective* (Dublin: Gill and Macmillan, 1978)

Molyneaux, James, 'Accountable Democracy at Westminster', *Unionist Voice*, no. 12 (October 1994)

Nagel, Thomas, *The View From Nowhere* (Oxford: Oxford University Press, 1986)

Nelson, Sarah, *Ulster's Uncertain Defenders: Loyalists and the Northern Ireland Conflict* (Belfast: Appletree Press, 1984)

Nesbitt, Desmond, *Unionism Restated: An Analysis of the Ulster Unionist Party's 'Statement of Aims'* (Belfast: Ulster Unionist Information Institute, 1995)

Noble, C.A.M., 'The Constitutional Significance of Britain's Protestant Heritage', *New Protestant Telegraph* (March 1996)

Nozick, Robert, *Anarchy, State and Utopia* (New York: Basic Books, 1974)

Nussbaum, Martha, 'Aristotelian Social Democracy', in R.B. Douglass *et al.* (eds.), *Liberalism and the Good* (New York: Routledge, 1990)

O Connor, Fionnuala, *In Search of a State: Catholics in Northern Ireland* (Belfast: Blackstaff Press, 1993)

O'Halloran, Clare, *Partition and the Limits of Irish Nationalism* (Dublin: Gill and Macmillan, 1988)

O'Leary, Brendan and McGarry, John, *The Politics of Antagonism: Understanding Northern Ireland* (London: Athlone Press, 1993)

O'Malley, Padraig, *Biting at the Grave: The Irish Hunger Strikes and*

the Politics of Despair; (Boston: Beacon Press; Belfast: Blackstaff
Press, 1990)

Northern Ireland: Questions of Nuance (Belfast: Blackstaff
Press, 1990)

The Uncivil Wars: Ireland Today (Belfast: Blackstaff Press, 1983)

Paisley, Ian, 'Flawed Visions for the Union', *News Letter*, 30 June
1995

'Why I Oppose the Downing Street Deal', *Belfast Telegraph*,
6 December 1995

Pakenham, Thomas, *The Year of Liberty: The Great Irish Rebellion of
1798* (London: Hodder and Stoughton, 1969)

*Paths to a Political Settlement in Ireland: Policy Papers Submitted to
the Forum for Peace and Reconciliation* (Belfast: Blackstaff Press,
1995)

Pollak, Andy (ed.), *A Citizens' Inquiry: The Opsahl Report on
Northern Ireland* (Dublin: Lilliput Press, 1993)

Rawls, John, *Political Liberalism* (New York: Columbia University
Press, 1993)

A Theory of Justice (Oxford: Oxford University Press, 1972)

Reed, Gary F., 'Berlin and the Division of Liberty', *Political Theory*,
vol. 8, no. 3 (August 1980)

Robinson, Peter, *The Union Under Fire: United Ireland Framework
Revealed* (Belfast, 1995)

Roche, Patrick and Birnie, Esmond, *An Economics Lesson for Irish
Nationalists and Republicans* (Belfast: Ulster Unionist
Information Institute, 1995)

Rorty, Richard, *Philosophy and the Mirror of Nature* (Princeton,
New Jersey: Princeton University Press, 1979)

Sabine, George, *A History of Political Theory*, 3rd rev. edn (London:
George Harrap, 1951)

Sandel, Michael, *Liberalism and the Limits of Justice* (Cambridge:
Cambridge University Press, 1983)

Shankill Think Tank, *A New Beginning*, Island Pamphlets No. 13
(Belfast: Island Publications, 1995)

Ulster's Protestant Working Class, Island Pamphlets No. 9

(Belfast: Island Publications, 1994)

Skinner, Quentin, *The Foundations of Modern Political Thought*, vol. 2, *The Age of Reformation* (Cambridge: Cambridge University Press, 1978)

'On Justice, the Common Good and Liberty', in Chantal Mouffe (ed.), *Dimensions of Radical Democracy: Pluralism, Citizenship, Community* (London: Verso, 1992)

Smith, Adam, *The Wealth of Nations* (Harmondsworth: Penguin, 1986)

Stewart, A.T.Q., *The Narrow Ground: Patterns of Ulster History* (Belfast: Pretani Press, 1986)

The Ulster Crisis (London: Faber and Faber, 1967)

Tamir, Yael, *Liberal Nationalism* (Princeton, New Jersey: Princeton University Press, 1993)

Taylor, Charles, 'Alternative Futures: Legitimacy, Identity and Alienation in Late Twentieth Century Canada', in Alan Cairns and Cynthia Williams (eds.), *Constitutionalism, Citizenship and Society in Canada* (Toronto: University of Toronto Press, 1985)

'Cross-Purposes: The Liberal–Communitarian Debate', in N. Rosenblum (ed.), *Liberalism and the Moral Life* (Cambridge, MA: Harvard University Press, 1989)

Hegel (Cambridge: Cambridge University Press, 1975)

Multiculturalism and 'The Politics of Recognition' (Princeton, New Jersey: Princeton University Press, 1992)

Philosophical Arguments (Cambridge, MA: Harvard University Press, 1995)

Philosophical Papers, vol. 1, *Human Agency and Language* (Cambridge: Cambridge University Press, 1985)

Philosophical Papers, vol. 2, *Philosophy and the Human Sciences* (Cambridge: Cambridge University Press, 1985)

Sources of the Self: The Making of the Modern Identity (Cambridge: Cambridge University Press, 1989)

'Two Theories of Modernity', *Hastings Center Report*, vol. 25, no. 2 (March–April 1995)

Tocqueville, Alexis de, *Democracy in America*, edited by R.D.

Heffner (New York: Mentor Press, 1984)

Ulster Young Unionist Council, *Selling Unionism Home and Away* (Belfast: Ulster Young Unionist Council, 1995)

Walker, Brian M., *Ulster Politics: The Formative Years 1868–1886* (Belfast: Ulster Historical Foundation and Institute of Irish Studies, 1989)

Walker, Graham, *The Politics of Frustration: Harry Midgley and the Failure of Labour in Northern Ireland* (Manchester: Manchester University Press, 1985)

Walzer, Michael, 'The Idea of Civil Society: A Path to Social Reconstruction', *Dissent* (Spring 1991)

White, Stephen K., *Political Theory and Postmodernism* (Cambridge: Cambridge University Press, 1991)

Whyte, John, *Interpreting Northern Ireland* (Oxford: Clarendon Press, 1990)

Wilson, Tom, *Ulster: Conflict and Consent* (Oxford: Blackwell, 1989)

Wolin, Sheldon, *Politics and Vision: Continuity and Innovation in Western Political Thought* (Boston: Little, Brown and Company, 1960)

INDEX

individual rights, 45, 103, 191–2, 197
language of, 103
political claims, and, 196–7
protection of, 179
Protestantism and, 101–9
right to march, 195
Robinson, Peter
parity of esteem, and, 125
Roche, Patrick, 138
Rushdie, Salman, 194

Sandel, Michael, 114
Sands, Bobby, 76, 78
Scottish Covenanters, 111
sectarianism, 4, 73, 189, 194
secular consent argument, 113, 114–15, 116,
117–18
security institutions
political vision of civic unionism, 179
self-determination, right of
liberal unionists' view, 135, 136, 143, 144
self-interpretations, 13–14, 189
dialogue, 14–15
unionist, 17–18
siege, language of, 132
siege mentality, 55, 57, 62, 63
siege of Derry (1689), 87
Sinn Féin, 35, 36, 37, 44, 122, 176
refusal to talk with, 26
Skinner, Quentin, 107
Smith, Adam, 202
social changes, 43
social justice, 204, 207
socio-economic concerns, 6, 7, 42, 179, 207
sovereignty see British sovereignty
state
civil society and, 201–9
common good, 206–8
institutional welfare, 208
unity in, 206
state of nature argument, 112–14
Stewart, A.T.Q., 177
Stormont regime, 43–4, 51, 85, 86, 108, 131
discriminatory practices, 123, 157
loyalty to, 124
Protestantism, privileging of, 86, 124–5
substantive identity
citizenship and, 156, 157–9, 161–2, 164
Sunningdale Agreement, 33, 86, 122
loyalist workers' opposition to, 116

symbols, 166, 179, 182

Taylor, Charles, 88–9, 163, 190–1, 192
Tocqueville, Alexis de, 205
totality of relationships, 175
Trimble, David, 8, 9, 138

UK state see British state
Ulster Democratic Party (UDP), 25
Ulster dimension of unionism, 152
Ulster Says No campaign, 26
Ulster-Scots identity, 89, 90
'Ulster' unionism
challenges, response to, 60–4
cultural unionism, 63–4; see also cultural
unionism
identity, 62–4
non-negotiability, 86–7
preferred institutional arrangements, 62, 86
Protestant-British ethos, 63, 72, 83–4, 87–90
way of life see 'Ulster unionist' way of life
Ulster Unionist Party (UUP), 5, 8, 23, 24–5
formal link with Orange Order, 9
liberal unionism, 20
minimalism, 21
'Ulster unionist' way of life, 19, 62, 84–91
British elements, 85
political dimension, 85–6
Ulster Volunteer Force, 116
Ulster Workers' Council strike (1974), 33, 87
Ulster's Solemn League and Covenant
(1912), 87, 116, 129
liberal unionists and, 130
ultra–Protestantism, 4
understanding
conditions of, 11–13
cultural parity of esteem, 46
dialogue, 13
historicality of, 12, 15
Union, the
British government commitment to, 30–2,
136
civic unionist view of, 169–70
defence of, 169
liberal unionist view of, 132–7
unionism; see also 'British' unionism; civic
unionism; cultural unionism; liberal
unionism; 'Northern Irish' unionism;
unionist identity; unionist politics;
unionist unity